Better Homes and Gardens®

Grillin' & Chillin'

Meredith® Books
Des Moines, Iowa

Better Homes and Gardens® *Grillin' and Chillin'*

Editor: Jessica Saari
Contributing Editor: Annie Krumhardt
Contributing Graphic Designer: Sundie Ruppert
Editorial Assistant: Sheri Cord
Book Production Manager: Mark Weaver
Contributing Copy Editor: Ali Cybulski
Contributing Proofreaders: Stephanie Boeding, Candy Meier, Lois White
Contributing Indexer: Elizabeth Walker
Test Kitchen Director: Lynn Blanchard
Test Kitchen Culinary Specialists: Marilyn Cornelius, Juliana Hale, Maryellyn Krantz, Jill Moberly, Colleen Weeden, Lori Wilson
Test Kitchen Nutrition Specialists: Elizabeth Burt, R.D., L.D.; Laura Marzen, R.D., L.D.

Meredith® Books

Editorial Director: John Riha
Deputy Editor: Jennifer Darling
Managing Editor: Kathleen Armentrout
Brand Manager: Janell Pittman
Group Editor: Jan Miller
Copy Chief: Doug Kouma
Senior Copy Editors: Kevin Cox, Elizabeth Keest Sedrel, Jennifer Speer Ramundt
Assistant Copy Editor: Metta Cederdahl

Executive Director, Sales: Ken Zagor
Director, Operations: George A. Susral
Director, Production: Douglas M. Johnston
Business Director: Janice Croat
Vice President and General Manager, SIM: Jeff Myers

Better Homes and Gardens® Magazine

Editor in Chief: Gayle Goodson Butler
Deputy Editor, Food and Entertaining: Nancy Wall Hopkins

Meredith Publishing Group

President: Jack Griffin
Executive Vice President: Doug Olson

Meredith Corporation

Chairman of the Board: William T. Kerr
President and Chief Executive Officer: Stephen M. Lacy
In Memoriam: E.T. Meredith III (1933–2003)

All of us at Meredith® Books are dedicated to providing you with information and ideas to enhance your life. We welcome your comments and suggestions. Write to us at: Meredith Books Editorial Department, 1716 Locust St., Des Moines, IA 50309-3023.

Cover Photography:
Front cover: Ribeyes with Summer Salsa (page 43)

Our seal assures you that every recipe in *Grillin' and Chillin'* has been tested in the Better Homes and Gardens® Test Kitchen. This means that each recipe is practical and reliable, and meets our high standards of taste appeal. We guarantee your satisfaction with this book for as long as you own it.

Grab your tongs and fire up the grill!

Long summer days mean warm breezes, backyard picnics, and—of course—delicious flavors penetrating sizzling meals from the grill. If you're the master cook at your house, you know how refreshing it is to take your cooking endeavors outdoors. You also know easily the same old grilled meals can lose their luster. That's why we've loaded this book with more than 200 summertime favorites, each recipe promising to bring something fresh and tasty your family and friends will love.

Besides grilled meat, poultry, and fish featured in dozens of fabulous dishes, you'll discover an assortment of veggie dishes, breads, and appetizers to toss on the grill. And when hot summer days have you craving something cool, you'll find plenty of refreshing summer drinks, salads, and icy cold desserts that make chilling out tastier than ever. Plus, for those who love to entertain, we've included a chapter all about throwing the perfect grilling bash. With options for serving 12, 25, or 50 grill-out guests, this barbecue-style meal is complete with a timetable to ensure your success in pulling off an awesome party.

So go ahead and enjoy the great outdoors—you're sure to have plenty of delicious food and a whole lot of fun!

—the editors

contents

10

28

70

62

104

40

142

172

ready, set, grill!

Cooking over glowing coals should be easy and carefree. Just follow these guidelines so your grill and coals are ready to go.

fire up!

Whether you grill with charcoal or gas, setting up the grill is easy.

For a charcoal grill:

About 25 to 30 minutes before cooking, remove the grill cover and open all the vents. Place the briquettes on the lower charcoal grate.

For **direct cooking,** use enough briquettes to cover the charcoal grate completely with one layer. Then pile these briquettes in a pyramid in the center of the grate.

For **indirect cooking,** the number of briquettes you need is based on your grill size. Check out the chart, *below.*

Grill diameter in inches	Briquettes needed to start	Briquettes to add if coals start to cool during longer grill times
26¾	60	18
22½	50	16
18½	32	10

Light the coals as described in "Lighting the Coals," *page 8*, and let them burn until they are lightly covered with gray ash. Using long-handle tongs, arrange the coals according to the cooking method you want to use.

For **direct cooking,** spread the coals evenly across the bottom of the grill so the coals reach 3 inches beyond all sides of the food you will cook.

For **indirect cooking,** arrange coals at one side of the grill; place a drip pan on the other side. Or place the drip pan in the center of the grill and arrange coals into two piles on opposite sides of the pan. Install the grill rack and check the temperature.

For a gas grill:

Open the lid. Turn on the gas valve and turn the burners to high. Ignite as directed by the manufacturer. Close the lid and preheat the grill (usually with all burners on high for 10 to 15 minutes).

For **indirect cooking,** turn off the burners below where the food will grill. For direct cooking and indirect cooking, adjust burner controls to the temperature needed for cooking.

strive for the best flavor

More often than not, anyone who has spent time over a grill has developed his or her own methodology and grilling techniques. Some are secrets to success, and others are ingredients to failure. Here are a few tried-and-true tricks to help you correct your grilling blunders or continue your achievements at the grill.

Use quality meat. Make sure your steaks are thick and well-marbled. The streaks of fat create wonderful, juicy flavor in meat, but be sure to trim large amounts of visible fat from around the outer edges of the meat. This reduces the dripping grease that causes flare-ups.

Pat meat dry. Pat meat dry with paper towels to eliminate all moisture on the meat's surface; otherwise, you will boil and braise your meat instead of grilling it.

Use fresh herbs. Throw a few sprigs of fresh thyme or rosemary over the coals just before you remove food from the grill. Or use an herb bouquet to baste your meat and veggies with sauce, giving them an added flavor punch.

Marinate. Marinades don't need to be complicated. Simply use a store-bought salad dressing or blend a few ingredients found in your spice rack and fridge. Combine juice, wine or other alcohol, fresh herbs, spices, garlic, onion, and peppers. Marinate the meat or poultry in a nonaluminum container to prevent off-flavors.

Add wood chunks and chips. The wood you choose—apple, cherry, hickory, oak, or other—is a matter of preference. Each type imparts a subtle smoky flavor to the meat. Think of smoke as a spice; too much of a good thing ruins the meal. Start off with a minimal amount of wood, and never add wood during the last half of grilling time.

Don't poke the meat. As tempting as it is to poke, mash, and play with meat while it grills, each poke only causes flavor and moisture loss as the juices drip to the bottom of the grill.

Don't flip your food too soon. Allow adequate time to sear the food before you move it from one spot to the other. Searing gives the food its rich caramelized color and flavor.

Let meat stand. Cutting into meat immediately after it's pulled from the grill causes all the flavorful juices to run out onto the plate. Let your meat stand 5 to 10 minutes to allow the meat to absorb its flavorful components.

testing doneness

Many factors help determine the amount of time needed to grill a given food. Direct grilling requires a lot less time than indirect grilling, but it also requires that you take your food off the grill at the right time. Factors that affect the amount of time needed to grill a food include the outside temperature, the food thickness, the food temperature, the desired doneness, and other conditions. Use the poke test to help you determine when your meat is done. Mimic the movements, below, and gently poke the fleshy section at the base of your thumb. The tension in your hand should match that of the meat, giving you a good indication of its doneness.

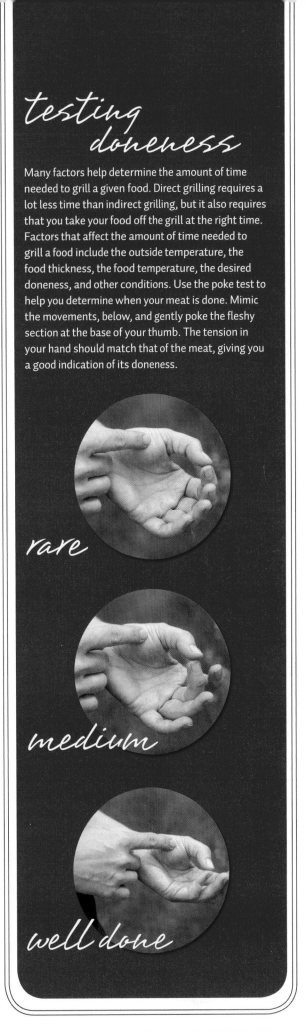

rare

medium

well done

ready or not?

Coals are ready for grilling when they are covered with gray ash, typically 25 to 30 minutes after you light them.

To check the temperature of the coals, use a built-in or separate flat grill thermometer. Or carefully place the palm of your hand above the grill at the cooking level and count the number of seconds you can hold it there. With your hand above the grill, say, "One, I love grilling; two, I love grilling ...; " and so on. Then check the chart, *below*, to determine the grill's temperature. (Note: When you use indirect grilling, hot coals provide medium-hot heat, and medium-hot coals provide medium heat.)

Hand-Holding Time	Thermometer	Temperature	Visual
2 seconds	400°F to 450°F	Hot (high)	Coals glowing and lightly covered with gray ash
3 seconds	375°F to 400°F	Medium-High	
4 seconds	350°F to 375°F	Medium	Coals glowing through a layer of ash
5 seconds	325°F to 350°F	Medium-Low	
6 seconds	300°F to 325°F	Low	Coals burning down and covered with a thick layer of ash

lighting the coals

If you're a charcoal grill aficionado, your first step to a tantalizing cookout is lighting and preheating the coals properly. (If you own a gas grill, just follow the manufacturer's directions and stop reading here.)

1. To start your charcoal grill, mound briquettes on the charcoal grate. You can also put the coals in a metal chimney to consolidate them for more efficient and faster heating. You'll need approximately 30 briquettes per pound of meat or enough to cover an area about 3 inches larger than the diameter of the food you plan to cook.
2. Apply some type of starter to the cold coals. If you use an electric starter, place the starter under the coals and plug it in, following the manufacturer's directions. For a chemical starter, you can choose from instant-lighting briquettes, lighter fluid, fire-starter gels, or paraffin fire starters. A word of caution: If you use a chemical starter, do not apply more once you have tried to light the fire.
3. Light the coals with a long match. Leave the grill uncovered as it preheats.
4. Let the coals burn until they turn ash gray (by day) or glow red (by night). This usually takes 25 to 30 minutes.
5. Once the coals are ready, use tongs to spread them for either direct or indirect cooking (see "Fire Up!" *page 6*).

to cover or not to cover?

That's the burning question. With its lid closed, a grill is like an oven. It reflects heat and cooks the food from all sides, thereby reducing cooking time. With a charcoal grill, it is important to keep the vents open to feed oxygen to the fire. Open the vents more to increase the temperature or partially close them to reduce the temperature. While there are no hard and fast rules, the following guidelines cover the topic:

Cover the Grill ...

... when you grill larger food items using indirect grilling so they cook evenly on all sides.

... to control flare-ups by reducing the supply of oxygen fueling the fire.

... when you smoke foods so the smoke infuses the food with flavor.

Uncover the Grill ...

... to prevent overcooking when you direct-cook thinner, smaller foods with short cooking times.

... when you need to monitor foods that could burn, such as steaks with brushed-on sauces.

tame the flame

Controlling the temperature of your coals during grilling is key to tender, juicy results. Tame or increase the flame in these ways:

* Adjust the vents in the grill's bottom or sides. Close them to restrict airflow and dampen the heat. Open them to promote heat. Leave the vents in the grill cover open at all times during cooking or the fire will be smothered.
* On a gas grill, adjust the temperature with the turn of a dial.
* To lower the temperature of charcoal, spread out the hot coals and let them burn down for 5 to 10 minutes.
* To build a hotter charcoal fire, use more coals and don't let them burn down. If you want more heat from burning coals, gently tap them with long-handle tongs to shake off excess ash, then move the coals closer together.
* If you grill for a long period (more than one hour) and the grill starts losing heat, use tongs to replenish the coals, adding eight to 10 coals every 30 to 45 minutes. If you use presoaked wood chips, add them whenever you add coals to the grill.

Take the guesswork out of deciding when your food is ready to take off the grill. Turn to this easy-to-use chart as a guide to capture perfectly grilled food.

Cut	Thickness/ Weight	Grill Temperature	Doneness	Direct Grilling Time	Indirect Grilling Time	
Flank steak	¾ inch–1 inch thick	medium	medium (160°F)	17–21 minutes	23–28 minutes	**beef**
Hamburgers	¾ inch thick	medium	well (170°F)	14–18 minutes	20–24 minutes	
Porterhouse steak	1 inch thick	medium	medium (160°F)	12–15 minutes	20–24 minutes	
Ribeye, sirloin, and T-bone steaks; tenderloin	1½ inches thick	medium	medium (160°F)	18–23 minutes	25–28 minutes	
Chop	1 inch thick	medium	medium rare (145°F) medium (160°F)	12–14 minutes 15–17 minutes	16–18 minutes 18–20 minutes	**lamb**
Chop	1 inch thick	medium	medium (160°F)	12–15 minutes	19–23 minutes	**veal**
Whole fish (dressed)	½ lb.–1½ lb.	medium	flakes when tested with fork	6–9 minutes per 8 oz.	15–20 minutes per 8 oz.	
Fillets, steaks	½ inch–1 inch thick	medium	flakes when tested with fork	4–6 minutes per ½-inch thickness	7–9 minutes per ½-inch thickness	**fish**
Sea scallops	12–15 per pound	medium	opaque	5–8 minutes	11–14 minutes	
Shrimp	medium-size large-size	medium medium	opaque opaque	5–8 minutes 7–9 minutes	8–10 minutes 9–11 minutes	
Broiler, fryer	1½ lb.–1¾ lb., halves 12 oz.–14 oz., quarters	medium medium	180°F 180°F	40–50 minutes 40–50 minutes	1–1¼ hours 50–60 minutes	
Boneless, skinless chicken breast	4 oz.–5 oz.	medium	170°F	12–15 minutes	15–18 minutes	**poultry**
Chicken pieces	2½ lb.–3 lb. total	medium	180°F	35–40 minutes	50–60 minutes	
Turkey tenderloin	8 oz.–10 oz.	medium	170°F	16–20 minutes	25–30 minutes	
Bone-in chop	1¼–1½ inches thick	medium	160°F	16–20 minutes	35–40 minutes	
Boneless chop	1¼–1½ inches thick	medium	160°F	14–18 minutes	30–35 minutes	**pork**
Sausages, cooked		medium		3–7 minutes		
Tenderloin	¾ lb.–1 lb.	medium-high	155°F		30–35 minutes	

9

summer chillers

When the summer heat is on and your thirst has you craving something refreshingly cool, quench it with an icy-good beverage. Any of these fruity favorites will provide the necessary cooldown.

3 nectarine-berry blitzes

1 ginger-pineapple punch

2 tangy citrus lemonade

4 summer fruit daiquiris

5 strawberry and sage shrub

6 spiced fruit tea

7 double-apricot margaritas

8 raspberry mojito punch

9 tropical sippers

ginger-pineapple punch

This company-pleasing cooler gets a double dose of ginger from grated fresh ginger and ginger ale.

Prep: 20 minutes   Chill: 2 hours   Makes: 12 (6-ounce) servings

    2   cups orange juice
    2   cups unsweetened pineapple juice
    2   tablespoons grated fresh ginger
    1   1-liter bottle diet or regular ginger ale, chilled
        Ice cubes
        Fresh pineapple wedges (optional)

1. In a large pitcher, combine orange juice, pineapple juice, and ginger. Cover and chill for 2 to 24 hours.

2. Using a fine-mesh sieve, strain mixture; discard ginger and pulp. Slowly pour ginger ale into juice mixture. Serve in ice-filled glasses. If desired, garnish with pineapple wedges.

Per Serving: 48 cal., 0 g fat, 0 mg chol., 22 mg sodium, 12 g carbo., 0 g fiber, 1 g pro.

berry-basil milk shakes

Sweetly sophisticated with a wine-and-basil-infused syrup, this frosty treat is for adults only.

Prep: 15 minutes   Makes: 4 servings

    2   cups (1 pint) strawberry ice cream
    2   cups (1 pint) strawberry sorbet
    1½   cups cold milk
    ¼   cup Basil Syrup
    ½   cup fresh raspberries
    ½   cup fresh blackberries
          Fresh raspberries and/or blackberries (optional)

1. In a large blender, combine ice cream, sorbet, milk, and Basil Syrup. Cover and pulse blender until mixture is smooth. Add raspberries and blackberries and pulse to break up berries.

2. Pour mixture into chilled glasses and, if desired, garnish with additional raspberries and/or blackberries.

Basil Syrup: In a medium saucepan, combine ¾ cup sugar and 1 cup dry white wine. Stir over low heat to dissolve the sugar. When sugar completely dissolves, bring mixture to a gentle boil, reduce heat to low, and simmer for 3 minutes. Remove from heat; add 2 cups basil leaves and stir to immerse basil completely in liquid. Cover and allow to stand at room temperature for 30 minutes. Using a fine-mesh sieve, pour mixture into a bowl. Discard basil leaves; cover bowl and chill for at least 1 hour and up to 5 days.

Per Serving: 347 cal., 8 g fat (5 g sat. fat), 26 mg chol., 88 mg sodium, 64 g carbo., 3 g fiber, 6 g pro.

tangy citrus lemonade

Lemons and limes combine in this thirst-quenching summer favorite.

Prep: 25 minutes   Chill: 2 hours
Makes: 8 to 10 (6- to 8-ounce) servings

    6   large lemons, juiced (1½ cups juice)
    3   medium limes, juiced (⅓ cup juice)
    ¾   to 1 cup honey or 1 cup sugar
    6   cups water
    2   cups fresh or frozen raspberries
          Ice cubes
          Lemon and/or lime slices (optional)
          Honey or sugar (optional)
          Fresh raspberries (optional)

1. In a 2½-quart pitcher, combine lemon juice, lime juice, and ¾ to 1 cup honey or 1 cup sugar. Add the water and 2 cups raspberries. Cover and chill for at least 2 hours or up to 24 hours.

2. Just before serving, gently stir mixture to combine. Pour mixture into ice-filled glasses. If desired, add lemon and/or lime slices and sweeten to taste with additional honey or sugar. If desired, garnish with additional raspberries.

Lemonade Tea: Add equal parts fresh-brewed iced tea and Tangy Citrus Lemonade to ice-filled glasses. Sweeten to taste with additional honey or sugar.

Per Serving: 119 cal., 0 g fat, 0 mg chol., 6 mg sodium, 33 g carbo., 3 g fiber, 1 g pro.

hit-the-spot lemon water

Amazing and refreshing flavors pop when you soak lemons and fresh herbs in water for an hour or so. No need to add sugar for pure, thirst-quenching goodness.

Prep: 15 minutes   Chill: 1 hour
Makes: 6 to 8 (about 8-ounce) servings

    4   lemons, sliced
    1½   cups firmly packed fresh mint or basil leaves
    6   to 8 cups water
          Fresh mint or basil sprigs
          Ice cubes

1. Place lemon slices in a large pitcher. Carefully rub the 1½ cups mint leaves between the palms of your hands to slightly bruise the leaves. Add mint to pitcher. Pour in water. Cover; chill for 1 to 8 hours.

2. Strain lemon-water mixture. Discard mint. Divide lemon slices and additional fresh mint leaves among six to eight tall glasses. Add ice cubes to each glass; fill with lemon water.

Per Serving: 11 cal., 0 g fat, 0 mg chol., 8 mg sodium, 4 g carbo., 1 g fiber, 0 g pro.

nectarine-berry blitzes

Add a swizzle stick or straw to this cranberry-topped slushy nectarine drink so guests can swirl the two great flavors together.

Start to Finish: 15 minutes   Makes: 4 (about 6-ounce) servings

- 1 cup sliced, pitted, and peeled nectarines
- 1 cup orange juice
- 1/3 cup plain or vanilla yogurt
- 1 cup ice cubes
- 1/2 cup frozen cranberry-raspberry juice concentrate, thawed
    Fresh nectarine slices (optional)

1. In a blender, combine 1 cup nectarines, orange juice, and yogurt. Cover; blend until smooth. With blender running, gradually add ice cubes through opening in lid until mixture becomes almost smooth.

2. Pour nectarine mixture over additional *ice cubes* in tall glasses. Pour 2 tablespoons of the juice concentrate in each glass to get a layered effect. If desired, garnish with nectarine slices.
Per Serving: 121 cal., 0 g fat, 1 mg chol., 14 mg sodium, 29 g carbo., 1 g fiber, 1 g pro.

summer fruit daiquiris

Pick your fruit, either peaches or strawberries. Both are bursting with full-of-flavor goodness when they are in peak season. When they're not, frozen fruit makes a sweet substitute.

Start to Finish: 15 minutes   Makes: 6 to 8 (4- to 5-ounce) servings

- 3 cups sliced, pitted, and peeled fresh peaches; frozen unsweetened peach slices; or fresh or frozen unsweetened strawberries
- 1/2 of a 12-ounce can frozen limeade or lemonade concentrate, thawed
- 1/4 cup light rum or orange juice
- 2 tablespoons powdered sugar
- 2 to 3 cups ice cubes
    Carambola (star fruit) slices, fresh peach chunks, or small fresh strawberries (optional)

1. In a blender, combine 3 cups fruit, limeade concentrate, rum, and powdered sugar. Cover and blend until smooth. With blender running, gradually add ice cubes, 1 cup at a time, through opening in lid until mixture reaches desired thickness.

2. Pour mixture into chilled glasses. If desired, garnish with fruit.
Per Serving: 138 cal., 0 g fat, 0 mg chol., 1 mg sodium, 30 g carbo., 2 g fiber, 1 g pro.

strawberry and sage shrub

Refreshingly light, this sparkling champagne sipper provides a perfect drink for large-group toasting.

Prep: 40 minutes   Stand: 1 hour   Chill: up to 3 days
Makes: 14 to 16 (about 8-ounce) servings

- 3 16-ounce packages frozen unsweetened whole strawberries or three 12-ounce packages frozen red raspberries
- 1 cup sugar
- 3/4 cup honey
- 1/2 cup water
- 1 tablespoon finely shredded lemon peel
- 1/2 cup lemon juice
- 2 teaspoons whole pink peppercorns (optional)
- 1/2 cup fresh sage leaves or 2 tablespoons dried sage, crushed
- 4 to 6 cups ice cubes
- 2 750-milliliter bottles champagne or two 1-liter bottles club soda, chilled
    Fresh sage leaves (optional)
    Fresh strawberries or raspberries (optional)

1. In a 4-quart Dutch oven, combine frozen strawberries, sugar, honey, the water, lemon peel, lemon juice, and, if desired, peppercorns. Cook, uncovered, over medium heat until mixture just begins to boil, stirring frequently. Remove from heat. Stir in sage. Let mixture stand, uncovered, for 1 hour.

2. Using a fine-mesh sieve, strain mixture; discard solids (you should have 4 to 5 cups syrup). Syrup may be covered and chilled for up to 3 days.

3. To serve, in a punch bowl, combine syrup and the ice cubes. Slowly pour the champagne or club soda down the side of the punch bowl. If desired, garnish individual servings with additional fresh sage leaves and fresh berries.
Per Serving: 220 cal., 0 g fat, 0 mg chol., 3 mg sodium, 41 g carbo., 2 g fiber, 1 g pro.

The fruit garnishes are extra, but they provide a sweet treat for a little munching.

spiced fruit tea

If you wish, when you make ice cubes to serve with the tea, add small slices of orange to the ice cube trays before pouring in a small amount of tea.

Prep: 15 minutes   Chill: 4 hours   Freeze: 4 hours
Makes: 8 to 10 (about 8-ounce) servings

6

5	cups boiling water
5	bags orange-flavor spiced herb tea
1/3	cup sugar
1/4	teaspoon ground cinnamon
1	46-ounce can unsweetened pineapple juice
2	cups cranberry juice cocktail
1/3	cup lime juice
	Orange slices, fresh pineapple chunks, and/or mint sprigs (optional)

1. Pour the boiling water into an extra-large bowl. Add the tea bags. Let steep for 5 minutes. Remove and discard tea bags. Stir in sugar and cinnamon until sugar dissolves. Stir in pineapple juice, cranberry juice, and lime juice. Remove 3 cups of the mixture. Cover and chill the remaining mixture for at least 4 hours or up to 3 days.

2. Pour the reserved 3 cups tea mixture into two clean ice cube trays. Cover and freeze until tea mixture is firm.

3. To serve, divide prepared ice cubes among glasses. Add chilled tea mixture. If desired, garnish with fruit and/or mint.

Per Serving: 157 cal., 0 g fat, 0 mg chol., 9 mg sodium, 39 g carbo., 0 g fiber, 1 g pro.

chill out

On hot summer days, even the iciest beverage loses its chill in a matter of minutes. Maximize the chill factor by refrigerating all the liquid ingredients for a few hours before you blend them into the beverage. Then, for an additional burst of cold, serve the individual drinks in chilled glasses. For extremely frosty treats, pour the beverage into glasses that have been stored in the freezer.

double-apricot margaritas

Start to Finish: 10 minutes   Makes: 8 (4-ounce) servings

7

	Coarse salt
	Lime wedges
1	15-ounce can unpeeled apricot halves, drained
1/2	cup tequila
1/4	cup sugar
1/4	cup lime juice
1/4	cup apricot nectar
3	cups ice cubes

1. Place salt in a shallow dish. Rub rims of eight margarita glasses or other 6-ounce glasses with lime wedges. Invert glasses into dish to coat rims with salt. Shake off any excess salt and set glasses aside.

2. In a blender, combine apricot halves, tequila, sugar, lime juice, and apricot nectar. Cover and blend until smooth. With blender running, gradually add ice cubes, 1 cup at a time, through opening in lid until mixture is slushy.

3. To serve, pour mixture into prepared glasses.

Per Serving: 91 cal., 0 g fat, 0 mg chol., 244 mg sodium, 15 g carbo., 1 g fiber, 0 g pro.

Nonalcoholic Double-Apricot Coolers: Prepare Double-Apricot Margaritas as directed, except omit tequila and increase apricot nectar to 3/4 cup.

raspberry mojito punch

You'll love the addition of raspberry to this mint-lime taste sensation.

Start to Finish: 15 minutes   Makes: 8 (8-ounce) servings

8

1/3	cup sugar
1/4	cup lightly packed fresh mint leaves
3	cups cold water
1	12-ounce can frozen raspberry juice blend concentrate, thawed
1/2	cup fresh lime juice, chilled
24	ounces (3 cups) club soda, chilled
1	cup ice cubes
1	lime, thinly sliced
1	cup fresh raspberries

1. In a punch bowl, combine sugar and mint. Using the back of a wooden spoon, lightly mash the mint by pressing it against the side of the bowl. Add the water, raspberry juice blend, and lime juice, stirring until sugar dissolves. Stir in club soda, ice cubes, lime, and raspberries. Serve at once.

Per Serving: 139 cal., 0 g fat, 0 mg chol., 38 mg sodium, 34 g carbo., 1 g fiber, 0 g pro.

pink rhubarb punch

Tart rhubarb joins juicy lemon in this spin on pink lemonade.

Prep: 20 minutes Cook: 5 minutes Chill: 4 to 24 hours

Makes: 10 (about 6-ounce) servings

- 6 cups fresh rhubarb, cut into $1/2$-inch pieces, or 6 cups frozen unsweetened, sliced rhubarb (24 ounces)
- 3 cups water
- 1 cup sugar
- $1/2$ of a 12-ounce can frozen pink lemonade concentrate ($3/4$ cup), thawed
- $1/4$ cup lemon juice
- 1 1-liter bottle carbonated water, chilled
  Crushed ice
  Fresh mint leaves and/or lemon slices (optional)

1. In a saucepan, combine rhubarb and water. Bring to boiling; reduce heat. Simmer, covered, for 5 minutes. Remove from heat; cool slightly. Strain mixture into a large pitcher, pressing to remove all juices. Discard pulp. Add sugar, lemonade concentrate, and lemon juice to rhubarb juice, stirring to dissolve sugar. Cover; chill for 4 to 24 hours.

2. To serve, stir in carbonated water. Serve in glasses over crushed ice. If desired, garnish with fresh mint and/or lemon slices.

Per Serving: 122 cal., 0 g fat, 0 mg chol., 7 mg sodium, 31 g carbo., 1 g fiber, 1 g pro.

berry-lemonade spritzer

For those who enjoy an alcoholic beverage, add a splash of rum, vodka, or gin to this thirst quencher.

Start to Finish: 10 minutes Makes: 8 (8-ounce) servings

- 1 6-ounce can (or $1/2$ of a 12-ounce can) frozen pink lemonade concentrate, thawed
- 1 6-ounce can (or $1/2$ of a 12-ounce can) frozen pineapple juice concentrate, thawed
- $3/4$ cup frozen strawberry daiquiri mix, thawed
- $3/4$ cup water
- 1 1-liter bottle lemon-lime carbonated beverage, chilled
- 8 whole fresh strawberries
  Ice cubes
  Lemon or orange wedges

1. In a large pitcher, stir together lemonade, pineapple juice, strawberry daiquiri mix, and the water. Slowly pour the carbonated beverage down side of pitcher. Stir with up-and-down motion to mix.

2. To serve, place a strawberry in each of eight large wine goblets or tall glasses. Add ice cubes, then pour in lemonade mixture. Garnish each glass with a lemon or orange wedge.

Per Serving: 175 cal., 0 g fat, 0 mg chol., 28 mg sodium, 46 g carbo., 0 g fiber, 0 g pro.

Quickly turn ice cubes into crushed ice by placing them in a heavy resealable plastic bag and pounding them with the flat side of a meat mallet.

tropical sippers

Freeze any leftover fresh ginger if you wish to preserve it. Slice or grate the frozen ginger when you want to use it in another recipe.

Prep: 25 minutes Makes: 16 (8-ounce) servings

   Sugar Syrup
- 1 64-ounce carton refrigerated pineapple-orange-banana juice
- 1 6-ounce can lemonade concentrate, thawed
- 1 1-liter bottle lemon-lime carbonated beverage, chilled
- 3 cups light-color rum
  Crushed ice (optional)
  Orange slices and/or kiwi slices (optional)

1. In a large punch bowl, stir together Sugar Syrup, pineapple-orange-banana juice, and lemonade concentrate. Slowly pour the carbonated beverage and rum down the side of the punch bowl. Gently stir to mix. If desired, serve over crushed ice and garnish with orange and/or kiwi slices.

Sugar Syrup: In a small saucepan, combine $1/2$ cup water, $1/3$ cup sugar, 12 inches stick cinnamon, two $1/4$-inch-thick slices ginger, and $1/2$ teaspoon whole cloves. Bring to boiling; reduce heat. Cover and simmer for 10 minutes. Remove from heat. Transfer to a small bowl. Cover and chill for 2 hours. Using a fine-mesh sieve, strain spices from the sugar syrup; discard spices.

Per Serving: 226 cal., 0 g fat, 0 mg chol., 22 mg sodium, 33 g carbo., 0 g fiber, 0 g pro.

sizzling
starters

Kick off your backyard get-together with a fresh, hot appetizer. As guests gather, toss a little something tasty over the coals and get the party started. While you meet and greet, let everyone enjoy a sampling of hot-off-the-grill, bite-size morsels. Serve spunky seafood cocktail, roasted vegetables with salsa, smoky Brie with peach relish, or another one of our zippy bites to fire up appetites for the great grilled favorites to follow.

calypso shrimp cocktail
(recipe, page 21)

*spicy chicken wings
with blue cheese dressing*

spicy chicken wings with blue cheese dressing

The heat is on! For a milder version of these pepper-coated wings, use the lower amount of the range of each seasoning, and sprinkle the spices on one side instead of shaking the wings in a bag of seasonings.

Prep: 35 minutes Chill: 6 hours Grill: 20 minutes
Makes: 12 (2-wing) servings

24	whole chicken wings (about 4 pounds)
3	to 4 teaspoons garlic salt
3	to 4 teaspoons cayenne pepper
3	to 4 teaspoons ground black pepper
1	tablespoon dried oregano, crushed
	Carrot and celery sticks
	Blue Cheese Dressing

1. Tuck under wing tips. Place chicken wings in a heavy resealable plastic bag set in a shallow dish. In a small dish, combine garlic salt, cayenne pepper, black pepper, and oregano. Sprinkle over chicken wings; seal bag. Shake bag to coat wings with seasonings. Chill in the refrigerator for 6 to 24 hours.

2. For a charcoal grill, arrange medium-hot coals around a drip pan. Test for medium heat above the pan. Place chicken wings on grill rack over drip pan. Cover and grill for 20 to 25 minutes or until chicken is no longer pink, turning once. (For a gas grill, preheat grill. Reduce heat to medium. Adjust for indirect cooking. Grill chicken as above.)

3. To serve, transfer wings to a serving bowl or platter with carrot and celery sticks and use Blue Cheese Dressing as a dipping sauce.

Blue Cheese Dressing: In a small bowl, combine 1 cup mayonnaise, 1 cup crumbled blue cheese (4 ounces), 2/3 cup evaporated milk, 1 tablespoon red wine vinegar, 1 tablespoon lemon juice, 1/4 teaspoon garlic salt, and 1/4 teaspoon celery seeds. Cover and chill for up to 1 week.

Per Serving: 372 cal., 32 g fat (8 g sat. fat), 87 mg chol., 580 mg sodium, 3 g carbo., 0 g fiber, 18 g pro.

Spread any extra of this condiment-style salsa on a sandwich or a wrap.

salsa romesco

Particularly good with roasted vegetables, this lively salsalike sauce also tastes delicious served with grilled pork.

Prep: 15 minutes   Stand: 15 minutes   Cook: 16 minutes

Makes: 14 (2-tablespoon) servings

- 2 dried New Mexico or ancho chile peppers
- 1/2 cup blanched almonds
- 1/2 cup olive oil
- 1 slice French bread, about 1/2 inch thick (about 3/4 ounce)*
- 1 small chile de arbol, seeded and crumbled, or 1/2 teaspoon crushed red pepper
- 1 cup chopped, seeded, and peeled tomatoes (2 medium)
- 6 cloves garlic, sliced
- 1/4 cup red wine vinegar
- 3/4 teaspoon salt
- 3 tablespoons olive oil

1. In a small bowl, cover dried peppers with boiling water. Let stand for 15 minutes. Drain. Remove stems and seeds from peppers and discard. Coarsely chop peppers.** Set aside. In a small skillet, roast almonds over medium-low heat about 8 minutes or until nuts are lightly toasted, shaking pan frequently. Set aside.

2. In a large skillet, heat the 1/2 cup oil over medium heat. Add bread; cook about 1 minute on each side until browned. Remove bread from skillet and set aside. In the same oil, cook the New Mexico and chile de arbol peppers for 1 minute. Add tomatoes and garlic; cook for 5 minutes more, stirring occasionally. Remove pan from heat and cool mixture slightly.

3. Transfer the tomato mixture, including the oil, to a food processor. Cover and process mixture with several on/off turns. Add almonds and bread; process to make a thick puree. Add vinegar, salt, and the 3 tablespoons olive oil. Process until combined. Serve with Roasted Vegetables (see recipe, right).

Note: For a thicker mixture that can be used as a spread, use two slices of French bread.

**Note:* Because hot chile peppers contain volatile oils that can burn your skin and eyes, avoid direct contact with chiles as much as possible. When working with chile peppers, wear plastic or rubber gloves. If your bare hands do touch the chile peppers, wash your hands well with soap and water.
Per Serving: 141 cal., 14 g fat (2 g sat. fat), 0 mg chol., 139 mg sodium, 4 g carbo., 1 g fiber, 2 g pro.

roasted vegetables with salsa romesco

Let the vegetables steam in a paper bag to loosen the skins and make them easier to peel off.

Prep: 15 minutes   Grill: 15 minutes   Stand: 15 minutes

Makes: 8 to 10 servings

- 4 Japanese eggplants
- 4 red sweet peppers
- 2 sweet onions, quartered
- 2 tablespoons extra virgin olive oil
- 1 tablespoon red wine vinegar
- 2 teaspoons snipped fresh rosemary
  Salsa Romesco (see recipe, left)

1. For a charcoal grill, place vegetables on the grill rack directly over medium coals. Cover and grill eggplants for 10 minutes, turning once. Grill peppers and onions for 15 to 20 minutes or until skin is charred, turning every 5 minutes. (For a gas grill, preheat grill. Reduce heat to medium. Place vegetables on the grill rack over heat. Grill as above.) Place a large paper bag on a tray; put vegetables in bag. Close bag and let stand for 15 minutes.

2. Remove vegetables from the bag; peel off and discard burnt skin. Seed the peppers and cut them into strips. Cut eggplants into chunks and separate onions. Arrange all vegetables on a platter.

3. In a small bowl, combine oil, vinegar, and rosemary; drizzle over vegetables. Serve vegetables with Salsa Romesco.
Per Serving: 320 cal., 27 g fat (3 g sat. fat), 0 mg chol., 247 mg sodium, 18 g carbo., 6 g fiber, 5 g pro.

grilled black bean and
sweet potato quesadillas

grilled black bean and sweet potato quesadillas

Turning over these loaded tortillas on a hot grill can be a bit tricky. For best results, use a wide metal spatula to get underneath the entire tortilla and carefully flip it over.

Prep: 25 minutes   Grill: 7 minutes   Makes: 8 (2-wedge) servings

- 1/2   cup chopped onion
- 2   cloves garlic, minced
- 1   tablespoon olive oil
- 1   15 1/2-ounce can black beans, rinsed and drained
- 1   tablespoon freshly squeezed lime juice
- 1   teaspoon dried oregano, crushed
- 1   teaspoon ground cumin
- 4   10-inch flour tortillas
- 1 1/2   cup mashed cooked sweet potatoes*
- 1   cup shredded Monterey Jack cheese (4 ounces)
- 1 1/2   cups tightly packed baby fresh spinach
- 1/2   to 3/4 cup purchased tomato salsa, corn salsa, and/or guacamole

1. In a large skillet, cook onion and garlic in hot oil until tender. Stir in black beans, lime juice, oregano, and cumin; heat through. Set aside.

2. Place one tortilla each on four large plates. Layer one-fourth of the sweet potatoes, 2 tablespoons of the cheese, one-fourth of the bean mixture, one-fourth of the spinach, and another 2 tablespoons cheese over half of each tortilla. Fold each tortilla over filling, pressing gently.

3. For a charcoal grill, slide quesadillas from plates onto the grill rack directly over low coals. Grill, uncovered, for 3 to 4 minutes or until cheese begins to melt; carefully turn. Grill second side for 4 to 5 minutes or until tortillas are crisp and filling is heated. (For a gas grill, preheat grill. Reduce heat to low. Place quesadillas on the grill rack over heat. Cover and grill as above.)

4. Using a pizza wheel, cut each quesadilla into four wedges. Serve warm with tomato salsa, corn salsa, and/or guacamole.

For mashed sweet potatoes: Wash, peel, and cut off woody portions and ends of about 12 ounces sweet potatoes. Cut into quarters. Cook, covered, in enough boiling salted water to cover for 25 to 30 minutes or until tender. (Or place in a casserole with 1/2 cup water. Microwave, covered, on 100% power [high] for 8 to 10 minutes or until tender, stirring once.) Drain and mash with a potato masher.

Per Serving: 223 cal., 8 g fat (3 g sat. fat), 13 mg chol., 484 mg sodium, 32 g carbo., 5 g fiber, 8 g pro.

calypso shrimp cocktail

Sail right by old-fashioned shrimp cocktail. This breezy lime-and-mint rendition features the zip of cumin, cayenne pepper, and jalapeño pepper. Pictured on page 17.

Prep: 25 minutes   Chill: 30 minutes   Grill: 5 minutes
Makes: 8 servings

- 1   pound fresh or frozen jumbo shrimp with tails
- 3   tablespoons olive oil
- 2   tablespoons snipped fresh mint
- 1/4   teaspoon salt
- 1/8   to 1/4 teaspoon cayenne pepper
- 1/8   teaspoon ground cumin
- 1/4   cup lime juice
- 1   cup yellow and/or red cherry tomatoes, halved and/or quartered
- 2   tablespoons thinly sliced green onion (1)
- 1   fresh jalapeño chile pepper, seeded and finely chopped*
- 6   cups torn mixed salad greens

1. Thaw shrimp, if frozen. Peel and devein shrimp, leaving tails intact if desired. Rinse shrimp; pat dry with paper towels. In a medium bowl, combine shrimp, 1 tablespoon of the oil, 1 tablespoon of the mint, the salt, cayenne pepper, and cumin. Cover and chill for 30 minutes.

2. Meanwhile, in a small bowl, combine remaining 2 tablespoons oil, remaining 1 tablespoon mint, and the lime juice; set aside. In another medium bowl, combine tomatoes, green onion, jalapeño pepper, and a dash *salt*; set aside.

3. Thread shrimp onto metal or wooden** skewers, leaving a 1/4-inch space between shrimp. Transfer skewers to a baking pan. For a charcoal grill, place skewers on the grill rack directly over medium coals. Grill, uncovered, for 5 to 8 minutes or until shrimp turn opaque, turning once halfway through grilling. (For a gas grill, preheat grill. Reduce heat to medium. Place skewers on the grill rack over heat. Cover and grill as above.) Remove shrimp from skewers.

4. Toss tomato mixture and greens together. Divide greens mixture among martini glasses or salad plates. Top with shrimp. Drizzle with lime juice mixture.

Note: Because hot chile peppers, such as jalapeños, contain volatile oils that can burn your skin and eyes, avoid direct contact with chiles as much as possible. When working with chile peppers, wear plastic or rubber gloves. If your bare hands do touch the chile peppers, wash your hands well with soap and water.

**Note:* If using wooden skewers, soak them in water for 30 minutes while the shrimp chills. Drain skewers before using.
Per Serving: 103 cal., 6 g fat (1 g sat. fat), 65 mg chol., 143 mg sodium, 3 g carbo., 1 g fiber, 9 g pro.

grilled yellow peppers with herb-caper sauce

Serve the sweet and smoky grilled peppers with an intriguing caper topper on sourdough bread strips.

Prep: 40 minutes   Grill: 10 minutes   Stand: 10 minutes
Makes: 8 servings

- 4 medium yellow sweet peppers
- 8 large 1/2-inch-thick slices whole wheat or white sourdough peasant bread
- 3 tablespoons olive oil
- 2 cloves garlic, halved
  Herb-Caper Sauce
  Freshly cracked black pepper
  Fresh chive blossoms or garlic chive blossoms (optional)

1. Quarter sweet peppers lengthwise. Remove and discard seeds and membranes. Brush sweet peppers and bread slices with oil. For a charcoal grill, place sweet peppers, cut sides up, on the grill rack directly over medium-hot coals. Grill, uncovered, about 10 minutes or until pepper skins are blistered and dark. (For a gas grill, preheat grill. Reduce heat to medium-high. Place peppers on the grill rack over heat. Cover and grill as above.) Remove sweet peppers from grill. Wrap sweet peppers tightly in foil; let stand for 10 to 15 minutes or until cool enough to handle.

2. Meanwhile, for a charcoal grill, place bread slices on the grill rack directly over medium-hot coals. Grill, uncovered, for 1 to 2 minutes or until golden, turning once halfway through grilling. (For a gas grill, place bread slices on rack over heat. Grill as above.) Rub bread slices with garlic halves; set aside.

3. Unwrap sweet peppers when they are cooled. Using a paring knife, gently pull the skin off sweet peppers. Cut sweet peppers into 1-inch-wide strips. Cut bread into 1-inch-wide strips. Spoon Herb-Caper Sauce onto peppers. Season peppers to taste with black pepper and serve with grilled bread strips. If desired, garnish with chive blossoms.

Herb-Caper Sauce: In a small bowl, combine 1/4 cup olive oil; 4 anchovy fillets, drained and finely chopped; 2 tablespoons snipped fresh parsley; 2 tablespoons finely chopped shallots; 1 tablespoon capers, finely chopped; 1 teaspoon snipped fresh tarragon; 1 teaspoon snipped fresh oregano; 1 teaspoon snipped fresh thyme; and 1 clove garlic, minced. Stir in 1 teaspoon white wine vinegar and dash salt.

Per Serving: 200 cal., 13 g fat (2 g sat. fat), 2 mg chol., 244 mg sodium, 17 g carbo., 3 g fiber, 5 g pro.

cedar-planked brie with peach relish

When fresh peaches are not in their prime, opt for thawed and chopped frozen peach slices.

Prep: 25 minutes   Soak: 1 hour   Cook: 45 minutes
Cool: 1 hour   Grill: 13 minutes   Makes: 12 servings

- 1 15×7×1/2-inch cedar grill plank
- 1 pound peaches, peeled, seeded, and chopped (2 1/2 cups)
- 3/4 cup packed brown sugar
- 3/4 cup cider vinegar
- 1/4 cup golden raisins
- 2 tablespoons finely chopped red onion
- 2 tablespoons finely chopped pickled ginger
- 1 teaspoon chili powder
- 1/4 teaspoon curry powder
- 1 tablespoon pickling spices
- 1 teaspoon mustard seeds
- 1 13- to 15-ounce round Brie cheese
  Grilled bread slices or assorted crackers

1. For at least 1 hour before grilling, soak plank in enough water to cover. Weigh down plank to keep it submerged during soaking. Drain plank.

2. For peach relish, in a medium nonreactive saucepan, combine peaches, brown sugar, vinegar, raisins, onion, ginger, chili powder, and curry powder. Place pickling spices and mustard seeds on a 6-inch square of 100%-cotton cheesecloth, bring up corners, and tie with clean 100%-cotton kitchen string (or place spices and seeds in a tea ball); add to mixture in saucepan. Bring peach mixture to boiling; reduce heat. Simmer, uncovered, stirring frequently, about 45 minutes or until thickened. Remove from heat and cool for 1 to 2 hours. Remove and discard spice bag.

3. For a charcoal grill, place the plank on the grill rack directly over medium coals until it begins to char and pop (about 3 to 5 minutes). Turn plank over. Place Brie on charred side of plank. Cover grill and cook for 10 to 12 minutes or until Brie softens and sides just begin to droop. (For a gas grill, preheat grill. Reduce heat to medium. Place plank on grill rack. Cover and grill as above.)

4. Serve Brie on plank. Serve with grilled bread slices or crackers and peach relish.

Per Serving: 188 cal., 8 g fat (5 g sat. fat), 31 mg chol., 204 mg sodium, 21 g carbo., 1 g fiber, 7 g pro.

cedar-planked brie
with peach relish

grilled cherry tomatoes with garlic

If your oven is heated up but your grill is not, bake these juicy bites at 350°F for 4 to 5 minutes or until they are heated through.
Prep: 20 minutes Grill: 4 minutes Makes: 12 servings

24	cherry tomatoes, 1 to 1¹/₂ inches in diameter
4	cloves garlic, cut into slivers
1	tablespoon olive oil
1	teaspoon snipped fresh rosemary or parsley
1	teaspoon sugar
¹/₄	teaspoon salt, coarse sea salt, or kosher salt

1. Remove stems, if necessary, from tomatoes. Using the tip of a sharp knife, pierce tomatoes. Carefully insert a sliver of garlic into each tomato.

2. Place tomatoes in the center of an 18×12-inch piece of foil. Drizzle tomatoes with olive oil; sprinkle with rosemary, sugar, and ¹/₄ teaspoon salt. Bring together the two long sides of the foil and seal with a double fold. Fold remaining edges together to completely enclose tomatoes.

3. For a charcoal grill, place tomatoes on the grill rack directly over medium coals. Grill, uncovered, for 4 to 5 minutes or until heated through. (For gas grill, preheat grill. Reduce heat to medium. Place tomatoes on the grill rack over heat. Cover and grill as above.)

4. To serve, carefully open hot, steamy foil packet. Transfer tomatoes to serving plate or platter. Sprinkle with additional salt.
Per Serving: 55 cal., 3 g fat (1 g sat. fat), 5 mg chol., 103 mg sodium, 5 g carbo., 1 g fiber, 2 g pro.

tomato-brie potato skins

A savvy cook never lets food go to waste. In this case, after you scoop out the potato flesh, mash it with a little milk, butter, and salt. Serve the mashed potatoes alongside your favorite grilled meat.
Prep: 30 minutes Grill: 25 minutes Makes: 10 servings

5	4- to 6-ounce potatoes and/or sweet potatoes
1	tablespoon olive oil
1	clove garlic, minced
1	4¹/₂-ounce round Brie cheese, cut into ¹/₂-inch pieces
1	cup cherry tomatoes, quartered
¹/₄	cup walnuts, toasted and chopped
¹/₄	cup snipped fresh Italian (flat-leaf) parsley
¹/₈	to ¹/₄ teaspoon crushed red pepper

1. Scrub potatoes; cut each potato in half lengthwise. In a small bowl, combine the oil, garlic, and ¹/₄ teaspoon *salt*. Brush cut surfaces of the potatoes with the oil mixture.

2. For a charcoal grill, place potatoes, cut sides down, on the grill rack directly over medium coals. Grill, uncovered, for 20 to 25 minutes or until tender, turning once halfway through grilling. (For a gas grill, preheat grill. Reduce heat to medium. Place potatoes, cut sides down, on the grill rack over heat. Cover and grill as above.)

3. Carefully scoop out the inside of each potato half, leaving a ¹/₂-inch-thick shell (reserve scooped-out potato flesh for another use). In a medium bowl, combine Brie pieces, cherry tomatoes, walnuts, parsley, and crushed red pepper. Spoon mixture into potato shells. Return potato shells, filled sides up, to grill; grill 5 to 7 minutes more or until cheese is softened and filling is heated through.
Per Serving: 111 cal., 7 g fat (3 g sat. fat), 13 mg chol., 85 mg sodium, 9 g carbo., 1 g fiber, 4 g pro.

tomato-brie potato skins

eggplant dip

eggplant dip

Prep: 45 minutes   Grill: 13 minutes
Makes: about 20 (¹⁄₄-cup) servings

1	bulb garlic (about 15 cloves)
¹⁄₂	cup extra virgin olive oil
2	1-pound eggplants, sliced ³⁄₄ inch thick
2	medium red sweet peppers, seeded and quartered lengthwise
1	teaspoon salt
¹⁄₃	cup lemon juice
¹⁄₄	cup snipped fresh Italian (flat-leaf) parsley
2	tablespoons snipped fresh oregano
	Oregano leaves (optional)
	Purchased flatbreads, broken

1. Using a sharp knife, cut off about ¹⁄₂ inch from top of the bulb to expose the ends of the individual cloves. Leaving the garlic bulb whole, remove any loose, papery layers. Fold a 20×12-inch piece of heavy foil in half crosswise. Place garlic bulb, cut end up, in center of foil; drizzle with 1 tablespoon of the olive oil. Bring up opposite edges of foil and seal with a double fold. Fold remaining edges together to completely enclose garlic, leaving space for steam to build.

2. Drizzle ¹⁄₄ cup olive oil over eggplant slices and red sweet peppers and sprinkle with salt; toss to coat. For a charcoal grill, place garlic packet on the grill rack directly over medium coals. Grill, uncovered, for 5 minutes. Add eggplant and pepper slices to grill. Grill for 8 to 10 minutes more or until garlic cloves are soft when pressed, eggplant is tender, and peppers are tender and lightly charred, turning garlic packet and eggplant and peppers once halfway through grilling time. (For a gas grill, preheat grill. Reduce heat to medium. Place garlic packet, eggplant, and pepper slices on grill rack over heat. Cover and grill as above.)

3. Coarsely chop eggplant and pepper slices; transfer to a large glass bowl. Squeeze garlic pulp from cloves into a small bowl; use a potato masher to mash the pulp. Add remaining 3 tablespoons oil and lemon juice to garlic; whisk to combine. Add garlic mixture, parsley, and snipped oregano to eggplant mixture; toss to combine.

4. Serve immediately or let mixture stand, covered, up to 1 hour before serving. Or cover and chill mixture up to 3 days; let stand at room temperature 30 minutes before serving. If desired, garnish with oregano leaves. Serve with flatbread pieces.

Per Serving: 111 cal., 6 g fat (1 g sat. fat), 0 mg chol., 199 mg sodium, 13 g carbo., 2 g fiber, 2 g pro.

creamy apricot and onion dip

To make the fruit wedges easier to turn on the grill, thread a few of them onto two side-by-side skewers, leaving space between each piece.

Prep: 15 minutes Grill: 14 minutes Cool: 10 minutes
Makes: 12 (1/4-cup) servings

- 4 apricots or 2 nectarines (about 3/4 pound), pitted and each cut into 8 wedges
- 2 teaspoons olive oil
- 3/4 teaspoon chili powder
- 1 large sweet onion, cut into 1/2-inch-thick slices
- 3/4 cup dairy sour cream
- 1/3 cup mayonnaise
- 1/2 teaspoon salt
- 1/8 teaspoon ground coriander
- 1/8 teaspoon cayenne pepper
  Baguette slices
- 2 tablespoons snipped fresh chives (optional)

1. In a medium bowl, toss apricot wedges with 1 teaspoon of the oil and the chili powder to coat. Brush the onion slices with the remaining 1 teaspoon oil.

2. For a charcoal grill, place apricot wedges on the grill rack directly over medium coals. Grill, uncovered, for 3 to 4 minutes per side or until apricots have grill marks and are tender but still hold their shape. Grill the onion slices, uncovered, for 7 to 8 minutes per side or until they have grill marks and are tender. (For a gas grill, preheat grill. Reduce heat to medium. Place apricots and onions on the grill rack over heat. Cover and grill as above.) Transfer apricots and onion slices to a cutting board and cool for 10 minutes.

3. Meanwhile, in a medium bowl, combine the sour cream, mayonnaise, salt, coriander, and cayenne pepper. When the apricots and onion are cool, chop onion into small pieces and stir onion pieces into the sour cream mixture. Coarsely chop apricots and spoon over dip. Stir apricots into dip just before serving. Serve immediately, or for more flavor, cover and chill dip at least 1 hour. Serve with baguette slices sprinkled with chives, if desired.

Per Serving: 86 cal., 8 g fat (3 g sat. fat), 7 mg chol., 138 mg sodium, 3 g carbo., 0 g fiber, 1 g pro.

dijon pork skewers with apple-apricot chutney

The crisp texture and lively flavor of tart apples, such as Granny Smith apples, make the Apple-Apricot Chutney a tangy-sweet partner for the cider-splashed pork.

Prep: 45 minutes Grill: 6 minutes Makes: 18 to 20 servings

- 3 tablespoons apple cider or apple juice
- 2 tablespoons Dijon-style mustard
- 1/2 teaspoon dried thyme, crushed
- 1 1/4 pounds boneless pork loin
  Apple-Apricot Chutney

1. In a small bowl, stir together apple cider, mustard, and thyme; set aside. Trim fat from pork. Cut pork across the grain into thin slices; cut slices into strips about 1 inch wide. Loosely thread two pork strips, accordion-style, onto each of 18 to 20 skewers.* Transfer skewers to a baking pan. Brush the mustard mixture on all sides of pork.

2. For a charcoal grill, place skewers on the grill rack directly over medium-hot coals. Grill, uncovered, for 6 to 8 minutes or until pork is cooked through, turning once. (For a gas grill, preheat grill. Reduce heat to medium-high. Place skewers on the grill rack over heat. Cover and grill as above.)

3. To serve, transfer skewers to a serving platter; serve with Apple-Apricot Chutney.

Apple-Apricot Chutney: In a medium saucepan, stir together 1/2 cup packed brown sugar; 1/4 cup white wine vinegar; 1 small clove garlic, minced; 1/2 teaspoon grated fresh ginger; and 1/4 teaspoon ground cinnamon. Stir in 2 cups peeled, cored, chopped tart cooking apples (about 2 medium); 1/2 cup snipped dried apricots; and 1/4 cup chopped onion. Bring to boiling; reduce heat. Cover; simmer 10 minutes. Uncover and boil gently about 15 minutes more or until only a small amount of liquid remains. Remove from heat. Cool slightly. To serve immediatly, transfer to a bowl. (Or to store, transfer to an air-tight container. Cover and chill for up to 2 days; let stand at room temperature for 30 minutes before serving.)

Note: If using wooden skewers, soak them in water for 30 minutes before grilling. Drain skewers before using.

Per Serving: 83 cal., 1 g fat (0 g sat. fat), 20 mg chol., 57 mg sodium, 11 g carbo., 1 g fiber, 7 g pro.

In the dog days of summer, a couple of hearty grilled appetizers make a great meal.

toasty breads

Next time you need something toasty to fill out your grilled dinner, think outside the ordinary bread box. Reach beyond basic dinner rolls and grab a loaf of Italian ciabatta, a French baguette, or soft breadsticks. With a few tasty stir-together ingredients, you can whip up a spread to slather between slices or to brush over the outside. Once you dress up the bread, grill it over fiery coals to create a toasty crust on the outside and oozing yummy goodness on the inside.

cheesy garlic bread on a stick
(recipe, page 31)

cheddar-bacon loaf

parmesan-pesto bread

A cupful of Parmigiano-Reggiano gives this grilled bread a cheesy gusto.

Prep: 15 minutes   Grill: 12 minutes   Makes: 12 servings

1	16-ounce loaf ciabatta or Italian bread
1/4	cup extra virgin olive oil
1/2	cup purchased basil pesto
4	ounces Parmigiano-Reggiano cheese, grated (about 1 cup)

1. Using a serrated knife, slice bread in half horizontally. Brush cut surfaces with olive oil. Spread pesto on bottom half of bread; sprinkle with cheese. Replace top half of loaf. Wrap loaf tightly in heavy foil.

2. For a charcoal grill, place loaf on the grill rack directly over medium-low coals. Grill, uncovered, about 12 minutes or until heated through, turning once. (For a gas grill, preheat grill. Reduce heat to medium-low. Place loaf on grill rack over heat. Cover and grill as above.)

Per Serving: 233 cal., 13 g fat (4 g sat. fat), 12 mg chol., 459 mg sodium, 21 g carbo., 1 g fiber, 8 g pro.

parmesan-pesto bread

cheddar-bacon loaf

Besides being rich and buttery, this cheesy loaf gets a tangy boost from a smidgen of mustard.

Prep: 10 minutes   Grill: 10 minutes   Makes: 12 servings

1	16-ounce loaf baguette-style French bread
1/2	cup butter, softened
1	cup shredded sharp cheddar cheese (4 ounces)
6	slices bacon, crisp-cooked, drained, and crumbled
1/4	cup sliced green onions (2)
2	teaspoons yellow mustard
1	teaspoon freshly squeezed lemon juice

1. Using a serrated knife, cut bread crosswise into 1-inch slices, cutting to but not through the bottom crust.

2. In a small bowl, stir together butter, cheese, bacon, onions, mustard, and lemon juice. Spread mixture on both sides of each bread slice. Wrap loaf tightly in heavy foil.

3. For a charcoal grill, place loaf on the grill rack directly over medium coals. Grill, uncovered, about 10 minutes or until cheese melts and bread is heated through, turning once. (For a gas grill, preheat grill. Reduce heat to medium. Place loaf on the grill rack over heat. Cover and grill as above.)

Per Serving: 238 cal., 13 g fat (8 g sat. fat), 35 mg chol., 461 mg sodium, 22 g carbo., 1 g fiber, 10 g pro.

cheesy garlic bread on a stick

Cubes of bread drizzled with garlic butter and tossed in Asiago cheese make a fun presentation when threaded on skewers and grilled to golden perfection. Pictured on page 29.

Prep: 20 minutes   Grill: 5 minutes   Makes: 6 to 8 servings

1/4	cup olive oil
1/4	cup butter
3	cloves garlic, minced
1	16-ounce loaf baguette-style French bread
1/3	cup freshly grated Asiago cheese

1. In a small saucepan, combine olive oil, butter, and garlic. Cook and stir over low heat until butter melts.

2. Using a serrated knife, cut bread into 1½-inch cubes. Place bread cubes in an extra-large bowl. Drizzle garlic mixture over bread cubes; toss to coat. Sprinkle with Asiago; toss to coat. Thread bread cubes on six to eight 10-inch skewers.* Transfer skewers to a baking pan.

3. For a charcoal grill, place skewers on the grill rack directly over medium coals. Grill, uncovered, for 5 to 10 minutes, turning often to brown evenly. (For a gas grill, preheat grill. Reduce heat to medium. Place skewers on the grill rack over heat. Cover and grill as above.) Serve immediately.

*Note: If using wooden skewers, soak them in water for at least 30 minutes before grilling. Drain skewers before using.

Per Serving: 392 cal., 20 g fat (8 g sat. fat), 26 mg chol., 614 mg sodium, 43 g carbo., 2 g fiber, 13 g pro.

toasted bread with creamy garlic spread

If you don't have fresh herbs on hand, substitute a pinch each of crushed dried thyme and rosemary.

Prep: 15 minutes   Grill: 32 minutes   Makes: 24 servings

1	bulb garlic (about 15 cloves)
1	tablespoon olive oil
1	12- to 16-ounce loaf baguette-style French bread
1/4	cup butter, softened
1	3-ounce package cream cheese, softened
1/2	teaspoon snipped fresh thyme
1/2	teaspoon snipped fresh rosemary

1. Using a sharp knife, cut off the top 1/2 inch of the garlic bulb to expose the ends of the individual cloves. Leaving the garlic bulb whole, remove any loose, papery outer layers.

2. Fold a 20×12-inch piece of heavy foil in half crosswise. Place garlic bulb, cut end up, in center of foil. Drizzle garlic with olive oil. Bring up opposite edges of foil and seal with a double fold. Fold remaining edges together to completely enclose garlic, leaving space for steam to build.

3. For a charcoal grill, arrange preheated coals around edge of grill. Test for medium heat. Place garlic on the grill rack in center of grill. Grill, covered, about 30 minutes or until garlic feels soft when packet is squeezed. (For a gas grill, preheat grill. Reduce heat to medium. Adjust heat for indirect cooking. Cover and grill as above.)

4. Using a serrated knife, cut bread into 1/2- to 3/4-inch slices. Grill bread slices directly over medium coals for 2 to 3 minutes or until golden, turning once halfway through grilling.

5. Let garlic cool before removing foil. For spread, squeeze garlic pulp from cloves into a small bowl. Stir in butter, cream cheese, thyme, and rosemary. Serve spread with grilled bread slices.

Per Serving: 78 cal., 4 g fat (2 g sat. fat), 9 mg chol., 117 mg sodium, 9 g carbo., 0 g fiber, 2 g pro.

In whatever form, bread and butter make a perfect serve-along for any grilled meat.

brandied blue cheese bread

If you find a bottle of brandy in your cupboard, add a splash. If not, the bread will still possess a wonderful blue cheese flavor without it.

Prep: 15 minutes   Grill: 10 minutes   Makes: 12 servings

1	12- to 16-ounce baguette-style French bread
1/2	cup butter, softened
1/2	cup crumbled blue cheese (2 ounces)
1	tablespoon brandy (optional)
1	tablespoon snipped fresh chives
1/8	teaspoon cayenne pepper

1. Using a serrated knife, cut bread diagonally into 1-inch slices, cutting to but not through the bottom crust.

2. In a small bowl, stir together butter, blue cheese, brandy (if using), chives, and cayenne pepper. Spread butter mixture between slices of bread. Wrap loaf tightly in heavy foil.

3. For a charcoal grill, place loaf on the grill rack directly over medium coals. Grill, uncovered, for 10 to 12 minutes or until bread is hot and cheese melts, turning occasionally. (For a gas grill, preheat grill. Reduce heat to medium. Place loaf on the grill rack over heat. Cover and grill as above.)

Per Serving: 166 cal., 10 g fat (6 g sat. fat), 24 mg chol., 305 mg sodium, 16 g carbo., 1 g fiber, 5 g pro.

italian breadsticks

Grilling breadsticks directly over the coals imbues them with a rustic flavor similar to that given by a brick oven.

Prep: 10 minutes   Grill: 2 minutes   Makes: 8 breadsticks

1/2	cup grated Parmesan cheese
1¼	teaspoons dried Italian seasoning, crushed
1/4	teaspoon crushed red pepper
8	purchased soft breadsticks
3	tablespoons butter, melted

1. In a shallow dish, combine Parmesan cheese, Italian seasoning, and red pepper. Brush each breadstick with melted butter and roll it in the Parmesan mixture to coat.

2. For a charcoal grill, place breadsticks on the grill rack directly over medium coals. Grill, uncovered, for 2 to 3 minutes or until golden, turning occasionally to brown evenly. (For a gas grill, preheat grill. Reduce heat to medium. Grill breadsticks on the grill rack over heat. Cover and grill as above.) Serve warm.

Per Breadstick: 194 cal., 7 g fat (4 g sat. fat), 16 mg chol., 430 mg sodium, 25 g carbo., 1 g fiber, 7 g pro.

toasted bread with creamy garlic spread

fire-baked flatbreads

Crisp, toasty flatbreads, topped with savory vegetables and cheeses or fresh summer fruit, grace the grill with the makings for meltingly magnificent light suppers, sides, or desserts.

grilled flatbreads

Prep: 45 minutes   Rise: 45 minutes   Grill: 5 minutes
Makes: 4 flatbreads

1¼	cups warm water (105°F to 115°F)
2	tablespoons olive oil
1	package active dry yeast
1	teaspoon sugar
3¼	to 3¾ cups all-purpose flour
1	teaspoon salt
	Cornmeal
	Olive oil (optional)

1. In a medium bowl, combine the warm water, the 2 tablespoons oil, the yeast, and sugar. Stir to dissolve yeast. Let stand about 10 minutes or until foamy.

2. Meanwhile, in a large bowl, combine 3 cups of the flour and the salt. Stir yeast mixture into flour mixture until combined. Stir in as much of the remaining flour as you can.

3. Turn dough out onto a lightly floured surface. Knead in enough of the remaining flour to make a soft dough that is smooth but slightly sticky (about 5 minutes total).

4. Place dough in an oiled bowl, turning once to grease surface of dough. Cover and let rise in a warm place until double in size (about 45 minutes).

5. Punch dough down. Turn dough out onto a lightly floured surface. Divide dough into four equal portions. Cover and let rest for 10 minutes. Roll each portion into a 10-inch circle. (It's okay if shapes are irregular; this adds to the rustic charm.) Prepare and grill one flatbread at a time, or stack and store dough rounds until ready to use.*

6. Sprinkle a baking sheet or pizza peel with cornmeal. Place a dough round on the baking sheet or peel. (When the baking sheet or peel is moved back and forth, the dough should move freely.)

7. For a charcoal grill, use the baking sheet or peel to transfer the dough round to the grill rack directly over medium coals (or gently pick up the dough and carefully place it on the grill rack). Grill, uncovered, about 3 minutes or until the bottom is lightly browned. (For a gas grill, preheat grill. Reduce heat to medium. Place dough round on grill rack over heat. Cover and grill as directed above.) Using wide spatulas, remove the flatbread from grill. Turn flatbread over; return to baking sheet or peel. If desired, brush flatbread lightly with additional oil. Add desired topping (see following recipes).

8. Return flatbread to the grill. Cover and grill for 2 to 3 minutes more or until bottom of flatbread is lightly browned and desired topping is heated through. Repeat with the remaining flatbreads.

To make ahead: Place one dough round on a baking sheet sprinkled lightly with cornmeal. Sprinkle top lightly with cornmeal and top with parchment paper. Continue stacking flatbreads, sprinkling each with cornmeal and topping with parchment paper. Cover stack with plastic wrap or foil and chill for up to 4 hours.

bacon-onion topping

Start to Finish: 25 minutes   Makes: 6 appetizer servings

2	slices bacon
1	large Vidalia or other sweet onion, thinly sliced (about 1½ cups)
⅓	cup crumbled blue cheese
	Fresh thyme leaves

1. In a large skillet, cook bacon over medium heat until crisp. Drain bacon on paper towels, reserving drippings in the skillet. Crumble bacon; set aside.

2. Add onion to reserved drippings. Cook for 15 to 20 minutes or until onion is very tender and golden brown, stirring occasionally.

3. Arrange onion on browned side of a flatbread (see Grilled Flatbreads, *left*). Sprinkle with blue cheese and bacon before returning flatbread to the grill. Sprinkle with thyme before serving. Cut into wedges.

Per Serving (including flatbread): 186 cal., 9 g fat (3 g sat. fat), 14 mg chol., 314 mg sodium, 20 g carbo., 1 g fiber, 4 g pro.

bacon-onion topping

cheesy roasted garlic topping

cheesy roasted garlic topping

Prep: 10 minutes   Roast: 25 minutes   Oven: 425°F
Makes: 6 appetizer servings

- 1   whole garlic bulb
- 2   teaspoons olive oil
- 3   ounces provolone cheese, shredded (³/₄ cup)
      Snipped fresh flat-leaf parsley

1. Preheat oven to 425°F. With a sharp knife, cut off the top ¹/₂ inch of the garlic bulb to expose the ends of the individual cloves. Leaving garlic bulb whole, remove any loose, papery outer layers. Place the garlic bulb, cut end up, in a custard cup. Drizzle with 1 teaspoon of the oil. Cover with foil and roast in preheated oven for 25 to 35 minutes or until garlic feels soft when pressed. When cool enough to handle, squeeze out the garlic pulp from individual cloves. If desired, cover and chill garlic pulp for up to 3 days.

2. Spread garlic pulp over browned side of a flatbread (see Grilled Flatbreads, *page 35*). Drizzle with the remaining 1 teaspoon oil and sprinkle with cheese before returning flatbread to the grill. Sprinkle with parsley before serving. Cut into wedges.

Per Serving (including flatbread): 150 cal., 7 g fat (3 g sat. fat), 10 mg chol., 224 mg sodium, 17 g carbo., 1 g fiber, 5 g pro.

herbed margherita topping

With just a few easy-to-find ingredients, this simple yet sophisticated grilled bread topper is a true favorite.

Start to Finish: 15 minutes   Makes: 6 appetizer servings

- ¹/₂   of a 4- to 5.2-ounce container semisoft cheese with garlic and herbs
- 1   medium roma tomato, thinly sliced
- ¹/₂   cup cherry, teardrop, and/or grape tomatoes, halved or quartered
- 1   tablespoon olive oil
       Fresh small basil leaves

1. Spread cheese over browned side of a flatbread (see Grilled Flatbreads, *page 35*). Top with tomatoes and drizzle with oil before returning flatbread to the grill. Sprinkle with basil before serving. Cut into wedges.

Per Serving (including flatbread): 140 cal., 7 g fat (3 g sat. fat), 9 mg chol., 100 mg sodium, 16 g carbo., 1 g fiber, 3 g pro.

herbed margherita topping

*balsamic-glazed cremini
and goat cheese topping*

grilled plum dessert topping

balsamic-glazed cremini and goat cheese topping

Start to Finish: 20 minutes   Makes: 6 appetizer servings

- 1   tablespoon olive oil
- 2   cups sliced fresh cremini mushrooms
- 1/4 teaspoon salt
- 1/4 teaspoon ground black pepper
- 2   tablespoons balsamic vinegar
- 1/3 cup crumbled goat cheese (chèvre)
- 1   tablespoon snipped fresh marjoram

1. In a large skillet, heat oil over medium heat. Add mushrooms; cook until tender, stirring occasionally. Sprinkle with salt and pepper. Stir in balsamic vinegar. Cook, uncovered, until vinegar evaporates, stirring occasionally. If desired, cover and chill cooked mushrooms for up to 3 days.

2. Spread cooked mushrooms over browned side of a flatbread (see Grilled Flatbreads, *page 35*). Sprinkle with cheese before returning flatbread to the grill. Sprinkle with marjoram before serving. Cut into wedges.

Per Serving (including flatbread): 138 cal., 6 g fat (2 g sat. fat), 7 mg chol., 220 mg sodium, 16 g carbo., 1 g fiber, 4 g pro.

grilled plum dessert topping

Sweet, tender plums are great for grilling. They stand up regally to high heat, and their flavor is magnified when heated.

Start to Finish: 20 minutes   Makes: 6 dessert servings

- 2   medium plums, halved lengthwise and pitted
- 1/4 cup mascarpone cheese
- 1   tablespoon honey
- 2   tablespoons sliced almonds, toasted
- 1   tablespoon crystallized ginger
       Honey (optional)

1. For a charcoal grill, place plums, cut sides down, on the grill rack directly over medium-hot coals. Grill, uncovered, for 5 to 8 minutes or until plums are tender and lightly browned. (For a gas grill, preheat grill. Reduce heat to medium-high. Place plums on grill rack over heat. Cover and grill as above.) Slice plums when they are cool enough to handle.

2. In a small bowl, combine mascarpone cheese and the 1 tablespoon honey. Spread mascarpone mixture over browned side of a flatbread (see Grilled Flatbreads, *page 35*). Add plums and sprinkle with almonds and ginger before returning flatbread to the grill. If desired, drizzle with additional honey before serving. Cut into wedges.

Per Serving (including flatbread): 158 cal., 7 g fat (3 g sat. fat), 12 mg chol., 104 mg sodium, 22 g carbo., 1 g fiber, 3 g pro.

grill kings

Through the years, thick, juicy steaks and chops have reigned as kings of the cuts to cook over an open flame. A hot sear to the outside locks tenderness and flavor inside a steak or chop, resulting in a taste sensation fit for royalty. Though just fine with a sprinkling of salt and pepper, steaks and chops become sensational with the royal treatment of a marinade, sauce, or condiment. Whether you choose beef, pork, or lamb, there's a recipe here that may become the specialty of your castle.

ribeyes with summer salsa
(recipe, page 43)

three-herb steaks

three-herb steaks

Any steak benefits from this recipe's summery fresh herb rub. Try it on T-bone, sirloin, and ribeye steaks, too.

Prep: 20 minutes Chill: 1 hour Grill: 15 minutes
Stand: 10 minutes Makes: 6 servings

- $1/2$ cup snipped fresh parsley
- $1/4$ cup olive oil
- $1/4$ cup snipped fresh basil
- 1   tablespoon snipped fresh oregano
- 1   to 2 tablespoons cracked black pepper
- $1/2$ teaspoon salt
- 2   beef top loin steaks, cut $1^{1}/_{2}$ inches thick
- 2   medium red or yellow sweet peppers cut into $1/2$-inch rings, seeds removed
- 1   tablespoon olive oil
    Salt
    Ground black pepper

1. For rub, in a small bowl, combine parsley, $1/4$ cup olive oil, basil, oregano, cracked black pepper, and $1/2$ teaspoon salt. Trim fat from meat. Using half of the rub mixture, sprinkle rub on both sides of each steak; rub in with your fingers. Cover and chill steaks for 1 hour. Meanwhile, brush pepper rings with 1 tablespoon olive oil. Season lightly with salt and black pepper.

2. For a charcoal grill, place steaks on the grill rack directly over medium coals. Grill, uncovered, until steaks reach desired doneness, turning once. Allow 15 to 19 minutes for medium rare (145°F) or 18 to 23 minutes for medium (160°F). Grill pepper rings next to the steaks the last 8 to 10 minutes of grilling, or until peppers are tender, turning once. (For a gas grill, preheat grill. Reduce heat to medium. Place steaks on grill rack over heat. Cover and grill steak and peppers as above.) Remove steaks from grill and sprinkle with remaining herb mixture. Cover and let stand for 10 minutes.

3. To serve, slice steaks across the grain. Serve with sweet peppers.
Per Serving: 307 cal., 19 g fat (5 g sat. fat), 77 mg chol., 313 mg sodium, 3 g carbo., 1 g fiber, 29 g pro.

ribeyes with summer salsa

With its chili powder rub and fresh salsa, this Tex-Mex-inspired dish is reminiscent of **carne asada**. *If you wish, slice the steak and wrap it and some salsa in warmed flour tortillas. Pictured on page 41.*

Prep: 25 minutes   Chill: 2 hours   Grill: 10 minutes
Stand: 10 minutes   Makes: 8 servings

1	pound tomatoes, seeded and chopped
1/2	cup chopped red onion
1/4	cup snipped fresh parsley
2	tablespoons lime juice
2	cloves garlic, minced
1	to 2 serrano chile peppers, seeded and minced*
1/4	teaspoon salt
1/4	cup ancho chili powder
2	tablespoons paprika
6	cloves garlic, minced
1	teaspoon salt
1	teaspoon coarsely ground black pepper
2	tablespoon olive oil
4	10- to 12-ounce beef ribeye steaks, cut 1 inch thick
	Snipped fresh parsley

1. For salsa, in a medium bowl, combine tomatoes, onion, 1/4 cup parsley, lime juice, 2 cloves garlic, serrano peppers, and 1/4 teaspoon salt. Cover and chill salsa for 2 hours.

2. For rub, in a small bowl, combine ancho chili powder, paprika, 6 cloves garlic, 1 teaspoon salt, and pepper. Stir in olive oil to make a paste that clings to meat. Trim fat from meat. Coat both sides of each steak with spice rub; rub in with your fingers. Cover and chill steaks for 1 hour.

3. For a charcoal grill, place steaks on the grill rack directly over medium coals. Grill, uncovered, until steaks reach desired doneness, turning once halfway through grilling. Allow 10 to 12 minutes for medium rare (145°F) or 12 to 15 minutes for medium (160°F). (For a gas grill, preheat grill. Reduce heat to medium. Place meat on the grill rack over heat. Cover and grill as above.)

4. Allow meat to stand 10 minutes before serving. Sprinkle with parsley and serve with salsa.

Note: Because hot chile peppers, such as serranos, contain volatile oils that can burn your skin and eyes, avoid direct contact with chiles as much as possible. When working with chile peppers, wear plastic or rubber gloves. If your bare hands do touch the chile peppers, wash your hands well with soap and water.
Per Serving: 310 cal., 16 g fat (5 g sat. fat), 83 mg chol., 490 mg sodium, 10 g carbo., 5 g fiber, 31 g pro.

steaks with nectarines

Juicy nectarines, tossed with a sweet-hot spice blend, sear on the grill alongside the steaks. The taste sensation explodes when the roasted fruit and juicy steaks meet crispy smoked bacon.

Prep: 20 minutes   Grill: 12 minutes   Makes: 4 servings

4	6- to 8-ounce boneless beef ribeye steaks, cut 1/2 inch thick
1	tablespoon sugar
1	to 1 1/2 teaspoons chili powder
1 1/2	teaspoons salt
1	teaspoon ground cumin
1/2	teaspoon freshly ground black pepper
1/8	to 1/4 teaspoon cayenne pepper
2	medium firm but ripe nectarines, pitted and cut into 8 wedges each
2	teaspoons water
4	slices bacon, preferably hickory-smoked

1. Trim fat from steaks. In a small bowl, combine sugar, chili powder, salt, cumin, black pepper, and cayenne pepper; reserve 1 teaspoon of the mixture. Sprinkle remaining spice mixture evenly over both sides of each steak; rub in with your fingers. Set aside. In a medium bowl, combine the nectarines, the reserved 1 teaspoon spice mixture, and the water; toss to coat. Set aside.

2. For a charcoal grill, place bacon slices in a large cast-iron skillet. Place skillet on the grill rack directly over medium coals. Grill, uncovered, for 8 to 10 minutes or until bacon is crisp-cooked and browned, turning very frequently. Carefully remove skillet from grill. Remove bacon from skillet and drain on paper towels.

3. Place steaks on the grill rack directly over the coals. Grill, uncovered, until steaks reach desired doneness, turning once halfway through grilling. Allow 4 to 6 minutes for medium rare (145°F) or 5 to 7 minutes for medium (160°F). Place nectarine wedges directly on grill rack alongside the steaks the last 3 to 5 minutes of grilling or until nectarines are lightly browned and warmed through, turning often. (For a gas grill, preheat grill. Reduce heat to medium. Cover and grill bacon, steaks, and nectarines as above.)

4. Transfer steaks to dinner plates and top each with a slice of bacon and four nectarine wedges.
Per Serving: 353 cal., 17 g fat (6 g sat. fat), 108 mg chol., 1,155 mg sodium, 11 g carbo., 1 g fiber, 38 g pro.

sausage-and-pepper-
smothered steak

bacon-wrapped tenderloin

Bison is a lean, tender option to beef steak. If you are lucky enough to have a bison vendor in your area, give it a try.

Prep: 25 minutes Marinate: 2 hours Grill: 10 minutes
Makes: 4 servings

4	beef tenderloin steaks or bison ribeyes, cut 1 inch thick (8 to 10 ounces each)
1/4	cup soy sauce
2	tablespoons olive oil
2	tablespoons ketchup
2	teaspoons snipped fresh thyme
1	clove garlic, minced
1/4	teaspoon dry mustard
4	teaspoons steak seasoning
8	slices hickory-smoked bacon, partially cooked
	Oven-Roasted Fingerling Potatoes
	Blue cheese dip or blue cheese salad dressing
1	large green onion, thinly bias-sliced
	Fresh thyme or oregano sprigs (optional)
	Steak seasoning (optional)
	Steak sauce (optional)

1. Trim fat from steaks. (If using bison, trim silver skin from steaks.) Place steaks in a heavy resealable plastic bag set in a shallow dish.

2. For marinade, in a small bowl, combine soy sauce, olive oil, ketchup, snipped thyme, garlic, and dry mustard. Pour over steaks; seal bag. Marinate in the refrigerator for 2 to 4 hours, turning bag occasionally. Drain meat, discarding marinade.

3. Sprinkle some of the 4 teaspoons steak seasoning over both sides of each steak; rub in with your fingers. Wrap the edge of each steak with two slices of partially cooked bacon, securing the ends with wooden toothpicks.

4. For a charcoal grill, place steaks on the grill rack directly over medium coals. Grill, uncovered, until steaks reach desired doneness, turning once halfway through grilling. Allow 10 to 12 minutes for medium rare (145°F) or 12 to 15 minutes for medium (160°F). (For a gas grill, preheat grill. Reduce heat to medium. Place steaks on the grill rack over heat. Cover and grill as above.) Before serving, discard toothpicks.

5. Serve steaks with the Oven-Roasted Fingerling Potatoes. Top potatoes with blue cheese dip or dressing and green onion. If desired, garnish steaks with thyme or oregano sprigs and serve with additional steak seasoning and steak sauce.

Oven-Roasted Fingerling Potatoes: Preheat oven to 450°F. In a greased 9×9×2-inch baking pan, place 12 fingerling potatoes (small, long, and finger-shape potatoes), halved, or 12 tiny new potatoes (about 1 pound), halved. In a small bowl, combine 2 tablespoons herb oil or olive oil and 2 teaspoons steak seasoning. Drizzle mixture over potatoes, tossing to coat. Roast in the preheated oven for 25 to 30 minutes or until potatoes are tender and browned on the edges, stirring once.

Per Serving: 552 cal., 24 g fat (7 g sat. fat), 164 mg chol., 2,136 mg sodium, 22 g carbo., 2 g fiber, 59 g pro.

sausage-and-pepper-smothered steak

Top a simple flank steak with a sassy combo of hearty onions, spicy sausage, and colorful sweet peppers, and you have a real yum factor.

Prep: 30 minutes Chill: 1 hour Grill: 17 minutes
Makes: 6 to 8 servings

1	2-pound beef flank steak
	Salt
	Freshly ground black pepper
2	teaspoons finely shredded lime peel
4	ounces bulk Italian sausage
1 1/2	cups chopped onions (2 large)
1 1/2	cups chopped red, yellow, and/or green sweet peppers (2 medium)
3	cloves garlic, minced
1/4	cup snipped fresh cilantro
1/4	cup cider vinegar

1. Trim fat from steak. Score both sides of steak in a diamond pattern, making shallow diagonal cuts at 1-inch intervals. Sprinkle steak with salt, black pepper, and lime peel. Wrap in plastic wrap and chill for 1 hour.

2. For a charcoal grill, place steak on the grill rack directly over medium coals. Grill, uncovered, for 17 to 21 minutes for medium doneness (160°F), turning once halfway through grilling. (For a gas grill, preheat grill. Reduce heat to medium. Place steak on the grill rack over heat. Cover and grill as above.)

3. Meanwhile, preheat a large cast-iron skillet next to steak directly over medium coals. Add sausage; cook, stirring occasionally, for 3 minutes. Add onions, sweet peppers, and garlic. Cook, stirring occasionally, for 8 to 10 minutes more or until vegetables are crisp-tender. Stir in cilantro and vinegar. Remove from heat.

4. To serve, thinly slice steak. Spoon pepper mixture on top of steak.

Per Serving: 351 cal., 19 g fat (7 g sat. fat), 76 mg chol., 321 mg sodium, 8 g carbo., 2 g fiber, 36 g pro.

steaks with squash and arugula

If you like foods with a peppery note, you'll love the salad green arugula. For a bit milder option, choose baby spinach.

Prep: 30 minutes   Grill: 8 minutes   Stand: 20 minutes
Makes: 4 servings

- 1/4 cup white wine vinegar or white balsamic vinegar
- 2 cloves garlic, minced
- 1/2 teaspoon kosher or sea salt or 1/4 teaspoon salt
- 1/4 cup extra virgin olive oil
- 1 medium yellow summer squash or zucchini, very thinly sliced
- 1 cup baby pattypan squash, halved
- 1 cup yellow or red pear tomatoes or cherry tomatoes, halved
- 1/4 cup finely chopped yellow sweet pepper
- 4 boneless beef ribeye steaks, cut 3/4 to 1 inch thick (2 1/2 to 3 pounds)
- Sea salt, kosher salt, or salt
- Freshly ground black pepper
- 5 cups loosely packed arugula or baby spinach
- 2 tablespoons snipped fresh Italian (flat-leaf) parsley

1. In a small bowl, combine vinegar, garlic, and the 1/2 teaspoon salt. Cover and let stand at room temperature 20 minutes. Whisk in olive oil. Add summer squash, pattypan squash, tomatoes, and sweet pepper. Toss gently. Set aside. Season steaks with additional salt and black pepper.

2. For a charcoal grill, place steaks on the grill rack directly over medium coals. Grill, uncovered, until steaks reach desired doneness, turning once halfway through grilling. Allow 8 to 12 minutes for medium rare (145°F) or 10 to 15 minutes for medium (160°F). (For a gas grill, preheat grill. Reduce heat to medium. Place steak on grill rack over heat. Cover and grill as above.)

3. Just before serving, add arugula and parsley to squash mixture; toss gently to combine. Serve vegetable mixture with grilled steaks.
Per Serving: 602 cal., 36 g fat (10 g sat. fat), 165 mg chol., 470 mg sodium, 6 g carbo., 2 g fiber, 59 g pro.

flat-iron steaks with avocado butter

Showcased first on restaurant menus and now available in meat markets across the country, flat-iron steaks trail only beef tenderloin in tenderness.

Prep: 25 minutes   Grill: 7 minutes   Makes: 6 servings

- 6 beef shoulder top blade (flat-iron) steaks or boneless ribeye steaks, cut 3/4 inch thick
- 1 tablespoon olive oil
- 1 tablespoon herbes de Provence, crushed
- 1/2 teaspoon salt
- 1/2 teaspoon freshly ground black pepper
- Avocado Butter

1. Trim fat from steaks. Brush steaks with olive oil. For rub, in a small bowl, combine herbes de Provence, salt, and pepper. Sprinkle evenly over both sides of each steak; rub in with your fingers. If desired, cover and chill for up to 24 hours.

2. For a charcoal grill, place steaks on the grill rack directly over medium coals. Grill, uncovered, until steaks reach desired doneness, turning once halfway through grilling. Allow 7 to 9 minutes for medium rare (145°F) or 10 to 12 minutes for medium (160°F). (For a gas grill, preheat grill. Reduce heat to medium. Place steaks on the grill rack over heat. Cover and grill as above.)

3. Serve steaks with Avocado Butter.

Avocado Butter: Halve, pit, peel, and chop 1 ripe avocado. In a medium bowl, combine the chopped avocado, 1/4 cup softened butter, 3 tablespoons lime juice, 2 tablespoons snipped fresh chervil or parsley, 1 tablespoon snipped fresh tarragon, 1/4 teaspoon salt, and, if desired, 1/8 teaspoon cayenne pepper. Using a fork, gently mash the ingredients together until thoroughly combined (if desired, leave mixture somewhat chunky). Spoon mixture into a small bowl; chill until almost firm.
Per Serving: 387 cal., 27 g fat (10 g sat. fat), 111 mg chol., 492 mg sodium, 3 g carbo., 2 g fiber, 34 g pro.

flat as an iron

Although it comes from the chuck, which is generally considered a less tender part of the animal, the flat-iron steak is one of the most tender cuts of beef available. Marketed to consumers as "beef shoulder top blade steak (flat iron)," this cut is generally less expensive than other, more popular steaks such as ribeyes. Because flat-iron steaks are well marbled and yield wonderful flavors, they don't require marinating and are great for grilling. The flat-iron steak is equally good cut into strips and skewered or used in stir-fries.

flat-iron steaks
with avocado butter

chipotle steaks and tomatoes

chipotle steaks and tomatoes

Another time, change the dressing for these steaks. Omit the oil and vinegar from the recipe, and stir the chipotle pepper into ½ cup bottled ranch-style salad dressing.

Prep: 10 minutes   Grill: 10 minutes   Makes: 4 servings

2   beef shoulder petite tenders or beef ribeye steaks (6 to 8 ounces each)
    Salt
    Ground black pepper
1   canned chipotle pepper in adobo sauce, finely chopped, plus 2 teaspoons adobo sauce
¼   cup olive oil
¼   cup vinegar
3   medium tomatoes (1 pound), thickly sliced
2   medium avocados, halved, pitted, peeled, and sliced
½   of a small red onion, very thinly sliced (½ cup)

1. Sprinkle steaks lightly with salt and black pepper. Spread each steak with 1 teaspoon of the adobo sauce.

2. For a charcoal grill, place steaks on the grill rack directly over medium coals. Grill, uncovered, until steaks reach desired doneness, turning once. Allow 10 to 12 minutes for medium rare (145°F) or 12 to 15 minutes for medium (160°F). (For a gas grill, preheat grill. Reduce heat to medium. Place steaks on the grill rack over heat. Cover and grill as above.)

3. Meanwhile, for dressing, in a screw-top jar, combine the chopped pepper, olive oil, and vinegar. Shake to combine.

4. Slice steaks and arrange on dinner plates with tomato and avocado slices. Top with onion slices and drizzle with dressing.
Per Serving: 421 cal., 33 g fat (6 g sat. fat), 50 mg chol., 221 mg sodium, 13 g carbo., 7 g fiber, 20 g pro.

lamb chops
with garlic and lavender

If you have trouble finding dried lavender, use finely shredded lemon peel instead. A splash of fresh lemon flavor pairs perfectly with the lamb.

Prep: 45 minutes   Grill: 12 minutes   Chill: 4 hours
Makes: 8 to 10 servings

16 to 20 lamb rib or loin chops, cut 1 inch thick (4 to 5 pounds total)
1   tablespoon dried lavender or finely shredded lemon peel
1   tablespoon dried Italian seasoning, crushed
1½ teaspoons freshly ground black pepper
1   teaspoon sea salt or salt
2   tablespoons extra virgin olive oil
4   whole bulbs garlic, separated into cloves and peeled
2   lemons, halved (optional)
    Fresh lavender (optional)

1. Trim fat from chops. For rub, in a small bowl, combine dried lavender, Italian seasoning, pepper, and sea salt. Sprinkle rub evenly over both sides of each chop; rub in with your fingers. Cover and chill chops for up to 4 hours.

2. In a medium skillet, heat oil over medium heat. Add garlic cloves and cook for 15 to 20 minutes or until golden and soft, stirring occasionally and turning down heat if oil splatters. Remove from heat; cover and keep warm.

3. Meanwhile, for a charcoal grill, place chops on the grill rack directly over medium coals. Grill, uncovered, until chops reach desired doneness, turning once halfway through grilling. Allow 12 to 14 minutes for medium rare (145°F) and 15 to 17 minutes for medium (160°F). (For a gas grill, preheat grill. Reduce heat to medium. Place chops on the grill rack over heat. Cover and grill as above.)

4. To serve, transfer chops to serving plates. Spoon garlic cloves on grilled chops. If desired, squeeze fresh lemon juice on chops and top with fresh lavender.
Per Serving: 215 cal., 12 g fat (3 g sat. fat), 64 mg chol., 263 mg sodium, 6 g carbo., 2 g fiber, 21 g pro.

take one turn

Restrain yourself from turning foods on the grill time and time again. When you're grilling directly over coals, it's best to turn food only once so you don't lose perfectly good juices. Most of our recipes call for turning the meat halfway through the suggested cooking time. However, when grilling with indirect heat, you usually don't need to turn the food at all.

summer pork chops
with corn-mango salsa

Get creative and play around with the fruit in this salsa. When they're in season, try peaches, nectarines, or even plums in place of the mango.

summer pork chops with corn-mango salsa

When combined with a few other ingredients, the snappy combo of corn and mango makes a tantalizing topper for blackened chops.
Prep: 40 minutes Marinate: 12 hours Grill: 14 minutes
Makes: 6 servings

- $1/3$ cup olive oil
- 2 tablespoons blackened steak seasoning
- 2 teaspoons garlic powder
- 1 large onion, thinly sliced
- 6 boneless pork loin chops, cut 1 inch thick
  Corn-Mango Salsa
  Steamed green and yellow beans (optional)

1. For marinade, in a heavy resealable plastic bag, combine oil, steak seasoning, and garlic powder; mix well. Add onion; mix well. Add chops; seal bag and turn to coat chops. Place bag in a large bowl. Marinate in the refrigerator for 12 hours or overnight, turning bag occasionally. Drain chops; discard marinade.

2. For a charcoal grill, place chops on the grill rack directly over medium heat. Grill, uncovered, for 14 to 18 minutes or until chops are slightly pink in center and juices run clear (160°F), turning once halfway through grilling. (For a gas grill, preheat grill. Reduce heat to medium. Place chops on the grill rack over heat. Cover and grill as above.) Serve chops with Corn-Mango Salsa and, if desired, green and yellow beans.

Corn-Mango Salsa: Husk 2 ears fresh sweet corn and brush with olive oil, coating all kernels. Place corn on the grill rack directly over medium heat. Grill, uncovered, until kernels are tender and just begin to brown, turning often. Remove ears from grill; cool. Cut kernels from ears. In a medium bowl, combine corn kernels; 1 medium mango, seeded, peeled, and finely chopped; $1/2$ cup finely chopped red sweet pepper; $1/4$ cup chopped sweet onion; $1/4$ cup fresh lemon juice; 2 tablespoons cooking oil; 2 tablespoons snipped fresh mint; 1 tablespoon snipped fresh cilantro; and $1/4$ teaspoon salt. Toss gently to mix.
Per Serving: 479 cal., 22 g fat (4 g sat. fat), 124 mg chol., 758 mg sodium, 17 g carbo., 2 g fiber, 53 g pro.

peanut-crusted chops

Keep the grill cover handy for this one. You need to cover the grill after you add the peanut crust mixture so it gets slightly crispy.
Prep: 15 minutes Grill: 11 minutes Makes: 4 servings

- $1/3$ cup creamy peanut butter
- $1/3$ cup pineapple juice
- 2 tablespoons finely chopped green onion (1)
- 1 tablespoon soy sauce
- 1 tablespoon honey
- 1 teaspoon grated fresh ginger or $1/4$ teaspoon ground ginger
- $1/2$ teaspoon dry mustard
  Several dashes bottled hot pepper sauce
- $1/3$ cup finely chopped honey-roasted peanuts
- 2 tablespoons fine dry bread crumbs
- 1 tablespoon toasted sesame seeds
- 4 boneless pork sirloin chops, cut $3/4$ inch thick
- 4 ounces Chinese egg noodles or dried angel hair pasta

1. For peanut sauce, in a small saucepan, heat peanut butter until it melts; gradually whisk in pineapple juice, green onion, soy sauce, honey, ginger, mustard, and hot pepper sauce. Set aside 2 tablespoons of the peanut sauce. Keep remaining peanut sauce warm. For crust mixture, in a small bowl, combine peanuts, bread crumbs, and sesame seeds; set aside.

2. For a charcoal grill, place chops on the grill rack directly over medium coals. Grill, uncovered, for 6 minutes. Turn chops and brush with the reserved 2 tablespoons peanut sauce. Sprinkle chops with crust mixture. With the back of a metal spatula, press crust onto chops. Cover and grill for 5 to 7 minutes more or until chops are slightly pink in center and juices run clear (160°F). (For a gas grill, preheat grill. Reduce heat to medium. Place chops on the grill rack over heat. Cover and grill as above.)

3. Meanwhile, cook noodles according to package directions; drain. Toss noodles with the remaining peanut sauce. Serve with chops.
Per Serving: 510 cal., 23 g fat (5 g sat. fat), 89 mg chol., 518 mg sodium, 39 g carbo., 6 g fiber, 42 g pro.

beer-marinated pork chops
with cheddar

beer-marinated pork chops with cheddar

When grilling is almost complete, sprinkle a mixture of cheddar and nuts on the pork. It will melt into a luscious saucelike topping.

Prep: 25 minutes Marinate: 4 hours Grill: 37 minutes
Makes: 4 servings

- 4 bone-in pork loin chops or pork rib chops, cut 1¼ to 1½ inches thick (about 10 to 12 ounces each)
- 1 12-ounce bottle honey-wheat beer
- 2 cloves garlic, minced
- 1 tablespoon olive oil
- ¼ teaspoon salt
- ½ teaspoon coarsely ground black pepper
- 4 ounces white cheddar cheese, shredded, or blue cheese, crumbled (1 cup)
- 2 tablespoons chopped walnuts, toasted
- ¼ cup thinly sliced green onions (2)
  Fresh herb sprigs (optional)

1. Place pork chops in a 2-gallon heavy resealable plastic bag set in an extra-large bowl; set aside. In a small bowl, combine beer, garlic, olive oil, salt, and ¼ teaspoon of the pepper; pour over pork. Seal bag. Marinate in refrigerator for 4 to 24 hours, turning bag occasionally. Drain pork chops, discarding marinade.

2. For a charcoal grill, arrange medium-hot coals around a drip pan. Test for medium heat above the pan. Place chops on the grill rack over drip pan. Cover and grill for 35 to 40 minutes or until chops are slightly pink in center and juices run clear (160°F.) (For a gas grill, preheat grill. Reduce heat to medium. Adjust for indirect cooking. Place pork on grill rack. Cover and grill as above.)

3. Meanwhile, for topping, in a small bowl, stir together cheese, nuts, green onions, and remaining pepper. Carefully spoon mixture over chops on grill. Cover and grill for 2 to 3 minutes more or until cheese melts. Garnish with fresh herb sprigs, if desired.

Per Serving: 428 cal., 17 g fat (8 g sat. fat), 160 mg chol., 595 mg sodium, 2 g carbo., 0 g fiber, 61 g pro.

asian apricot-glazed chops

A little goes a long way. Handle the extra spicy Oriental chili-garlic sauce the same way you would hot pepper sauce.

Prep: 15 minutes Grill: 11 minutes Makes: 4 servings

- ⅓ cup apricot preserves
- 1 tablespoon Oriental chili-garlic sauce
- 2 teaspoons soy sauce
- ¼ teaspoon ground ginger
- 4 boneless pork sirloin chops, cut ¾ inch thick
  Salt and ground black pepper

1. For the glaze, place apricot preserves in a small bowl; snip any large pieces of fruit. Stir in chili-garlic sauce, soy sauce, and ginger. Set glaze aside. Sprinkle both sides of each chop with salt and pepper.

2. For a charcoal grill, place chops on the grill rack directly over medium coals. Grill, uncovered, for 11 to 13 minutes or until chops are slightly pink in center and juices run clear (160°F), turning once halfway through grilling and brushing with glaze during the last 2 to 3 minutes of grilling. (For a gas grill, preheat grill. Reduce heat to medium. Place chops on the grill rack over heat. Cover and grill as above.)

Per Serving: 317 cal., 9 g fat (3 g sat. fat), 106 mg chol., 515 mg sodium, 20 g carbo., 0 g fiber, 36 g pro.

grilled pork and pineapple

Complete this easy weekday meal with a tossed green salad or buttered asparagus spears and whole grain dinner rolls.

Prep: 15 minutes Grill: 7 minutes Makes: 4 servings

- 4 ¾-inch-thick boneless top loin pork chops (about 1¼ pounds total)
  Salt
  Ground black pepper
- 1 peeled and cored fresh pineapple
- 3 tablespoons orange marmalade
- ½ cup plain yogurt
- ¼ cup roasted, lightly salted cashew halves and/or pieces or toasted pecans, coarsely chopped
  Fresh thyme (optional)

1. Sprinkle both sides of each pork chop lightly with salt and pepper. Cut pineapple crosswise into ½-inch-thick slices; set aside.

2. For a charcoal grill, place chops on the grill rack directly over medium coals. Grill, uncovered, for 4 minutes. Turn chops; add pineapple to grill. Brush chops and pineapple with 2 tablespoons of the marmalade. Grill for 3 to 5 minutes more or until chops are slightly pink in center and juices run clear (160°F), turning pineapple once. (For a gas grill, preheat grill. Reduce heat to medium. Place chops on the grill rack over heat. Cover and grill as above.)

3. Meanwhile, in a small bowl, stir together yogurt and remaining 1 tablespoon marmalade. Season to taste with additional *ground black pepper.*

4. Arrange pineapple and chops on dinner plates. Spoon yogurt mixture over chops and pineapple; sprinkle with nuts and, if desired, garnish with thyme.

Per Serving: 317 cal., 7 g fat (2 g sat. fat), 80 mg chol., 313 mg sodium, 29 g carbo., 2 g fiber, 35 g pro.

smoked pork chops
with onion-blackberry relish

1. In a small saucepan, combine onions, the water, and ¼ teaspoon salt. Bring to boiling; reduce heat. Simmer, uncovered, for 3 minutes; drain onions. Cool slightly.

2. For relish, in a serving bowl, whisk together vinegar, chipotle pepper, and ¼ teaspoon salt. Stir in onions and blackberries. If desired, cover and chill for up to 24 hours. Let stand at room temperature for 1 hour before serving.

3. For a charcoal grill, place chops on the grill rack directly over medium coals. Grill, uncovered, about 5 minutes or until heated through, turning once halfway through grilling. (For a gas grill, preheat grill. Reduce heat to medium. Place chops on grill rack over heat. Cover and grill as above.)

4. To serve, stir the parsley and the green onions into relish. Serve chops with relish. If desired, garnish with parsley sprigs.
Per Serving: 198 cal., 7 g fat (2 g sat. fat), 60 mg chol., 1,752 mg sodium, 13 g carbo., 3 g fiber, 21 g pro.

beer-brined pork loin chops

Prep: 15 minutes   Marinate: 8 to 24 hours   Grill: 30 minutes
Makes: 4 servings

4	boneless pork top loin chops, cut 1½ inches thick
1¾	cups water
1¾	cups stout (dark beer)
3	tablespoons coarse salt
2	tablespoons mild-flavor molasses
2	teaspoons coarsely cracked black pepper
4	cloves garlic, minced

1. Trim fat from chops. Place chops in a heavy resealable plastic bag set in a shallow dish. For the brine, in a large bowl, combine water, stout, salt, and molasses; stir until salt dissolves. Pour brine over chops; seal bag. Marinate in refrigerator for 8 to 24 hours, turning bag occasionally.

2. Drain chops, discarding brine. Pat chops dry with paper towels. In a small bowl, combine pepper and garlic. Sprinkle pepper mixture evenly over both sides of each chop; rub in with your fingers.

3. For a charcoal grill, arrange medium-hot coals around a drip pan. Test for medium heat above the pan. Place chops on the grill rack over drip pan. Cover and grill for 30 to 35 minutes or until chops are slightly pink in center and juices run clear (160°F), turning once halfway through grilling. (For a gas grill, preheat grill. Reduce heat to medium. Adjust for indirect cooking. Place chops on the grill rack over heat. Cover and grill as above.)
Per Serving: 345 cal., 12 g fat (4 g sat. fat), 123 mg chol., 702 mg sodium, 3 g carbo., 0 g fiber, 50 g pro.

smoked pork chops
with onion-blackberry relish

Prep: 20 minutes   Stand: 1 hour   Grill: 5 minutes
Makes: 6 servings

2	cups coarsely chopped Vidalia, Walla Walla, or other sweet onions
1	cup water
¼	teaspoon salt
2	tablespoons red wine vinegar
1	canned chipotle chile pepper in adobo sauce, drained and chopped
¼	teaspoon salt
1	cup fresh blackberries or raspberries
6	cooked 4 to 6 ounce smoked boneless pork chops
¼	cup snipped fresh flat-leaf parsley
¼	cup sliced green onions (2)
	Fresh flat-leaf parsley sprigs (optional)

Brining in beer adds the earthy flavors of hops and grains to pork. Strong, dark beers—like stout—work best. Skip the wine and serve the sizzlers with ice-cold ale or pilsner.

beer-brined pork loin chops

greek honey-lemon pork chops

The marinade in this recipe not only makes chops sear beautifully but also provides enticing sweet-sour balance.

Prep: 15 minutes   Marinate: 4 to 24 hours   Grill: 11 minutes
Makes: 4 servings

- 4 bone-in pork rib chops, cut ¾ to 1 inch thick
- 2 tablespoons honey
- 2 teaspoons finely shredded lemon peel
- 2 tablespoons lemon juice
- 1 tablespoon snipped fresh mint or ½ teaspoon dried mint, crushed
- 1 tablespoon olive oil
- ½ teaspoon salt
- ¼ teaspoon cayenne pepper

1. Trim fat from chops. Place chops in a resealable plastic bag set in a shallow dish.

2. For marinade, in a small bowl, combine honey, lemon peel, lemon juice, mint, oil, salt, and cayenne pepper. Pour over chops. Seal bag; turn to coat chops. Marinate in the refrigerator for 4 to 24 hours, turning bag occasionally. Drain chops, discarding marinade.

3. For a charcoal grill, place chops on the grill rack directly over medium coals. Grill, uncovered, for 11 to 13 minutes or until chops are slightly pink in center and juices run clear (160°F), turning once halfway through grilling. (For a gas grill, preheat grill. Reduce heat to medium. Place chops on grill rack over heat. Cover and grill as above.)

Per Serving: 257 cal., 11 g fat (3 g sat. fat), 71 mg chol., 350 mg sodium, 10 g carbo., 0 g fiber, 29 g pro.

pork chops with hot pineapple salsa

Cook the salsa to intensify its sweet flavors. Try it with chicken breasts and grilled fish, too.

Prep: 20 minutes   Grill: 7 minutes   Makes: 4 servings

- 1 20-ounce can crushed pineapple (juice pack), undrained
- 1 15-ounce can black-eyed peas, rinsed and drained
- ½ cup finely chopped red onion
- ⅓ cup finely chopped red sweet pepper
- ¼ cup snipped fresh parsley
- 2 fresh jalapeño chile peppers, seeded and finely chopped*
- ½ teaspoon salt
- ¼ teaspoon ground cumin
- 4 boneless pork top loin chops, cut 1 inch thick
- 1 tablespoon olive oil
- ½ teaspoon dried thyme, crushed
- ½ teaspoon ground black pepper
- ½ teaspoon lemon juice

1. For salsa, in a medium saucepan, combine pineapple, black-eyed peas, onion, sweet pepper, parsley, jalapeño peppers, salt, and cumin. Cook over medium heat about 5 minutes or until heated through, stirring occasionally. Remove from heat; cover to keep warm.

2. Meanwhile, trim fat from chops. In a small bowl, combine oil, thyme, black pepper, and lemon juice. Brush oil mixture evenly over both sides of each chop.

3. For a charcoal grill, place chops on the grill rack directly over medium coals. Grill, uncovered, for 7 to 9 minutes or until chops are slightly pink in center and juices run clear (160°F), turning once halfway through grilling. (For a gas grill, preheat grill. Reduce heat to medium. Place chops on grill rack over heat. Cover and grill as above.)

4. Serve the chops with warm pineapple salsa.

Note: Because chile peppers contain volatile oils that can burn your skin and eyes, avoid direct contact with them as much as possible. When working with chile peppers, wear plastic or rubber gloves. If your bare hands do touch the peppers, wash your hands and nails well with soap and warm water.

Per Serving: 466 cal., 12 g fat (3 g sat. fat), 93 mg chol., 661 mg sodium, 43 g carbo., 7 g fiber, 44 g pro.

pork chops with hot pineapple salsa

greek honey-lemon
pork chops

grilled yogurt-marinated chops

grilled yogurt-marinated pork chops

Prep: 20 minutes   Marinate: 24 hours   Grill: 35 minutes
Makes: 4 servings

4	bone-in pork rib chops, cut 1¼ to 1½ inches thick
1½	cups plain low-fat yogurt
¼	cup snipped fresh cilantro
3	tablespoons finely chopped onion
3	tablespoons lemon juice
2	teaspoons ground coriander
4	cloves garlic, minced
1½	teaspoons salt
1	teaspoon ground cumin
1	teaspoon ground turmeric
1	teaspoon paprika
1	teaspoon dried marjoram, crushed
1	teaspoon freshly ground black pepper
¼	teaspoon saffron threads or ⅛ teaspoon ground saffron (optional)

1. Trim fat from chops. Place chops in a resealable plastic bag set in a shallow dish.

2. For marinade, in a medium bowl, combine yogurt, cilantro, onion, lemon juice, coriander, garlic, salt, cumin, turmeric, paprika, marjoram, pepper, and, if desired, saffron. Pour over chops. Seal bag; turn to coat chops.

3. Marinate in the refrigerator for 24 hours, turning bag occasionally. Remove chops from marinade, scraping off and discarding excess marinade.

4. For a charcoal grill, arrange medium-hot coals around a drip pan. Test for medium heat above the pan. Place chops on the grill rack over drip pan. Cover and grill for 35 to 40 minutes or until chops are slightly pink in center and juices run clear (160°F), turning once halfway through grilling. (For a gas grill, preheat grill. Reduce heat to medium. Adjust for indirect cooking. Place pork on grill rack. Cover and grill as above.)

Per Serving: 218 cal., 8 g fat (3 g sat. fat), 73 mg chol., 372 mg sodium, 3 g carbo., 0 g fiber, 30 g pro.

choosing chops

Enhanced or pure pork?
* **Enhanced pork** is a pretenderized, ready-to-go product that has been injected with a solution of water, sodium, phosphate, and sometimes flavorings and preservatives. Although higher in sodium than other pork, enhanced pork is nearly immune to overcooking, so it makes a great choice for novice grillers.
* **Pure pork chops** are the choice of most serious chefs because they have more pork flavor. They require close attention, however, because the line between perfect, juicy chops and dry, overcooked ones can be a fine one.

Thick or thin?
* **Thick chops** (1½-inches to 1¾-inches thick) work best for grilling. Thinner ones, however, are great when time is short—they grill quickly over direct heat.

Loin, rib, sirloin, or blade?
* **Loin chops** are the leanest pork chops.
* **Sirloin chops** offer the most marbling.
* **Rib chops** fall in the middle. Most professional chefs prefer bone-in rib chops for their enhanced flavor.
* **Blade chops,** cut from the shoulder, are well-marbled and flavorful but contain a large amount of bone.

achieving pork perfection

Pork is drier than red meat, but it absorbs other flavors marvelously. Several grilling enhancements capitalize on that chemistry.

* **Rubbing** Mixtures of herbs and spices can be rubbed directly on the meat to add flavor. They can be applied conveniently just before cooking.

* **Saucing** Bottled or homemade sauces offer variations of sweet, spicy, fruity, and smoky flavors. The trick with sweet sauces is to not let the sugars burn, so brush on the sauce at the last stage of cooking.

* **Marinating** Usually made up of a combination of acid, oil, and flavoring, a marinade is best applied several hours before grilling.

* **Brining** A form of heavy-duty marinating, brining means soaking pork in water, salt, and sugar to drive extra moisture into the meat.

* **Stuffing** Slice a pocket in the side of a chop and stuff it with any favorite dressing. Use small, water-soaked wood skewers to hold the meat securely together.

* **Topping** Relishes of chopped seasonal fruits, chiles, olives, and other fresh ingredients add zing to chops.

real ribs!

Manners, shmanners. Who needs them? Some foods are meant to be eaten with your fingers, and barbecued ribs are one of them. In fact, the mouthwatering, fall-off-the-bone tender meat seems to taste better eaten straight from the bone. Loved by folks unafraid to grab a bone, don a bib, and dig right in, ribs are the ultimate when rubbed with spices and bathed in sauce. Turn the page to find lip-smackin' real good ribs.

citrus-glazed baby back ribs
(recipe, page 62)

caribbean baby back ribs

citrus-glazed baby back ribs

These fork-tender ribs get a jump start in the oven, then finish on the grill under a glistening glaze. Pictured on page 61.

Prep: 10 minutes   Bake: 3 hours   Grill: 10 minutes   Oven: 300°F
Makes: 4 servings

4	pounds pork loin back ribs or meaty pork spareribs
	Salt
	Ground black pepper
2	tablespoons cornstarch
2	tablespoons brown sugar
1/2	teaspoon salt
2	cups orange juice
1	teaspoon finely shredded lime peel (set aside)
2	tablespoons lime juice
1	tablespoon snipped fresh mint
1	teaspoon finely shredded lemon peel

1. Preheat oven to 300°F. Place ribs in a large roasting pan (do not cut into smaller rib pieces). Season with salt and pepper. Cover and bake ribs in the preheated oven about 3 hours or until very tender.

2. Meanwhile, for sauce, in a medium saucepan, stir together the cornstarch, brown sugar, and 1/2 teaspoon salt. Stir in orange juice and lime juice. Cook and stir over medium heat until thickened and bubbly. Remove from heat. Stir in the mint, lime peel, and lemon peel.

3. Remove ribs from pan. Brush the ribs with some of the sauce. For a charcoal grill, place ribs on the grill rack directly over medium coals. Grill, uncovered, for 10 minutes, turning and brushing occasionally with sauce. (For a gas grill, preheat grill. Reduce heat to medium. Place ribs on the grill rack over heat. Cover and grill as above.) Serve ribs with remaining sauce.

Per Serving: 876 cal., 63 g fat (24 g sat. fat), 224 mg chol., 796 mg sodium, 24 g carbo., 0 g fiber, 46 g pro.

Although ribs provide a great meal, two-rib portions make great appetizers, too.

caribbean baby back ribs

The combination of pineapple rum and molasses gives these juicy baby backs a Caribbean touch. If you can't find pineapple rum, substitute an equal amount of rum or pineapple juice, or a mixture of the two.
Prep: 40 minutes   Chill: 2 hours   Grill: $1^1/_2$ hours
Makes: 6 servings

2	tablespoons packed brown sugar
1	to 2 tablespoons paprika
1	tablespoon garlic powder
2	to 4 teaspoons coarsely ground black pepper
$1^1/_2$	teaspoons salt
$^1/_2$	teaspoon ground cumin
$3^1/_2$	to 4 pounds pork loin back ribs
1	tablespoon cooking oil
$^1/_2$	cup chopped onion
1	clove garlic, minced
1	8-ounce can tomato sauce
$^1/_3$	cup pineapple rum
$^1/_3$	cup light-flavor molasses
2	tablespoons Worcestershire sauce
2	tablespoons vinegar
2	teaspoons dry mustard
2	teaspoons chili powder

1. For rub, in a small bowl, stir together brown sugar, paprika, garlic powder, pepper, salt, and cumin. Sprinkle rub evenly over both sides of ribs; rub in with your fingers. Cover and chill for 2 to 24 hours.

2. For a charcoal grill, arrange medium-hot coals around a drip pan. Test for medium heat above pan. If desired, place ribs in a rib rack. Place ribs, bone sides down, on a lightly oiled grill rack over drip pan. Cover and grill for $1^1/_2$ to $1^3/_4$ hours or until ribs are tender. (For a gas grill, preheat grill. Reduce heat to medium. Adjust for indirect cooking. Grill as above, except place ribs in a roasting pan.)

3. Meanwhile, for sauce, heat oil in a small saucepan over medium heat. Cook and stir onion and garlic in hot oil about 5 minutes or until tender. Stir in tomato sauce, pineapple rum, molasses, Worcestershire sauce, vinegar, dry mustard, and chili powder. Bring to boiling; reduce heat. Simmer, uncovered, about 20 minutes or until sauce is reduced to $1^1/_2$ cups, stirring occasionally.

4. To serve, cut ribs into six portions. Spoon sauce over ribs.
Per Serving: 467 cal., 21 g fat (7 g sat. fat), 84 mg chol., 904 mg sodium, 25 g carbo., 2 g fiber, 36 g pro.

spicy beer-brined ribs

Prep: 20 minutes   Marinate: 6 hours   Grill: $1^1/_2$ hours
Makes: 4 servings

3	12-ounce cans beer
3	tablespoons coarse kosher salt
3	tablespoons packed brown sugar
1	tablespoon celery seeds
1	tablespoon cayenne pepper
$1^1/_2$	teaspoons ground black pepper
1	teaspoon liquid smoke (optional)
4	pounds meaty pork spareribs or pork loin back ribs
	Honey-Beer Barbecue Sauce or bottled barbecue sauce

1. For brine, in a large bowl, combine beer, salt, brown sugar, celery seeds, cayenne pepper, ground black pepper, and, if desired, liquid smoke; stir until salt and brown sugar dissolve. Cut ribs into two-rib portions; place in a heavy resealable plastic bag set in a shallow dish. Pour brine over ribs; seal bag. Marinate in the refrigerator for 6 hours, turning bag occasionally.

2. Remove ribs from bag; discard brine. Pat ribs dry with paper towels.

3. For a charcoal grill, arrange medium-hot coals around a drip pan. Test for medium heat above pan. If desired, place ribs in a rib rack. Place ribs, bone sides down, on the grill rack over drip pan. Cover and grill for $1^1/_2$ to $1^3/_4$ hours or until ribs are tender, brushing with barbecue sauce during the last 5 minutes of grilling. Add more coals as needed to maintain temperature and smoke. (For a gas grill, preheat grill. Reduce heat to medium. Adjust heat for indirect cooking. Grill as above, except place ribs in a roasting pan.) Before serving, brush ribs with any remaining sauce.

Honey-Beer Barbecue Sauce: In a medium saucepan, cook $^1/_3$ cup chopped onion and 1 clove garlic, minced, in 1 tablespoon cooking oil until tender. Stir in $^3/_4$ cup bottled chili sauce, $^1/_2$ cup beer, $^1/_4$ cup honey, 2 tablespoons Worcestershire sauce, and 1 tablespoon yellow mustard. Bring to boiling; reduce heat. Simmer, uncovered, about 20 minutes or until sauce is desired consistency, stirring occasionally.

Make-Ahead Directions: Prepare as directed through Step 2. Cover and chill for up to 24 hours. Grill as directed in Step 3.
Per Serving: 853 cal., 63 g fat (20 g sat. fat), 221 mg chol., 1,354 mg sodium, 17 g carbo., 0 g fiber, 44 g pro.

tennessee pork ribs

Folks in Tennessee know that a good slab of ribs supplies one of life's greatest pleasures. In that part of the country, some of the best ribs are rubbed with a mixture of spices and mopped with a mustardy glaze.
Prep: 20 minutes Chill: 6 hours Soak: 1 hour Grill: 1¹/₂ hours
Makes: 4 to 6 servings

4	to 5 pounds pork loin back ribs or meaty pork spareribs
1	tablespoon paprika
1	tablespoon packed brown sugar
1	teaspoon ground black pepper
1	teaspoon ground cumin
1	teaspoon dry mustard
¹/₂	teaspoon garlic powder
¹/₂	teaspoon cayenne pepper
¹/₄	teaspoon celery seeds
1¹/₂	cups hickory wood chips
¹/₂	cup cider vinegar
2	tablespoons yellow mustard
¹/₄	teaspoon salt

1. Trim fat from ribs. For rub, in a small bowl, combine paprika, brown sugar, black pepper, cumin, dry mustard, garlic powder, cayenne pepper, and celery seeds. Sprinkle rub evenly over both sides of ribs; rub in with your fingers. Cover and chill for 6 to 24 hours.

2. For at least 1 hour before grilling, soak wood chips in enough water to cover. Drain wood chips. Meanwhile, in a small bowl, combine vinegar, yellow mustard, and salt.

3. For a charcoal grill, arrange medium-hot coals around a drip pan. Test for medium heat above pan. Sprinkle drained wood chips over coals. If desired, place ribs in a rib rack. Place ribs, bone sides down, on the grill rack over drip pan. Cover and grill for 1¹/₂ to 1³/₄ hours or until ribs are tender, brushing with mustard mixture three times during the last 30 minutes of grilling. Add more coals and wood chips as needed to maintain temperature and smoke. (For a gas grill, preheat grill. Reduce heat to medium. Adjust for indirect cooking. Grill as above, except place ribs in a roasting pan. Add wood chips according to manufacturer's directions.)
Per Serving: 485 cal., 21 g fat (7 g sat. fat), 135 mg chol., 336 mg sodium, 8 g carbo., 1 g fiber, 63 g pro.

Pile the meaty ribs on a platter and let your family dig right in.

kansas city pork spareribs

You'll need lots of napkins for these smoky, saucy ribs.
Prep: 20 minutes Soak: 1 hour Cook: 30 minutes
Grill: 1¹/₂ hours Makes: 4 servings

4	cups hickory, oak, or apple wood chips
4	pounds meaty pork spareribs or pork loin back ribs
1	tablespoon packed brown sugar
1	tablespoon garlic pepper
1	tablespoon paprika
1¹/₂	teaspoons chili powder
1	teaspoon salt
¹/₂	teaspoon celery seeds
¹/₄	cup cider vinegar
	Kansas City Barbecue Sauce

1. For at least 1 hour before grilling, soak wood chips in enough water to cover. Drain wood chips.

2. Trim fat from ribs. For rub, in a small bowl, stir together brown sugar, garlic pepper, paprika, chili powder, salt, and celery seeds. Brush ribs with vinegar. Sprinkle rub evenly over both sides of ribs; rub in with your fingers.

3. For a charcoal grill, arrange medium-hot coals around a drip pan. Test for medium heat above pan. Sprinkle drained wood chips over coals. If desired, place ribs in a rib rack. Place ribs, bone sides down, on the grill rack over drip pan. Cover and grill for 1¹/₂ to 1³/₄ hours or until ribs are tender. Add more coals and wood chips as needed to maintain temperature and smoke. (For a gas grill, preheat grill. Reduce heat to medium. Adjust for indirect cooking. Grill as above, except place ribs in a roasting pan. Add wood chips according to manufacturer's directions.)

4. Serve ribs with Kansas City Barbecue Sauce.

Kansas City Barbecue Sauce: In medium saucepan, cook ¹/₂ cup finely chopped onion and 2 cloves garlic, minced, in 1 tablespoon hot olive oil until onion is tender. Stir in ³/₄ cup apple juice, ¹/₂ of a 6-ounce can (¹/₃ cup) tomato paste, ¹/₄ cup vinegar, 2 tablespoons packed brown sugar, 2 tablespoons molasses, 1 tablespoon paprika, 1 tablespoon Worcestershire sauce, 1 teaspoon salt, and ¹/₂ teaspoon ground black pepper. Bring to boiling; reduce heat. Simmer, uncovered, about 30 minutes or until sauce is desired consistency, stirring occasionally. Stir in 1 tablespoon prepared horseradish.
Per Serving: 688 cal., 42 g fat (14 g sat. fat), 176 mg chol., 1,470 mg sodium, 34 g carbo., 2 g fiber, 46 g pro.

tennessee pork ribs

mustard-glazed ribs

Use this sassy glaze on spareribs or beef short ribs, too. If an earthier flavor is what you're looking for, substitute sage for the savory.

Prep: 25 minutes   Grill: 1¹/₂ hours   Makes: 4 servings

- 2 tablespoons cooking oil
- ¹/₃ cup chopped sweet onion
- 1 cup whole grain, spicy brown, or other mustard
- 2 tablespoons honey
- 2 tablespoons cider vinegar
- 1 teaspoon snipped fresh summer savory or ¹/₈ teaspoon dried summer savory, crushed
- 3 pounds pork country-style ribs
  Orange slices (optional)

1. For glaze, in a medium saucepan, heat oil over medium-high heat. Add onion and cook until golden brown. Reduce heat to low; stir in mustard, honey, and vinegar. Simmer for 3 minutes. Stir in savory; cook and stir for 1 minute more. Set aside, reserving about one third of glaze to serve with ribs.

2. Trim excess fat from ribs. For a charcoal grill, arrange medium-hot coals around a drip pan. Test for medium heat above the pan. If desired, place ribs in a rib rack. Place ribs, bone sides down, on lightly oiled grill rack over drip pan. Cover and grill for 1¹/₂ to 2 hours or until tender, brushing occasionally with glaze during the last 10 minutes of grilling. (For a gas grill, preheat grill. Reduce heat to medium. Adjust grill for indirect cooking. Grill as above, except place the ribs in a roasting pan.)

3. Heat and pass reserved glaze with ribs. Garnish with fresh orange slices, if desired.

Per Serving: 396 cal., 23 g total fat (5 g sat. fat), 101 mg chol., 904 mg sodium, 13 g carbo., 1 g dietary fiber, 34 g protein.

The combination of **sweet and savory** *flavors—such as honey and mustard or mango and chile pepper—tastes divine on succulent ribs.*

reggae baby back ribs

Prep: 15 minutes   Marinate: 8 to 24 hours   Grill: 1¹/₂ hours
Makes: 4 large servings

- ¹/₄ cup packed brown sugar
- 2 tablespoons grated fresh ginger
- 2 teaspoons salt
- 2 teaspoons finely shredded lime peel
- 1 teaspoon ground cumin
- ¹/₂ teaspoon ground cinnamon
- 4 pounds pork loin back ribs, cut into 6- to 8-rib portions
- ¹/₂ cup chicken broth
- ¹/₄ cup dark rum
- 3 tablespoons lime juice
- 1 tablespoon olive oil
- 1 small fresh habanero chile pepper, finely chopped
  Mango-Guava BBQ Sauce

1. In a small bowl, combine brown sugar, ginger, salt, lime peel, cumin, and cinnamon. Sprinkle mixture evenly over ribs; rub in with your fingers. Refrigerate for 8 to 24 hours.

2. For mop sauce, in a medium bowl, combine broth, rum, lime juice, oil, and habanero. Cover and chill for 8 to 24 hours.

3. For a charcoal grill, arrange medium-hot coals around a drip pan. Test for medium heat above pan. If desired, place ribs in a rib rack. Place ribs, bone sides down, on the grill rack over drip pan. Cover and grill for 1¹/₂ to 1³/₄ hours or until ribs are tender, brushing with mop sauce every 15 to 20 minutes. (For a gas grill, preheat grill. Reduce heat to medium. Adjust for indirect cooking. Grill as above, except place ribs in a roasting pan.)

4. While ribs are cooking, prepare Mango-Guava BBQ Sauce. About 15 minutes before ribs are done, brush some of the sauce over ribs. Serve the remaining sauce.

Mango-Guava BBQ Sauce: In a small saucepan, combine 1¹/₃ cups chopped mangoes; ²/₃ cup packed brown sugar; ²/₃ cup chopped onion; ¹/₃ cup lime juice; ¹/₄ cup olive oil; ¹/₄ cup guava paste; 3 tablespoons honey; 2 tablespoons tomato paste; 2 cloves garlic, minced; and ³/₄ teaspoon ground cumin. Bring to boiling; reduce heat. Cover and simmer for 15 minutes. Cool slightly. Transfer to a food processor or blender. Cover and process or blend until slightly chunky.

Per Serving: 1,315 cal., 76 g fat (27 g sat. fat), 223 mg chol., 1,585 mg sodium, 95 g carbo., 4 g fiber, 47 g pro.

reggae baby back ribs

chinese ribs

Spareribs have long graced the list of favorite traditional Chinese appetizers. This succulent recipe brings the same goodness to the main entrée.

Prep: 25 minutes   Chill: 6 hours   Soak: 1 hour   Grill: $1^1/_2$ hours
Makes: 4 to 5 servings

4	pounds pork loin back ribs or meaty pork spareribs
2	tablespoons granulated sugar
$^1/_2$	teaspoon salt
$^1/_4$	teaspoon paprika
$^1/_4$	teaspoon ground turmeric
$^1/_4$	teaspoon celery seeds
$^1/_4$	teaspoon dry mustard
$^1/_4$	cup ketchup
$^1/_4$	cup soy sauce
2	tablespoons packed brown sugar
2	tablespoons water
1	teaspoon grated fresh ginger or 1 teaspoon ground ginger
2	cups alder or oak wood chips

1. Trim fat from ribs. For rub, in a small bowl, combine granulated sugar, salt, paprika, turmeric, celery seeds, and dry mustard. Sprinkle rub evenly over both sides of ribs; rub in with your fingers. Cover and chill for 6 to 24 hours.

2. For sauce, in a small bowl, stir together ketchup, soy sauce, brown sugar, the water, and ginger. Cover and chill for 6 to 24 hours.

3. For at least 1 hour before grilling, soak wood chips in enough water to cover. Drain wood chips.

4. For a charcoal grill, arrange medium-hot coals around a drip pan. Test for medium heat above pan. Sprinkle drained wood chips over coals. If desired, place ribs in a rib rack. Place ribs, bone sides down, on the grill rack over drip pan. Cover and grill for $1^1/_2$ to $1^3/_4$ hours or until ribs are tender, brushing once with sauce during the last 15 minutes of grilling. Add more coals and wood chips as needed to maintain temperature and smoke. (For a gas grill, preheat grill. Reduce heat to medium. Adjust for indirect cooking. Grill as above, except place ribs in a roasting pan. Add wood chips according to manufacturer's directions.) Before serving, brush ribs with any remaining sauce.

Per Serving: 527 cal., 20 g fat (7 g sat. fat), 135 mg chol., 1,484 mg sodium, 17 g carbo., 0 g fiber, 65 g pro.

sweetly spiced barbecued pork ribs

Smothered with a glazelike sauce, these spice-rubbed ribs showcase an eclectic combination of ingredients and create a memorable taste sensation.

Prep: 20 minutes   Grill: $1^1/_2$ hours   Makes: 4 to 5 servings

4	to 5 pounds pork loin back ribs or meaty pork spareribs
1	tablespoon ground black pepper
2	teaspoons kosher salt or sea salt
2	teaspoons chili powder
1	teaspoon sugar
1	teaspoon onion powder
1	teaspoon garlic powder
1	teaspoon dried parsley flakes
1	teaspoon dried oregano, crushed
	Sweet-and-Sour Barbecue Sauce

1. Trim fat from ribs. For rub, in a small bowl, stir together pepper, salt, chili powder, sugar, onion powder, garlic powder, parsley, and oregano. Sprinkle rub evenly over both sides of ribs; rub in with your fingers. If desired, cut ribs into 2- or 3-rib portions.

2. Place rib portions, bone sides down, in a large roasting pan.* Pour Sweet-and-Sour Barbecue Sauce over ribs.

3. For a charcoal grill, arrange medium-hot coals around the edge of grill. Test for medium heat above center of grill. Place uncovered roasting pan on grill rack in center of grill. Grill, covered, for $1^1/_2$ to $1^3/_4$ hours or until ribs are tender, spooning sauce over ribs every 20 to 25 minutes. (For a gas grill, preheat grill. Reduce heat to medium. Adjust for indirect cooking. Place uncovered roasting pan on grill rack. Grill as above.)

*Note: To protect the roasting pan from blackening as the ribs cook, wrap the outside with heavy foil.

Sweet-and-Sour Barbecue Sauce: In a medium bowl, combine 1 cup dry red wine, 1 cup pineapple juice, $^1/_2$ cup honey, $^1/_2$ cup cider vinegar, $^1/_2$ cup soy sauce, $^1/_4$ cup yellow mustard, 2 tablespoons bourbon, and 1 teaspoon bottled hot pepper sauce.
Per Serving: 731 cal., 21 g fat (7 g sat. fat), 135 mg chol., 3,106 mg sodium, 52 g carbo., 2 g fiber, 68 g pro.

pearls of wisdom for perfect pork ribs

So you seek the secrets to creating fall-off-the-bone, tender, melt-in-your-mouth ribs like those at your favorite rib joint? Many pit masters claim they have cracked the secret code to great barbecue, but the truth is that many techniques work and all are tasty in their own way. The doneness, the flavoring, and the cut of meat all factor in creating the ultimate rack of ribs.

1. **Juicy Doneness** Whether ribs are cooked on the grill, in the oven, or in a smoker, the tear test offers the best way to determine if they are done. Pull the rack of ribs off the grill, then using tongs or your fingers, grab hold of two ribs located toward the center of the rack and give them a tug. If the meat tears easily with little or no resistance, your killer ribs are cooked to perfection.

2. **Smoky Flavoring** Sure, you can rub the meat down with a masterful blend of herbs and spices, infuse it with a tangy marinade, or mop it with a spunky sauce, but the true secret to a barbecued meat's flavor lies in the smoking process and the rich, smoky aromas produced by the wood used in the grill. Unlike direct grilling, smoking infuses the meat with an intense, robust, smoky scent and flavor. Depending on the type used, wood adds a sweet, spicy, or earthy scent. But not just any wood works—only hardwoods such as hickory, oak, apple, mesquite, cherry, alder, and pecan. Softwoods such as pine produce a harsh, bitter flavor. While most barbecue masters have their favorites, no specific hardwood is better than another. Various woods are more plentiful in different areas of the country, so the type you use depends on what's available, what you're accustomed to, and the intensity of flavor you want to create. In fact, many chefs use a combination of different woods to bring out a blend of aromatic flavors. Try combining woods based on some of their smoking characteristics listed below.

Oak
Hickory
Apple

✶ **Alder** sweet and delicate smoke
✶ **Apple** fruity, slightly sweet smoke
✶ **Cherry** fruity, slightly sweet smoke
✶ **Hickory** pungent, rich, bacon-scented smoke
✶ **Maple** mild, slightly sweet smoke

✶ **Mesquite** pungent, earthy smoke
✶ **Oak** heavy, strong smoke
✶ **Peach** woodsy, slightly sweet smoke
✶ **Pecan** mild smoke, similar to hickory
✶ **Walnut** heavy smoke, can be bitter

3. **The Perfect Cut** The exact number of pork rib cuts, styles, and varieties available is up for debate. Depending on where they live, people differ in opinion on the subject, but generally there are two basic cuts of pork ribs.

Spareribs come from the belly of the hog. Large and meaty, they contain more fat and flavor than pork loin back ribs. The cut is best known as the St. Louis-style sparerib.

Spareribs

Pork Loin Back Ribs

Pork Loin Back Ribs come from the loin of the hog. The most tender and lean portion, baby back ribs are the most expensive and weigh in at $1\frac{1}{4}$ to $2\frac{1}{4}$ pounds per rack.

magical poultry

It's time to zap the old birds with some new tricks. Just like magic, the wave of a wand, a spunky sauce, a zesty marinade, or a spicy rub transforms one of America's most popular grilled foods into a fantastic new dinnertime sensation. Abracadabra! Succulent grilled poultry—arranged in a salad, perched on a bed of rice, or wrapped in tortillas—turns into a complete meal. These pages hold a magical assortment of light, fresh, and flavorful chicken and turkey recipes, all sure to fill your mealtimes with the favorable surprise of empty plates!

peach-glazed chicken
(recipe, page 73)

dipping drumsticks

dipping drumsticks

Kids love to dip! Try these easy-fixing drumsticks or chicken breast halves and let your kids choose their favorite dipping sauces.

Prep: 15 minutes   Grill: 50 minutes   Makes: 4 servings

- **3   tablespoons white wine Worcestershire sauce**
- **2   cloves garlic, minced**
- **1/2   teaspoon poultry seasoning**
- **1/8   teaspoon ground black pepper**
- **8   chicken drumsticks***
- **Assorted dipping sauces (such as bottled ranch salad dressing, barbecue sauce, sweet-and-sour sauce, or creamy Dijon-style mustard blend)**

1. In a small bowl, combine Worcestershire sauce, garlic, poultry seasoning, and pepper. Remove the skin from chicken. Brush chicken with Worcestershire mixture.

2. For a charcoal grill, arrange medium-hot coals around a drip pan. Test for medium heat above the pan. Place chicken on the grill rack over the drip pan. Grill, covered, for 50 to 60 minutes or until chicken is no longer pink (180°F), turning once halfway through grilling. (For a gas grill, preheat grill. Reduce heat to medium. Adjust for indirect cooking. Place chicken pieces on the grill rack. Cover and grill as above.)

3. Serve drumsticks with desired dipping sauces.

*Note: If you prefer, use 4 skinless, boneless chicken breast halves (about 1 1/4 pounds total). Prepare as directed in Step 1. Place chicken breast halves on the grill rack directly over medium heat; grill for 15 to 18 minutes or until tender and no longer pink (170°F), turning once halfway through grilling. Cut chicken breasts into 1-inch-wide strips. Serve with desired dipping sauces.

Per Serving: 371 cal., 27 g fat (6 g sat. fat), 127 mg chol., 504 mg sodium, 5 g carbo., 0 g fiber, 29 g pro.

peach-glazed chicken

Whole chicken variation pictured on page 71.

Prep: 15 minutes   Grill: 50 minutes   Makes: 4 to 6 servings

2½   to 3 pounds meaty chicken pieces (breast halves,
     thighs, and drumsticks)*
     Salt and coarsely ground black pepper
½   cup peach preserves, large pieces snipped
1   tablespoon white wine vinegar
1   tablespoon prepared horseradish
1   teaspoon grated fresh ginger
½   teaspoon salt
½   teaspoon coarsely ground black pepper

1. If desired, remove the skin from chicken. Sprinkle chicken lightly with salt and pepper. For a charcoal grill, arrange preheated coals around a drip pan. Test for medium heat above the pan. Place chicken on the grill rack above the drip pan. Grill, covered, for 40 minutes. (For a gas grill, preheat grill. Reduce heat to medium. Adjust for indirect cooking. Place chicken on grill rack. Grill as above.)

2. Meanwhile, in a small microwave-safe bowl, combine preserves, vinegar, horseradish, ginger, ½ teaspoon salt, and ½ teaspoon pepper. Microwave, uncovered, on 100% power (high) for 30 to 60 seconds or until preserves melt, stirring once. Brush mixture over chicken pieces. Cover and grill for 10 to 20 minutes more or until chicken is no longer pink (170°F in breast halves, 180°F in thighs or drumsticks), brushing occasionally with sauce. Spoon any remaining preserve mixture over chicken.

*Whole Chicken Variation: Remove neck and giblets from the body cavity of a 4- to 5-pound whole roasting chicken; reserve for another use or discard. If desired, sprinkle the body cavity of chicken with salt and pepper. Pull neck skin to the back and fasten with a short skewer. Tie drumsticks to tail with 100-percent-cotton kitchen string. Twist the wing tips under the back. Sprinkle chicken with additional salt and pepper.

For a charcoal grill, arrange medium-hot coals around a drip pan. Test for medium heat above the pan. Place chicken, breast side up, on the grill rack over drip pan. Grill, covered, for 1 hour. Cut string between drumsticks. Cover and grill for 45 to 60 minutes more or until chicken is no longer pink (170°F in breast and 180°F in thigh). Meanwhile, prepare preserve mixture as directed above. Brush preserve mixture over chicken several times during the last 15 minutes of grilling. (For a gas grill, preheat grill. Reduce heat to medium. Adjust for indirect cooking. Place chicken on grill rack. Cover and grill as above.) Transfer chicken to serving platter; cover loosely with foil and let stand 15 minutes before serving.

Per Serving: 356 cal., 9 g fat (3 g sat. fat), 115 mg chol., 565 mg sodium, 28 g carbo., 1 g fiber, 37 g pro.

curried chicken strips with sweet mango chutney

For optimum flavor, prepare the chutney ahead so it can chill for at least 8 hours.

Prep: 25 minutes   Marinate: 2 hours   Chill: 8 hours
Soak: 1 hour   Grill: 8 minutes   Makes: 4 servings

1   pound skinless, boneless chicken breast halves
⅓   cup rice vinegar, dry white wine, or chicken broth
2   tablespoons cooking oil
1   tablespoon soy sauce
2   teaspoons finely shredded orange peel
1   tablespoon orange juice
2   teaspoons curry powder
1   teaspoon chili powder
½   teaspoon ground cumin
12   6-inch wooden skewers
    Nonstick cooking spray
    Sweet Mango Chutney
2   cups hot cooked rice

1. Cut chicken into long strips about ½ inch thick. Place chicken in a large resealable plastic bag set in a deep dish. For marinade, combine vinegar, oil, soy sauce, orange peel and juice, curry powder, chili powder, and cumin. Pour marinade over chicken in bag. Seal bag, turning to coat chicken. Marinate in the refrigerator 2 to 6 hours, turning bag occasionally. Drain chicken, discarding marinade.

2. Soak wooden skewers in water for 30 minutes before grilling. Drain skewers. Coat skewers with nonstick cooking spray. Thread chicken on skewers, accordion-style. Transfer skewers to a baking sheet.

3. For a charcoal grill, place skewers on rack directly over medium coals. Grill, uncovered, for 8 to 10 minutes or until chicken is no longer pink (170°), turning to brown evenly. (For a gas grill, preheat grill. Reduce heat to medium. Place skewers on the grill rack. Cover and grill as above.) To serve, stir 1 cup of the Sweet Mango Chutney into the rice. Spoon rice mixture onto a platter. Arrange chicken skewers over rice mixture. Spoon remaining chutney over the skewers.

Sweet Mango Chutney: In a large saucepan, combine 2 cups seeded, peeled, and chopped mangoes (2 large); 1 cup peeled, cored, and chopped pear or tart apple (1 medium); ½ cup chopped leek or onion; ½ cup honey; ⅓ cup rice vinegar; 1 tablespoon orange juice; 2 cloves garlic, minced; ¼ teaspoon salt; ¼ teaspoon crushed red pepper; and ¼ teaspoon ground ginger. Bring to boiling; reduce heat. Simmer, uncovered, for 20 to 25 minutes or until chutney is desired consistency, stirring occasionally. Remove from heat; cool. Transfer chutney to a tightly covered container and chill at least 8 hours before serving. Store any remaining chutney in the refrigerator up to 1 week. Serve chutney at room temperature.

Per Serving: 495 cal., 5 g fat (1 g sat. fat), 66 mg chol., 347 mg sodium, 82 g carbo., 4 g fiber, 30 g pro.

Toss a handful or two of leftover fresh herbs into a salad of mixed spring greens.

tex-thai chicken breasts

Expect your taste buds to heat up with this spicy chicken, but know that the crunchy cucumbers and mild mango offer a cooldown effect.

Prep: 30 minutes   Marinate: 1 hour   Grill: 12 minutes
Makes: 4 servings

- 3/4 cup bottled green salsa
- 1/4 cup unsweetened coconut milk
- 2 tablespoons thinly sliced green onion (1)
- 1/2 teaspoon finely shredded lime peel
- 1 tablespoon lime juice
- 1 tablespoon chopped fresh cilantro
- 1 tablespoon chopped fresh mint
- 1 teaspoon green curry paste
- 1 teaspoon grated fresh ginger
- 1 teaspoon soy sauce
- 1 clove garlic, minced
- 4 skinless, boneless chicken breast halves (about 1 1/4 pounds total)
- Chopped mango
- Chopped cucumber
- Fresh mint (optional)

1. For marinade, in a blender or food processor, combine salsa, coconut milk, green onion, lime peel and juice, cilantro, mint, curry paste, ginger, soy sauce, and garlic. Cover and blend or process until nearly smooth. Remove 1/3 cup of the mixture; cover and chill until serving time.

2. Place chicken in a large resealable plastic bag set in a shallow dish. Pour remaining marinade over chicken. Seal bag, turning to coat chicken. Marinate in refrigerator for 1 to 2 hours, turning bag occasionally. Drain chicken, reserving marinade.

3. For a charcoal grill, place chicken on the grill rack directly over medium coals. Grill, uncovered, for 12 to 15 minutes or until chicken is no longer pink (170°F), turning once and brushing with reserved marinade halfway through grilling. (For a gas grill, preheat grill. Reduce heat to medium. Place chicken on the grill rack over heat. Cover and grill as above.) Serve chicken with mango and cucumber. Drizzle with reserved 1/3 cup marinade mixture. If desired, garnish with mint.

Per Serving: 226 cal., 6 g fat (3 g sat. fat), 82 mg chol., 465 mg sodium, 8 g carbo., 1 g fiber, 34 g pro.

beer can chicken

The bird looks humorous sitting upright on the grill, but the moist, herb-seasoned chicken tastes sublime.

Prep: 30 minutes   Grill: 1 1/4 hours   Stand: 10 minutes
Makes: 4 to 6 servings

- 2 teaspoons packed brown sugar
- 2 teaspoons paprika
- 2 teaspoons salt
- 1 teaspoon dry mustard
- 1/2 teaspoon ground black pepper
- 1/2 teaspoon dried thyme, crushed
- 1/4 teaspoon garlic powder
- 1 12-ounce can beer
- 1 3 1/2- to 4-pound whole broiler-fryer chicken
- 2 tablespoons butter or margarine, softened
- 1 lemon wedge

1. In a small bowl, combine brown sugar, paprika, salt, dry mustard, pepper, thyme, and garlic powder. Drink or pour about half of the beer from the can. Add 1 teaspoon of the spice mixture to the half-empty can (beer will foam up).

2. Remove neck and giblets from chicken. Sprinkle 1 teaspoon of the spice rub inside the body cavity. Rub the outside of the chicken with butter and sprinkle on the remaining spice rub.

3. Hold the chicken upright with the opening of the body cavity at the bottom, and lower it onto the beer can so the can fits into the cavity. Pull the chicken legs forward so the bird rests on its legs and the can. Twist wing tips behind back. Stuff the lemon wedge in the neck cavity to seal in steam.

4. For a charcoal grill, arrange medium-hot coals around a drip pan. Test for medium heat above pan. Stand chicken upright on grill rack over drip pan. Grill, covered, for 1 1/4 to 1 3/4 hours or until chicken is no longer pink (180°F in thigh muscle). If necessary, place a tent of foil over chicken to prevent overbrowning. (For a gas grill, preheat grill. Reduce heat to medium. Adjust for indirect cooking. If necessary, remove upper grill racks so chicken will stand upright. Cover and grill as above.) Remove chicken from grill, holding by the can. Cover with foil; let stand for 10 minutes. Use a hot pad to grasp can and heavy tongs to carefully remove the chicken.

Per Serving: 635 cal., 45 g fat (15 g sat. fat), 217 mg chol., 1,180 mg sodium, 3 g carbo., 0 g fiber, 51 g pro.

in the can

While its origin is a mystery, Beer Can Chicken began popping up at barbecue cook-offs across the country in the early 1990s. The cooking technique perches a whole chicken vertically on top of an open can of beer, so flavor-infused steam penetrates the chicken, generating incredibly tender and juicy results. The upright position allows the bird to cook evenly with the fat running off, resulting in a crisp, golden skin.

beer can chicken

mushroom-stuffed chicken

mushroom-stuffed chicken

Tucked under the skin, Italian-scented mushrooms infuse the chicken with flavor.

Prep: 30 minutes   Cool: 10 minutes   Grill: 50 minutes
Makes: 4 to 6 servings

2	tablespoons olive oil
1	to 1¼ pounds chopped mixed mushrooms (4 cups)
1	clove garlic, minced
2	teaspoons snipped fresh oregano or ¼ teaspoon dried oregano, crushed
2	tablespoons dry Marsala (optional)
1	teaspoon anchovy paste or soy sauce
¼	teaspoon salt
¼	teaspoon freshly ground black pepper
2½	to 3 pounds meaty chicken pieces (breast halves, thighs, and drumsticks)
	Salt and freshly ground black pepper
	Lemon halves (optional)
	Fresh oregano sprigs (optional)

1. In a large skillet, heat olive oil over medium heat. Add mushrooms, garlic, and oregano. Cook mushrooms for 6 to 8 minutes or until lightly browned and tender, stirring occasionally. Remove from heat. Stir in Marsala (if desired), anchovy paste, ¼ teaspoon salt, and ¼ teaspoon pepper. Return to heat and cook and stir for 2 minutes more. Remove from heat and allow to cool slightly, about 10 minutes.

2. With your hands, loosen skin of each chicken piece on one side. Stuff mushroom mixture evenly beneath the skin of each chicken piece. Sprinkle chicken lightly with salt and pepper

3. For a charcoal grill, arrange medium-hot coals around a drip pan. Test for medium heat above the pan. Place chicken pieces, bone sides down, on the grill rack over drip pan. Grill, covered, for 50 to 60 minutes or until chicken is no longer pink (170°F in breast halves, 180°F in thighs and drumsticks). (For a gas grill, preheat grill. Reduce heat to medium. Adjust for indirect cooking. Place chicken pieces on the grill rack. Cover and grill as above.)

4. If desired, serve with fresh lemon and garnish with oregano.
Per Serving: 328 cal., 16 g fat (4 g sat. fat), 116 mg chol., 437 mg sodium, 4 g carbo., 1 g fiber, 41 g pro.

honey-glazed chicken
with roasted grapes

Prep: 20 minutes   Stand: 15 minutes   Grill: 50 minutes
Makes: 4 servings

4	bone-in chicken breast halves (2½ to 3 pounds total)
5	tablespoons balsamic vinegar
1	tablespoon extra virgin olive oil
3	garlic cloves, minced
¾	teaspoon salt
¼	teaspoon ground black pepper
¼	cup honey
2	teaspoons freshly shredded orange peel
1	bulb garlic (about 10 cloves) (optional)
2	teaspoons extra virgin olive oil (optional)
1	pound red and/or green seedless grapes, cut into 4 bunches
1	tablespoon honey
1	wedge blue cheese (optional)
1	tablespoon honey (optional)

1. Place chicken in a large resealable plastic bag set in a shallow dish. For marinade, in a small bowl, combine 2 tablespoons of the vinegar, 1 tablespoon oil, minced garlic, ½ teaspoon of the salt, and pepper. Pour marinade over chicken. Seal bag and turn bag to coat chicken. Set aside for 15 minutes.

2. Meanwhile, in another small bowl, stir together the remaining 3 tablespoons vinegar, ¼ cup honey, orange peel, and remaining ¼ teaspoon salt; set aside. Separate and peel garlic cloves (if using). Place garlic on an 8-inch square of heavy foil; drizzle with 2 teaspoons olive oil. Wrap foil around garlic to seal.

3. For a charcoal grill, arrange medium-hot coals around a drip pan. Test for medium heat above the pan. Remove chicken from bag, discarding marinade. Place chicken, skin sides down, on the grill rack over the drip pan. Place garlic packet (if using) next to chicken. Grill, covered, for 25 minutes. Remove garlic and cool. Turn chicken skin sides up; brush with some of the honey mixture. Cover and grill about 25 minutes more or until chicken is no longer pink (170°F), brushing occasionally with honey mixture up until the last 5 minutes of grilling. (For a gas grill, preheat grill. Reduce heat to medium. Adjust for indirect cooking. Place chicken, skin sides down, on the grill rack. Cover and grill as above.)

4. Meanwhile, drizzle grapes with 1 tablespoon honey. Place grapes on grill rack over coals or heat. Cover and grill for 2 to 3 minutes or until browned and softened, turning once. Transfer chicken and grapes to serving plates. If desired, serve with cheese topped with garlic and drizzled with honey.
Per Serving: 622 cal., 25 g fat (6 g sat. fat), 144 mg chol., 559 mg sodium, 49 g carbo., 1 g fiber, 49 g pro.

honey-dijon chicken

Marinating the chicken overnight frees up your time in the kitchen right before dinner.

Prep: 15 minutes Marinate: 8 to 24 hours Grill: 12 minutes
Makes: 8 servings

8	skinless, boneless chicken breast halves (about 2$^1/_2$ pounds total)
$^1/_2$	cup white Zinfandel wine, apple juice, or apple cider
$^1/_4$	cup olive oil
$^1/_4$	cup honey
$^1/_4$	cup Dijon-style mustard
4	cloves garlic, minced
$^1/_2$	teaspoon ground black pepper
$^1/_4$	teaspoon salt

1. Place chicken breasts in a resealable plastic bag set in a bowl. For marinade, in a small bowl, combine wine or apple juice, oil, honey, mustard, garlic, pepper, and salt. Pour marinade over chicken; seal bag. Marinate in the refrigerator for at least 8 hours or up to 24 hours, turning bag occasionally.

2. Drain chicken, discarding marinade. For a charcoal grill, place chicken on the grill rack directly over medium coals. Grill, uncovered, for 12 to 15 minutes or until done (170°F), turning once halfway through grilling. (For a gas grill, preheat grill. Reduce heat to medium. Place chicken on greased grill rack over heat. Cover and grill as directed above.)
Per Serving: 380 cal., 23 g fat (6 g sat. fat), 118 mg chol., 171 mg sodium, 3 g carbo., 0 g fiber, 37 g pro.

White Zinfandel wine and honey infuse these crowd-pleasing chicken breasts with a pleasant hint of sweetness.

chicken stuffed with spinach and sweet peppers

Prep: 20 minutes Marinate: 2 to 4 hours Grill: 45 minutes
Makes: 6 servings

6	bone-in chicken breast halves (about 3 pounds total)
$^1/_4$	cup honey mustard
2	tablespoons mayonnaise
1	tablespoon olive oil
1	tablespoon red wine vinegar
2	teaspoons snipped fresh oregano or 1 teaspoon dried oregano, crushed
2	teaspoons snipped fresh basil or 1 teaspoon dried basil, crushed
2	teaspoons snipped fresh rosemary or 1 teaspoon dried rosemary, crushed
1	cup finely shredded mozzarella cheese (4 ounces)
1	cup chopped fresh spinach
$^1/_2$	cup chopped red sweet pepper
3	cloves garlic, minced
$^1/_4$	teaspoon ground black pepper

1. Make a pocket in each chicken breast half by cutting horizontally from one side almost to the opposite side. Place chicken in a resealable plastic bag set in a shallow dish. For marinade, in a small bowl, combine mustard, mayonnaise, oil, vinegar, oregano, basil, and rosemary. Pour over chicken. Seal bag; turn to coat chicken. Marinate in the refrigerator for 2 to 4 hours, turning bag occasionally. Remove chicken from marinade, scraping off and discarding excess marinade.

2. Meanwhile, for stuffing, in a medium bowl, combine mozzarella cheese, spinach, sweet pepper, garlic, and black pepper. Divide stuffing among pockets in chicken. If necessary, secure the openings with wooden toothpicks.

3. For a charcoal grill, arrange medium-hot coals around a drip pan. Test for medium heat above the pan. Place chicken pieces, bone sides down, on the grill rack over drip pan. Cover and grill for 45 to 55 minutes or until chicken is no longer pink (170°F), turning once halfway through grilling. (For a gas grill, preheat grill. Reduce heat to medium. Adjust for indirect cooking. Place chicken pieces on the grill rack. Cover and grill as above.) Before serving, discard toothpicks.
Per Serving: 297 cal., 11 g total fat (3 g sat. fat), 103 mg chol., 282 mg sodium, 5 g carbo., 1 g fiber, 41 g pro.

chicken stuffed with spinach
and sweet peppers

cherry-chicken roll-ups

For a light meal, serve a side of fresh asparagus and wheat rolls with the roll-ups.

cherry-chicken roll-ups

Sink your fork into one of these plump rolls, and creamy cherry-dotted filling oozes out.

Prep: 30 minutes Grill: 20 minutes Makes: 4 servings

- 1/2 of an 8-ounce container mascarpone cheese or 1/2 of an 8-ounce tub (about 1/2 cup) cream cheese
- 1/3 cup snipped dried cherries
- 3 tablespoons thinly sliced green onions
- 4 skinless, boneless chicken breast halves (about 1 1/4 pounds total)
- 1 tablespoon packed brown sugar
- 1/2 teaspoon salt
- 1/4 teaspoon ground black pepper

1. For filling, in a small bowl, combine mascarpone cheese, dried cherries, and green onions. Set filling aside.

2. Place each chicken breast half between two pieces of plastic wrap. Using the flat side of a meat mallet, pound the chicken lightly into rectangles about 1/4 inch thick. Remove plastic wrap. Spread filling evenly over each chicken breast half to within 1/2 inch of edges. Fold in sides of each chicken piece; roll up from a short end. Secure with wooden toothpicks.

3. For rub, in a small bowl, combine brown sugar, salt, and pepper. Sprinkle rub over chicken roll-ups; rub in with your fingers.

4. For a charcoal grill, arrange medium-hot coals around a drip pan. Test for medium heat above the pan. Place chicken on the grill rack over drip pan. Grill, covered, for 20 to 25 minutes or until chicken is no longer pink (170°F). (For a gas grill, preheat grill. Reduce heat to medium. Adjust for indirect cooking. Place chicken on grill rack. Cover and grill as above.)

Per Serving: 459 cal., 15 g fat (8 g sat. fat), 118 mg chol., 400 mg sodium, 45 g carbo., 2 g fiber, 40 g pro.

turkey fajitas

Pile the ingredients on the tortillas and serve the fajitas ready-made, or lay out the makings on a platter and let diners assemble their own.

Prep: 20 minutes Marinate: 1 hour Grill: 12 minutes
Makes: 5 servings

- 12 ounces boneless turkey breast
- 1 cup bottled green taco sauce or green salsa (salsa verde)
- 2 tablespoons olive oil
- 10 8-inch flour tortillas
- 1 medium red onion, cut into 1/2-inch slices
- 2 medium zucchini and/or yellow summer squash, cut lengthwise into 1/2-inch slices
- 1 medium red sweet pepper, quartered and seeded
  Bottled green taco sauce or green salsa (salsa verde)
  Snipped fresh cilantro

1. Cut turkey into 1/2-inch slices. Place turkey in a large resealable plastic bag set in a shallow dish. For marinade, in a small bowl, combine the 1 cup taco sauce and oil. Pour 1/2 cup of marinade over turkey; seal bag. Marinate in the refrigerator for 1 hour, turning bag once. Reserve remaining marinade. Stack tortillas and wrap in foil.

2. Drain turkey, discarding marinade. Skewer onion slices with wooden toothpicks, inserting from one edge to the center. Brush onion, squash, and sweet pepper with reserved marinade.

3. For a charcoal grill, place turkey and vegetables on the grill rack directly over medium coals. Grill, uncovered, for 12 to 14 minutes or until turkey is no longer pink (170°F), turning once halfway through grilling. Place tortilla packet on the grill for the last 5 minutes of grilling. (For a gas grill, preheat grill. Reduce heat to medium. Place turkey, vegetables, and tortillas on grill rack over heat. Cover and grill as above.) Remove toothpicks from onion slices; discard toothpicks.

4. Cut turkey and vegetables into bite-size strips. On each tortilla, arrange some of the turkey, onion, squash, and red pepper. Drizzle each fajita with taco sauce and sprinkle with cilantro. Fold in sides; roll up tortillas.

Per Serving: 350 cal., 11 g fat (2 g sat. fat), 42 mg chol., 459 mg sodium, 40 g carbo., 3 g fiber, 22 g pro.

orange-balsamic turkey tenderloins

Less is more in this case. To be sure the turkey stays juicy and tender, refrigerate it in the brine no longer than 6 hours.

Prep: 10 minutes   Marinate: 4 to 6 hours   Grill: 12 minutes
Makes: 4 servings

2	turkey breast tenderloins
1/2	cup balsamic vinegar
2	cups orange juice
3	tablespoons coarse kosher salt
1	tablespoon sugar
1	tablespoon dried basil, crushed
1/2	teaspoon ground black pepper
1/4	cup orange marmalade

1. Split each tenderloin in half horizontally. Set aside 1 tablespoon of the vinegar. For brine, in a large bowl, combine remaining vinegar, the orange juice, salt, sugar, basil, and pepper. Place tenderloins in brine mixture. Cover and marinate in the refrigerator for at least 4 hours or up to 6 hours, turning tenderloins occasionally.

2. Drain tenderloins; discard brine. Rinse tenderloins and pat dry with paper towels. In a small bowl, combine the reserved vinegar and marmalade.

3. For a charcoal grill, place tenderloins on the grill rack directly over medium coals. Grill, uncovered, for 12 to 15 minutes or until turkey is no longer pink (170°F), turning once halfway through grilling and brushing with marmalade mixture during the last 2 minutes of grilling. (For a gas grill, preheat grill. Reduce heat to medium. Place tenderloins on grill rack over heat. Cover and grill as above.)

Per Serving: 196 cal., 2 g fat (1 g sat. fat), 68 mg chol., 789 mg sodium, 17 g carbo., 0 g dietary fiber, 27 g protein.

For a special dinner, make one of these turkey dishes—guests will love the amazing flavor the turkey acquires from the grill and just a handful of ingredients.

turkey breast stuffed with sausage, fennel, and figs

Prep: 20 minutes   Grill: 1 1/2 hours   Stand: 10 minutes
Makes: 10 to 12 servings

1	4- to 5-pound bone-in turkey breast
1/2	teaspoon salt
1/2	teaspoon ground black pepper
1	pound bulk or link sweet Italian sausage
12	green onions, thinly sliced
2/3	cup snipped dried figs
1 1/2	teaspoons fennel seeds
2	tablespoons olive oil
1/4	teaspoon salt
1/4	teaspoon ground black pepper

1. Remove bone from turkey (you may want to ask the butcher to remove the bone for you). Place turkey, skin side down, between two pieces of plastic wrap. Working from the center to the edges, pound lightly with the flat side of a meat mallet to an even thickness. Remove plastic wrap. Sprinkle turkey with the 1/2 teaspoon salt and the 1/2 teaspoon pepper.

2. For stuffing, remove casings from sausage, if present. In a medium bowl, combine sausage, green onions, figs, and fennel seeds.

3. Spoon stuffing over half of the turkey; fold other half of turkey over stuffing. Tie in several places with 100-percent-cotton kitchen string or secure with metal skewers. Rub skin with oil and sprinkle with the 1/4 teaspoon salt and the 1/4 teaspoon pepper.

4. For a charcoal grill, arrange medium-hot coals around a drip pan. Test for medium heat above the pan. Place turkey on the grill rack over the drip pan. Cover and grill for 1 1/2 to 2 hours or until turkey is no longer pink (170°F) and center of stuffing registers 165°F. (For a gas grill, preheat grill. Reduce heat to medium. Adjust for indirect cooking. Place turkey on the grill rack. Cover and grill as above.)

5. Remove turkey from grill. Cover with foil and let stand for 10 minutes before carving.

Per serving: 364 cal., 18 g fat (6 g sat. fat), 119 mg chol., 577 mg sodium, 8 g carbo., 2 g dietary fiber, 41 g protein.

turkey breast stuffed with sausage, fennel, and figs

For individual servings, arrange the colorful Cajun turkey salad on separate plates.

tahini turkey thighs

Rich-flavor tahini, a paste made from sesame seeds, is the color of peanut butter but much thicker. Use a whisk when combining it with the other ingredients.

Prep: 45 minutes   Grill: 50 minutes   Makes: 6 servings

4	turkey thighs (about 3$1/2$ to 4 pounds)
$1/2$	cup tahini (sesame seed paste)
$1/4$	cup water
2	tablespoons soy sauce
1	tablespoon lemon juice
1	tablespoon honey
1	tablespoon Asian chili-garlic sauce
1	teaspoon grated fresh ginger
	Chickpea Salad

1. If desired, remove skin from turkey. For sauce, in a medium bowl, whisk together tahini, the water, soy sauce, lemon juice, honey, chili-garlic sauce, and ginger until combined. Set sauce aside.

2. For a charcoal grill, arrange medium-hot coals around a drip pan. Test for medium heat above the pan. Place turkey thighs, bone sides up, on the grill rack over drip pan. Grill, covered, for 50 to 60 minutes or until turkey is no longer pink (180°F), turning once halfway through grilling and brushing frequently with sauce during the last 20 minutes of grilling. (For a gas grill, preheat grill. Reduce heat to medium. Adjust for indirect cooking. Cover and grill as above.) Discard any remaining sauce.

3. To serve, cut turkey meat from bones. Serve with Chickpea Salad.

Chickpea Salad: For dressing, in a small screw-top jar, combine 3 tablespoons olive oil, 3 tablespoons lemon juice, $1/4$ teaspoon salt, and $1/8$ teaspoon ground black pepper. Cover and shake well. Rinse and drain two 15-ounce cans garbanzo beans (chickpeas). In a large bowl, combine the beans; $3/4$ cup finely chopped yellow or red sweet pepper; $2/3$ cup snipped fresh parsley; $1/2$ cup finely chopped, seeded cucumber; $1/3$ cup snipped fresh mint; 2 chopped, seeded roma tomatoes; and $1/4$ cup finely chopped red onion. Add dressing; toss to combine. Cover and chill until ready to serve.

Per Serving: 600 cal., 32 g fat (6 g sat. fat), 119 mg chol., 985 mg sodium, 34 g carbo., 8 g fiber, 44 g pro.

cajun turkey cutlets
with fruit

Like an artist's palette, the plate presentation can change each time you serve this artful masterpiece, depending what fruit is in season.

Prep: 10 minutes   Grill: 12 minutes   Makes: 4 servings

2	turkey breast tenderloins (about 1 pound)
1	tablespoon olive oil
$1^1/2$	teaspoons Cajun seasoning
6	cups torn mixed greens
$1^1/2$	cups sliced cantaloupe
1	cup fresh blueberries
	Crumbled farmer cheese (optional)
	Purchased salad dressing of your choice

1. Using a sharp knife, cut each turkey breast tenderloin in half horizontally. Brush turkey pieces with olive oil. Sprinkle with Cajun seasoning.

2. For a charcoal grill, place turkey on the grill rack directly over medium coals. Grill, uncovered, for 12 to 15 minutes or until turkey is no longer pink (170°F), turning once halfway through grilling. (For a gas grill, preheat grill. Reduce heat to medium. Place turkey on grill rack over heat. Cover and grill as above.) Slice turkey.

3. On a serving platter, arrange greens along with the turkey, cantaloupe, and berries. If desired, sprinkle cheese over salad. Serve with dressing.

Per Serving: 359 cal., 22 g fat (4 g sat. fat), 68 mg chol., 161 mg sodium, 14 g carbo., 3 g fiber, 29 g pro.

mustard–dill fish
(recipe, page 93)

tuna with bean salad and anchovy-caper vinaigrette

tuna with bean salad and anchovy-caper vinaigrette

Prep: 30 minutes   Stand: 1 hour   Cook: 2 hours   Grill: 8 minutes
Makes: 6 servings

- 1 pound dried cannellini beans (white kidney beans) or three 19-ounce cans cannellini beans, rinsed and drained
- 1/2 cup fresh marjoram sprigs
- 6 tablespoons extra virgin olive oil
  Kosher salt and freshly ground black pepper
- 2 to 4 anchovy fillets, drained
- 1/3 cup finely chopped parsley
- 3 tablespoons capers, drained
- 2 cloves garlic, minced
- 1 teaspoon Dijon-style mustard
- 6 tablespoons lemon juice (2 lemons)
- 1/4 cup extra virgin olive oil
- 6 4-ounce fresh tuna steaks, about 3/4 inch thick*
- 6 1/2-inch slices red onion (2 large)

1. Rinse dried beans, if using. In a Dutch oven, combine rinsed beans and 8 cups water. Bring to boiling; reduce heat. Simmer, covered, for 2 minutes. Remove from heat. Let stand, covered, for 1 hour. (Or place beans in water in Dutch oven. Cover and let soak in a cool place for 6 to 8 hours or overnight.) Drain and rinse beans. Return beans to Dutch oven. Stir in 8 cups fresh water; add marjoram sprigs and 1 tablespoon of the olive oil. Bring to boiling; reduce heat. Simmer,

covered, 2 hours or until tender. Drain, discarding marjoram sprigs. Cool slightly. Toss beans with 4 tablespoons of the olive oil; season with salt and pepper. Cover; set aside. (If using canned beans, in a saucepan, combine beans, 1 1/2 to 2 tablespoons snipped fresh marjoram, 4 tablespoons olive oil, and salt and pepper to taste. Cook and stir over medium heat until heated; cover and keep warm.)

2. For vinaigrette, in a small bowl, mash anchovy fillets with a fork. Add parsley, capers, garlic, and mustard; mix thoroughly. Stir in 2 tablespoons of the lemon juice. Add the 1/4 cup olive oil, whisking to combine ingredients. Season to taste with additional salt. Set aside.

3. Brush tuna and onion slices with the remaining 1 tablespoon olive oil; sprinkle lightly with additional salt and pepper. For a charcoal grill, place fish and onions on the grill rack directly over medium coals. Grill, uncovered, for 8 to 9 minutes or until tuna is slightly pink in center and onions are tender, turning once halfway through grilling. (For a gas grill, preheat grill. Reduce heat to medium. Place tuna and onions on the grill rack over heat. Cover and grill as above.)

4. To serve, spoon beans onto six serving plates. Drizzle beans with remaining 4 tablespoons lemon juice. Place a fish steak on each plate. Drizzle each serving with vinaigrette. Serve with red onion slices. If desired, sprinkle with additional marjoram sprigs.

*Note: Skinless salmon fillets can be used in place of tuna steaks. Salmon is done when it flakes easily with a fork.
Per Serving: 603 cal., 25 g fat (4 g sat. fat), 52 mg chol., 734 mg sodium, 53 g carbo., 16 g fiber, 44 g pro.

mustard-dill fish

Choose ripe summer tomatoes for the tomato-dill relish. Quick-cooking them in a skillet on the grill brings out their sweet flavor. Pictured on page 91.

Prep: 15 minutes Grill: 5 minutes Makes: 4 servings

- 4   catfish fillets (about 1 1/2 pounds total)
      Salt and ground black pepper
- 1/4 cup Dijon-style mustard
- 2   tablespoons snipped fresh dill
- 1   tablespoon olive oil
- 3   cups cut-up assorted tomatoes
- 1   tablespoon snipped fresh dill
- 1   tablespoon olive oil
- 2   cloves garlic, thinly sliced
- 1   tablespoon olive oil
      Snipped fresh dill (optional)

1. Rinse fish; pat dry with paper towels. Sprinkle fish with salt and pepper.

2. In a small bowl, stir together mustard, 2 tablespoons dill, and 1 tablespoon olive oil. Spread mixture over both sides of each fillet.

3. In a bowl, combine tomatoes, 1 tablespoon dill, 1 tablespoon olive oil, and garlic. Season mixture to taste with salt and pepper.

4. For a charcoal grill, preheat a large cast-iron skillet on the grill rack directly over medium-hot coals. Add 1 tablespoon olive oil to skillet. Add fish to hot skillet. Grill, uncovered, for 4 to 6 minutes per 1/2-inch thickness of fish or until fish flakes easily when tested with a fork, turning fish once halfway through grilling. Using a large metal spatula, remove fish from skillet; keep warm. Add tomato mixture to skillet on grill. Grill, uncovered, for 1 to 2 minutes or until tomatoes are just heated, stirring often. (For a gas grill, preheat grill. Reduce heat to medium-high. Preheat skillet on grill rack over heat. Cover and grill fish and tomatoes as above.)

5. To serve, spoon tomato mixture onto a serving platter. Top with fish fillets. If desired, sprinkle with additional snipped fresh dill.

Per Serving: 358 cal., 23 g fat (4 g sat. fat), 79 mg chol., 602 mg sodium, 5 g carbo., 2 g fiber, 28 g pro.

salmon and asparagus with garden mayonnaise

A spoonful of lemony herbed mayonnaise puts the finishing touch on a bistro-style plate presentation.

Prep: 10 minutes Grill: 8 minutes Makes: 4 servings

- 4   6- to 8-ounce skinless salmon fillets, cut 1 inch thick
- 1   pound asparagus spears
- 1   tablespoon olive oil
      Sea salt or salt
      Freshly ground black pepper
- 1/2 cup finely chopped celery (1 stalk)
- 1/4 cup thinly sliced green onions (2)
- 1/3 cup mayonnaise
- 1   tablespoon lemon juice
- 2   teaspoons snipped fresh tarragon or 1/2 teaspoon dried tarragon, crushed
      Lemon wedges (optional)

1. Rinse fish; pat dry with paper towels. Snap off and discard woody bases from asparagus spears. Brush asparagus and both sides of each salmon fillet lightly with some of the oil. Sprinkle asparagus and salmon with salt and pepper.

2. Grease an unheated grill rack. For a charcoal grill, place salmon on the greased grill rack directly over medium coals. Place asparagus on grill rack next to salmon. Grill, uncovered, for 8 to 12 minutes or until asparagus is tender and fish flakes easily when tested with a fork, turning fish once halfway through grilling and turning asparagus occasionally. (For a gas grill, preheat grill. Reduce heat to medium. Place fish and asparagus on grill rack over heat. Cover; grill as above.)

3. Meanwhile, in a small bowl, stir together celery, green onions, mayonnaise, lemon juice, and tarragon.

4. To serve, arrange asparagus on four serving plates. Top each serving with a salmon fillet. Spoon mayonnaise mixture on top of salmon. If desired, serve with lemon wedges.

Per Serving: 501 cal., 37 g fat (7 g sat. fat), 107 mg chol., 313 mg sodium, 6 g carbo., 3 g fiber, 37 g pro.

cooked to perfection

Cooking fish too long causes it to become tough and dry. Follow these simple steps for moist and tender grilled fish.

✳ **If you grill fish with skin,** let the skin become crisp and brown and allow the fish to pull away from the grill before turning it.

✳ **Check the flesh at the thickest part** of the fillet. When the fish is cooked, it will be opaque, moist, and pull apart easily when tested with a fork.

✳ **For thicker, denser fish steaks** where the fork test is difficult, insert an instant-read thermometer horizontally into the steak. Remove the steak from the grill when it reaches an internal temperature of 140°.

grilled fish
with moroccan vinaigrette

Instead of greasing your grill rack, grill fish in foil packets. Fold four 24×18-inch pieces of heavy foil to make four 12×9-inch rectangles. Place a fish fillet in the center of each foil rectangle. Sprinkle with salt and freshly ground black pepper. Drizzle olive oil over fish. Bring up long sides of foil and seal with a double fold. Fold remaining edges together to completely enclose fish, leaving space for steam to build. Grill as directed.

Prep: 20 minutes   Grill: 6 minutes   Makes: 4 servings

1	1/4 to 1 1/2 pounds fresh or frozen red snapper, sea bass, grouper, or tuna fillets, cut into four 3/4-inch-thick portions
2	tablespoons olive oil
1/4	teaspoon kosher salt or sea salt
1/4	teaspoon freshly ground black pepper
1/2	cup red wine vinegar
2	tablespoons snipped fresh Italian (flat-leaf) parsley
2	tablespoons snipped fresh cilantro
2	tablespoons olive oil
1	tablespoon fresh lemon juice
1	large shallot, minced
1	clove garlic, minced
1/2	teaspoon kosher salt or sea salt
1/2	teaspoon paprika
1/4	teaspoon cayenne pepper
1/4	teaspoon ground cumin
	Hot cooked couscous
	Lemon wedges (optional)
	Mesclun (optional)
	Radish slivers (optional)

1. Thaw fish, if frozen. Rinse fish; pat dry with paper towels. Brush both sides of fish with some of the 2 tablespoons olive oil. Sprinkle both sides of fish with the 1/4 teaspoon salt and 1/4 teaspoon freshly ground black pepper.

2. For vinaigrette, in a screw-top jar, combine vinegar, parsley, cilantro, 2 tablespoons olive oil, lemon juice, shallot, garlic, the 1/2 teaspoon salt, paprika, cayenne pepper, and cumin. Cover and shake well. Set aside.

3. Grease an unheated grill rack. For a charcoal grill, place fish on the greased rack directly over medium coals. Grill, uncovered, for 6 to 9 minutes or until fish flakes easily when tested with a fork, gently turning once and brushing once with remaining oil halfway through grilling. (For a gas grill, preheat grill. Reduce heat to medium. Place fish on greased rack over heat. Cover and grill as above.)

4. To serve, thoroughly shake vinaigrette. Divide couscous among four serving plates or shallow bowls. Use a wide spatula to transfer fish to plates. Drizzle the vinaigrette over fish. If desired, garnish with lemon wedges, mesclun, and radish slivers. Serve immediately.

Per Serving: 501 cal., 37 g fat (7 g sat. fat), 107 mg chol., 313 mg sodium, 6 g carbo., 3 g fiber, 37 g pro.

grilled trout stuffed
with lemon and herbs

This is a simple, flavorful way to grill almost any whole fish. In this Greek recipe, the stuffing was created to flavor the fish from the inside as it cooks. Trout is more customary to this traditional recipe, but salmon and sea bass work just as well.

Prep: 20 minutes   Grill: 8 minutes   Makes: 4 servings

4	8- to 10-ounce fresh or frozen dressed rainbow trout or Coho salmon
1	tablespoon olive oil
1	teaspoon kosher salt
1/4	teaspoon freshly ground black pepper
2	lemons
2	tablespoons snipped fresh oregano, thyme, and/or chives or 2 teaspoons dried oregano or thyme, crushed
2	cloves garlic, minced
12	sprigs fresh oregano and/or thyme, and/or chive stems (omit if using dried herbs)

1. Thaw fish, if frozen. Rinse fish; pat dry with paper towels. If desired, remove the heads of the trout. Drizzle fish lightly with the olive oil; rub in with your fingers. Spread fish open. Sprinkle flesh of fish with salt and pepper; set aside.

2. Cut one of the lemons in half lengthwise, then cut each half into thin slices. Cut remaining lemon into wedges; set aside.

3. In a small bowl, combine snipped or dried herbs and the garlic. Sprinkle the flesh of fish with herb mixture. Arrange the lemon slices evenly along the inside of each fish. Arrange herb sprigs over lemon slices. Squeeze one of the lemon wedges over inside of each fish. Fold remaining side of each fish over lemon slices and herbs.

4. For a charcoal grill, place the fish on the rack directly over medium coals. Grill, uncovered, for 8 to 12 minutes or until fish flakes easily when tested with a fork, turning once halfway through grilling. (For a gas grill, preheat grill. Reduce heat to medium. Place fish on the grill rack over medium heat. Cover and grill as directed above.) Serve with remaining lemon wedges.

Per Serving: 356 cal., 16 g fat (4 g sat. fat), 133 mg chol., 564 mg sodium, 6 g carbo., 3 g fiber, 48 g pro.

grilled trout stuffed with lemon and herbs

grilled fish tacos

Fish can be fragile and fall apart on the grill, so be sure to grease the grill rack well and use a metal turner for flipping the fish.

Prep: 15 minutes   Marinate: 15 minutes   Grill: 4 minutes
Makes: 6 servings

   1   pound fresh or frozen skinless cod, sole, or flounder fillets, $1/2$ inch thick
   1   tablespoon lemon juice
   1   tablespoon olive oil
   1   teaspoon chili powder
 $1/2$ teaspoon ground cumin
 $1/4$ teaspoon salt
 $1/4$ teaspoon ground black pepper
  12   7- to 8-inch flour tortillas
       Pineapple Salsa

1. Thaw fish, if frozen. Rinse fish; pat dry with paper towels. Arrange fish in a 2-quart square baking dish; set aside. For marinade, in a small bowl, whisk together lemon juice, oil, chili powder, cumin, salt, and pepper. Pour over fish. Turn fish to coat with marinade. Cover and marinate in the refrigerator for 15 minutes. Drain fish, discarding any marinade. Stack tortillas and wrap in foil.

2. Grease an unheated grill rack. For a charcoal grill, place fish and tortillas on the greased grill rack directly over medium coals. Grill, uncovered, for 4 to 6 minutes or until fish flakes easily when tested with a fork and tortillas are warmed, turning tortilla packet once. (For a gas grill, preheat grill. Reduce heat to medium. Place fish and tortilla packet on greased grill rack over heat. Cover and grill as above.)

3. Transfer fish to a cutting board. Cut or flake fish into 1-inch pieces. Serve in warmed tortillas topped with Pineapple Salsa.

Pineapple Salsa: In a medium bowl, stir together 1 cup diced fresh pineapple, $1/4$ cup chopped red sweet pepper, $1/4$ cup chopped red onion, 2 tablespoons chopped fresh cilantro, 1 chopped fresh serrano or jalapeño chile pepper,* 1 teaspoon finely shredded lime peel, and $1/2$ teaspoon salt. Serve immediately or store in an airtight container in the refrigerator for up to 24 hours.

Note: Because hot chile peppers, such as serranos or jalapeños, contain volatile oils that can burn your skin and eyes, avoid direct contact with chiles as much as possible. When working with chile peppers, wear plastic or rubber gloves. If your bare hands do touch the chile peppers, wash your hands well with soap and water.
Per Serving: 322 cal., 3 g fat (0 g sat. fat), 33 mg chol., 1,017 mg sodium, 53 g carbo., 3 g fiber, 18 g pro.

grilled shrimp and romaine

If you own a grill wok, preheat it on the grill and toss in the shrimp instead of threading them on skewers. Grill, stirring often, for 5 to 8 minutes or until shrimp are opaque.

Prep: 15 minutes   Grill: 5 minutes   Makes: 4 servings

 $1/4$ cup olive oil
 $1/2$ teaspoon kosher salt or $1/4$ teaspoon salt
   1   pound fresh or frozen large shrimp, peeled and deveined
   2   hearts of romaine lettuce, halved lengthwise
 $1/4$ cup finely shredded Parmesan cheese
   2   lemons
       Olive oil
       Kosher salt or salt
       Freshly ground black pepper

1. In a small bowl, whisk together the $1/4$ cup olive oil and $1/2$ teaspoon kosher salt. Set aside. On four 10-inch metal or wooden skewers,* thread shrimp, leaving a $1/4$-inch space between shrimp. Brush oil mixture over cut sides of lettuce and the shrimp. Transfer skewers and lettuce to a baking sheet or tray.

2. For a charcoal grill, place shrimp on the grill rack directly over medium coals. Grill, uncovered, for 5 to 8 minutes or until shrimp are opaque, turning once halfway through grilling. Grill lettuce, cut sides down, for 2 to 4 minutes or until grill marks develop on the lettuce and lettuce is slightly wilted. (For a gas grill, preheat grill. Reduce heat to medium. Place shrimp on grill rack over heat. Cover and grill shrimp and lettuce as above.)

3. Place lettuce in serving bowl. Remove shrimp from the skewers. Place shrimp in bowl with lettuce and sprinkle with Parmesan cheese. Squeeze the juice of one of the lemons over the shrimp and lettuce and drizzle with additional olive oil. Sprinkle with additional kosher salt and freshly ground black pepper. Cut the remaining lemon in wedges and serve with the salad.

Note: If using wooden skewers, soak them in water for 30 minutes. Drain skewers before using.
Per Serving: 267 cal., 20 g fat (3 g sat. fat), 133 mg chol., 514 mg sodium, 2 g carbo., 0 g fiber, 19 g pro.

grilled shrimp and romaine

grilled shrimp in coconut milk sauce

grilled shrimp
in coconut milk sauce

Prep: 25 minutes   Marinate: 30 minutes   Cook: 15 minutes
Grill: 7 minutes   Makes: 4 servings

1	pound fresh or frozen extra-large shrimp
2	teaspoons lime juice
1	malagueta, tabasco, or bird chile pepper or chile de arbol, finely chopped*
2	cloves garlic, minced
	Salt and freshly ground black pepper
$1/2$	cup chopped red sweet pepper
$1/4$	cup finely chopped onion
1	tablespoon olive oil
1	cup chopped tomatoes (2 medium)
$1/2$	cup unsweetened coconut milk
1	tablespoon tomato paste

1. Thaw shrimp, if frozen. If using wooden skewers, soak them in water for 30 minutes before using. Peel and devein shrimp, leaving tails intact if desired. Rinse shrimp; pat dry with paper towels. Place shrimp in a large resealable plastic bag set in a shallow bowl.

2. For marinade, in a small bowl, stir together lime juice, half of the finely chopped chile pepper, and half of the garlic; add salt and black pepper to taste. Pour marinade over shrimp. Seal bag; turn to coat

shrimp. Marinate in refrigerator for 30 minutes to 1 hour, turning bag occasionally.

3. For sauce, in a medium skillet, cook sweet pepper, onion, remaining chile pepper, and remaining garlic in hot oil over medium heat about 10 minutes or until tender, stirring occasionally. Add tomatoes, coconut milk, and tomato paste. Bring to boiling; reduce heat. Simmer, uncovered, 5 minutes or until sauce reaches desired consistency. Season to taste with salt. Set aside and keep warm.

4. Thread shrimp onto skewers, leaving a $1/4$-inch space between pieces. Grease an unheated grill rack. For a charcoal grill, place skewers on greased rack directly over medium coals. Grill, uncovered, for 7 to 9 minutes or until shrimp are opaque, turning once halfway through grilling. (For a gas grill, preheat grill. Reduce heat to medium. Place skewers on greased grill rack over heat. Cover; grill as above.) Serve shrimp skewers with sauce.

*Note: Because hot chile peppers contain volatile oils that can burn your skin and eyes, avoid direct contact with chiles as much as possible. When working with chile peppers, wear plastic or rubber gloves. If your bare hands do touch the chile peppers, wash your hands well with soap and water.

Per Serving: 195 cal., 10 g fat (6 g sat. fat), 129 mg chol., 327 mg sodium, 6 g carbo., 1 g fiber, 19 g pro.

98
grillin' and chillin'

shrimp kabobs with cilantro-lime butter sauce

Prep: 40 minutes Grill: 5 minutes Makes: 4 servings

24	fresh or frozen large shrimp in shells
1/3	cup butter, melted
1/4	cup snipped fresh cilantro
2	tablespoons thinly sliced green onion (1)
1	teaspoon finely shredded lime peel
1	tablespoon lime juice
1/4	teaspoon smoked paprika or paprika
1/4	teaspoon garlic salt
1/4	of a fresh pineapple, cored and cut into 1/2-inch-thick wedges
	Nonstick cooking spray
	Cilantro-Scented Couscous
	Fresh lime wedges

1. Thaw shrimp, if frozen. Peel and devein shrimp, leaving tails intact if desired. Rinse shrimp; pat dry with paper towels. For sauce, in a small bowl, stir together melted butter, cilantro, green onion, lime peel, lime juice, paprika, and garlic salt. Set aside.

2. On four 8- to 10-inch metal skewers, thread shrimp, leaving a 1/4-inch space between pieces. Brush shrimp with some of the sauce. Thread pineapple wedges onto four 8- to 10-inch metal skewers. Transfer kabobs to a baking pan.

3. Lightly coat an unheated grill rack with nonstick spray. For a charcoal grill, place kabobs on the greased rack directly over medium coals. Grill shrimp kabobs, uncovered, for 5 to 8 minutes or until shrimp are opaque, turning once and brushing with some of the remaining sauce halfway through grilling. Grill pineapple kabobs for 5 minutes, turning once and brushing with sauce halfway through grilling. (For a gas grill, preheat grill. Reduce heat to medium. Place kabobs on greased grill rack over heat. Cover and grill as above.)

4. Remove shrimp and pineapple kabobs from grill. Serve kabobs over Cilantro-Scented Couscous. Serve with fresh lime wedges.

Cilantro-Scented Couscous: In a medium saucepan, cook 1/2 cup sliced green onions (4) in 1 tablespoon hot oil over medium heat until tender. Stir in 1/2 teaspoon smoked paprika or paprika; cook and stir for 30 seconds. Carefully add 1 cup reduced-sodium chicken broth and 2 tablespoons snipped fresh cilantro. Bring mixture to boiling; stir in 3/4 cup couscous. Remove from heat. Cover and let stand for 5 minutes. Fluff couscous with a fork before serving.

Per Serving: 508 cal., 20 g fat (10 g sat. fat), 105 mg chol., 390 mg sodium, 62 g carbo., 6 g fiber, 19 g pro.

spicy grilled shrimp

Cajun seasoning in the marinade and in the warm marmalade-honey sauce adds big zing to shrimp and rice.

Prep: 15 minutes Marinate: 1 hour Grill: 7 minutes
Makes: 4 servings

1 1/2	pounds fresh or frozen, peeled and deveined extra-large shrimp
1	tablespoon olive oil
1 1/2	to 2 1/2 teaspoons Cajun seasoning
1/4	cup orange marmalade
1/4	cup honey
1/2	teaspoon Cajun seasoning
2	cups hot cooked rice

1. Thaw shrimp, if frozen. If using wooden skewers, soak them in water for 30 minutes before using. Rinse shrimp; pat dry with paper towels. Place shrimp in a large resealable plastic bag set in a shallow bowl.

2. For marinade, in a small bowl, combine oil and 1 1/2 to 2 1/2 teaspoons Cajun seasoning. Pour marinade over shrimp. Seal bag; turn to coat shrimp. Marinate in the refrigerator for 1 hour, turning bag occasionally.

3. Meanwhile, for sauce, in a small saucepan, combine marmalade, honey, and 1/2 teaspoon Cajun seasoning; set aside.

4. Drain shrimp, discarding marinade. Thread shrimp onto skewers, leaving a 1/4-inch space between pieces. Transfer skewers to a pan.

5. Grease an unheated grill rack. For a charcoal grill, place skewers on the greased grill rack directly over medium coals. Grill, uncovered, for 7 to 9 minutes or until shrimp are opaque, turning once halfway through grilling. (For a gas grill, preheat grill. Reduce heat to medium. Place skewers on greased grill rack over heat. Cover; grill as above.)

6. Heat and stir sauce over low heat for 2 to 3 minutes or until melted. Serve shrimp on skewers with hot cooked rice and drizzle with sauce.

Per Serving: 430 cal., 7 g fat (1 g sat. fat), 259 mg chol., 357 mg sodium, 55 g carbo., 1 g fiber, 37 g pro.

the nose knows

When selecting fresh seafood, look for shiny, taut, bright skin and flesh that is firm and elastic with a moist appearance. Ask to smell the fish; avoid any selections with a strong fishy odor.

catfish with summer succotash salad

Finish this Southern-style meal with pieces of corn bread spread with butter or drizzled with honey.

Prep: 15 minutes   Grill: 6 minutes   Makes: 4 servings

2	cups frozen lima beans
4	4- to 6-ounce catfish fillets, about 1/2 inch thick
	Olive oil
	Garlic salt
	Ground black pepper
1	cup purchased corn relish
1	cup fresh baby spinach

1. Cook lima beans according to package directions. Drain beans in colander; rinse under cold water to cool quickly.

2. Meanwhile, rinse fish; pat dry with paper towels. Brush fish with oil and sprinkle with garlic salt and pepper. Place in a well-greased grill basket.

3. For a charcoal grill, place grill basket on the grill rack directly over medium coals. Grill, uncovered, for 6 to 9 minutes or until fish flakes easily when tested with a fork, turning basket once halfway through grilling. (For a gas grill, preheat grill. Reduce heat to medium. Place grill basket on the grill rack directly over heat. Cover; grill as above.)

4. Place fish on serving platter. In a large bowl, toss together cooked beans, corn relish, and spinach. Serve with fish.

Per Serving: 372 cal., 12 g fat (3 g sat. fat), 53 mg chol., 509 mg sodium, 41 g carbo., 5 g fiber, 24 g pro.

halibut with chutney cream sauce

This velvety, rich sauce perfectly partners with any type of white fish.

Prep: 20 minutes   Grill: 4 minutes per 1/2-inch thickness
Makes: 4 servings

4	fresh or frozen halibut steaks (about 1 3/4 pounds total)
1	tablespoon lime juice
	Salt
	Ground black pepper
1/2	cup mango chutney
1/3	cup dry white wine
1	tablespoon finely chopped shallot
2	tablespoons whipping cream
1/2	cup butter, cut into 8 slices
1	mango, seeded, peeled, and sliced
	Sliced green onions

1. Thaw halibut, if frozen. Rinse fish; pat dry with paper towels. Brush each steak with some lime juice and sprinkle with salt and pepper.

2. Lightly grease an unheated grill rack. For a charcoal grill, place fish on the greased grill rack directly over medium coals. Grill, uncovered, for 4 to 6 minutes per 1/2-inch thickness or until fish flakes easily when tested with a fork, turning fish once halfway through grilling. (For a gas grill, preheat grill. Reduce heat to medium. Place fish on greased grill rack over heat. Cover and grill as above.)

3. Meanwhile, for sauce, in a small saucepan, combine the chutney, wine, and shallot. Bring to boiling; reduce heat. Boil gently, uncovered, about 5 minutes or until thickened, stirring occasionally. Add cream; heat through. Whisk in butter, one piece at a time, until melted. Serve fish with sauce and mango slices; sprinkle with onions.

Per Serving: 562 cal., 32 g fat (18 g sat. fat), 139 mg chol., 517 mg sodium, 24 g carbo., 2 g fiber, 43 g pro.

clambake

Although traditionally clambakes occur on a beach, you can enjoy this version in your backyard.

Prep: 20 minutes   Soak: 45 minutes   Grill: 20 minutes
Makes: 4 servings

1	pound littleneck clams
1	pound mussels
1	pound cooked smoked chorizo, sliced 1/2 inch thick (optional)
1	pound small round red potatoes, cut into 1-inch pieces
4	ears fresh corn, husks and silks removed
4	6- to 8-ounce lobster tails
1/2	cup butter, melted

1. Scrub clams and mussels in shells under cold running water. Remove beards from mussels, if present. Place clams and mussels in a large bowl; add 1/3 cup *salt* and enough cold water to cover. Soak for 15 minutes; drain. Repeat two more times. Rinse in fresh cold water.

2. Place clams and mussels in the bottom of a 13×9×3-inch disposable foil pan. Place chorizo (if desired), potatoes, and corn on top; add lobster tails. Cover pan with foil, sealing well.

3. For a charcoal grill, place foil pan on the grill rack directly over medium coals. Grill, uncovered, for 20 to 30 minutes or until potatoes are tender. (For a gas grill, preheat grill. Reduce heat to medium. Place foil pan on the grill rack over heat. Cover and grill as above.)

4. Transfer clam mixture to a newspaper-lined surface or a platter, reserving cooking liquid. Discard clams and mussels that don't open. Serve seafood and vegetables with butter and cooking liquid.

Per Serving: 564 cal., 34 g fat (17 g sat. fat), 166 mg chol., 647 mg sodium, 44 g carbo., 4 g fiber, 25 g pro.

clambake

trout with mushroom stuffing

Wild mushrooms and bacon create a savory stuffing. Grilled apples, although not a must, provide a sweet accompaniment to the trout.

Prep: 25 minutes   Soak: 1 hour   Cook: 8 minutes
Grill: 20 minutes   Makes: 4 servings

- 1 cup apple or alder wood chips or chunks
- 4 10- to 12-ounce fresh or frozen pan-dressed trout
- 4 slices bacon, chopped
- 2 cups sliced assorted wild mushrooms (such as cremini, shiitake, chanterelle, oyster, porcini, and/or cèpes)
- 3 tablespoons butter, melted
- 1/2 teaspoon salt
- 1/2 teaspoon coarsely ground black pepper
- 3 large cloves garlic, peeled and thinly sliced
- 8 sprigs fresh thyme
- 1/4 cup dry white wine
  Grilled Apple Slices (optional)

1. For at least 1 hour before grilling, soak wood chips or chunks and several wooden toothpicks in enough water to cover. Drain before using.

2. Thaw fish, if frozen. Rinse fish; pat dry with paper towels. For stuffing, in a large skillet, cook bacon over medium heat for 3 to 4 minutes or until it softens and begins to brown. Add mushrooms; cook for 5 to 8 minutes or until mushrooms are tender and most of the liquid evaporates, stirring occasionally. Set aside.

3. Meanwhile, brush the outside and cavity of each fish with melted butter. Sprinkle each fish cavity with salt, pepper, and garlic slices. Place one-fourth of the mushroom mixture and 2 thyme sprigs in each fish cavity and sprinkle with 1 tablespoon wine. Secure stuffing inside fish with four to five short metal skewers or the soaked toothpicks. Place the fish on a sheet of heavy-duty foil.

4. For a charcoal grill, arrange medium-hot coals around a drip pan. Add drained wood chips or chunks to coals. Test for medium heat above the pan. Place foil with fish on grill rack over drip pan. Grill, covered, for 20 to 25 minutes or until fish flakes easily when tested with a fork. (For a gas grill, preheat grill. Reduce heat to medium. Add wood chips or chunks according to manufacturer's directions. Adjust for indirect cooking. Place fish on grill rack. Cover and grill as above.)

5. If desired, serve with Grilled Apple Slices.

Grilled Apple Slices: Remove the cores from 2 apples. Cut apples crosswise into 1/2-inch slices; brush slices with olive oil. Grill apple slices directly over medium coals for 5 to 6 minutes or until apples are tender, turning once. Serve warm with fish.
Per Serving: 544 cal., 29 g fat (12 g sat. fat), 198 mg chol., 614 mg sodium, 3 g carbo., 1 g fiber, 63 g pro.

pineapple and scallop skewers

Watch the ticking clock as the scallops soak in the marinade. Scallops get tough if they marinate too long.

Prep: 20 minutes   Stand: 15 minutes   Grill: 8 minutes
Makes: 4 servings

- 2 teaspoons finely shredded lime peel
- 1/4 cup lime juice
- 1/4 cup snipped fresh cilantro
- 2 small green and/or red fresh jalapeño chile peppers, seeded and finely chopped*
- 2 teaspoons sugar
- 1/2 teaspoon salt
- 1/2 teaspoon ground black pepper
- 1/3 cup canola oil
- 16 sea scallops (about 1 1/2 pounds)
- 12 large fresh pineapple chunks
- 1 avocado, pitted, peeled, and cut into 8 chunks

1. In a small bowl, combine lime peel and juice, cilantro, jalapeño, sugar, salt, and black pepper. Slowly whisk in oil; set aside.

2. In a large bowl, combine scallops, pineapple, and avocado. Toss with 2 tablespoons of the lime juice mixture. Let stand for 15 minutes.

3. Alternately thread four scallops, three pineapple chunks, and two avocado chunks on each of four 12- to 16-inch skewers. Transfer skewers to a baking pan.

4. Grease an unheated grill rack. For a charcoal grill, place skewers on the greased grill rack directly over medium-hot coals. Grill, uncovered, about 8 minutes or until scallops are opaque, turning once halfway through grilling. (For a gas grill, preheat grill. Reduce heat to medium-high. Place skewers on the greased grill rack over heat. Cover and grill as above.)

5. Transfer skewers to a serving platter and serve with remaining lime juice mixture.

*Note: Because hot chile peppers, such as jalapeños, contain volatile oils that can burn your skin and eyes, avoid direct contact with chiles as much as possible. When working with chile peppers, wear plastic or rubber gloves. If your bare hands do touch the chile peppers, wash your hands well with soap and water.
Per Serving: 423 cal., 26 g fat (2 g sat. fat), 56 mg chol., 572 mg sodium, 19 g carbo., 4 g fiber, 30 g pro.

dressed up

A "dressed" fish is a whole fish that has been scaled, gutted, and had its gills removed. A "pan-dressed" fish is prepared the same but also has its head, tail, and fins removed.

pineapple and scallop skewers

simply smokin'

What began as an ancient culinary art form has evolved into today's barbecue phenomenon. Restaurant chefs and cook-off contestants across the country have raised the bar on grilling as they infuse a variety of foods with smoky, sweet flavor by cooking low and slow over flavorful woods. And they've expanded their smoking repertoires beyond the traditional ribs and fish to include chops, roasts, and more. With our inventive recipes, you can bring this cooking sensation to your own backyard. Pull out a smoker or grab some grilling planks for your grill and start smokin'.

brisket with
black bean and corn salsa
(recipe, page 106)

spiced and sassy beef ribs

Prep: 30 minutes Chill: 8 to 48 hours Soak: 1 hour
Smoke: 2¹/₂ hours Makes: 4 servings

- 4   pounds beef back ribs (about 8 ribs)
- 1   tablespoon paprika
- 1   tablespoon garlic salt
- 1¹/₂ teaspoons coarsely ground black pepper
- ¹/₂   teaspoon ground cumin
- ¹/₂   teaspoon dried thyme, crushed
- ¹/₂   teaspoon onion powder
- ¹/₄   teaspoon ground coriander
- ¹/₈   teaspoon cayenne pepper
- ¹/₈   teaspoon ground cardamom
- 8   to 10 mesquite or hickory wood chunks
- 2   tablespoons cooking oil
     Mustard Dipping Sauce

1. Trim fat from ribs. For rub, in a small bowl, combine the paprika, garlic salt, black pepper, cumin, thyme, onion powder, coriander, cayenne pepper, and cardamom. Sprinkle rub evenly over ribs; rub in with your fingers. Cover and chill for 8 to 48 hours.

2. For at least 1 hour before smoke cooking, soak wood chunks in enough water to cover. Drain before using. In a smoker, arrange preheated coals, drained wood chunks, and water pan according to the manufacturer's directions. Pour water into pan. Place ribs on the grill rack over the water pan. Smoke, covered, for 2¹/₂ to 3 hours or until tender. Add additional coals and water as needed to maintain temperature and moisture. Serve ribs with Mustard Dipping Sauce.

Mustard Dipping Sauce: In a small saucepan, whisk together ¹/₃ cup Dijon-style mustard, ¹/₄ cup honey, ¹/₄ cup apple juice, 4 teaspoons packed brown sugar, 1 tablespoon cider vinegar, and ¹/₈ teaspoon salt. Bring to boiling; reduce heat. Simmer, uncovered, for 3 minutes.
Per Serving: 393 cal., 25 g fat (8 g sat. fat), 88 mg chol., 843 mg sodium, 2 g carbo., 1 g fiber, 38 g pro.

brisket with black bean and corn salsa

Pictured on page 105.
Prep: 40 minutes Marinate: 6 hours Soak: 1 hour
Smoke: 5 hours Makes: 8 to 10 servings

- 1   3- to 3¹/₂-pound beef brisket
- 1   12-ounce bottle or can beer
- ³/₄   cup lime juice
- ¹/₂   cup chopped onion
- 3   tablespoons cooking oil
- 3   tablespoons steak sauce
- 2   teaspoons chili powder
- 2   teaspoons ground cumin
- 2   teaspoons bottled minced garlic
- 6   to 8 oak or hickory wood chunks
     Black Bean and Corn Salsa

1. Trim fat from brisket. Place brisket in a large resealable plastic bag. For marinade, in a medium bowl, combine the beer, lime juice, onion, oil, steak sauce, chili powder, cumin, and garlic; pour over brisket. Seal bag. Chill for 6 to 24 hours, turning bag occasionally.

2. For at least 1 hour before cooking, soak the wood chunks in enough water to cover. Drain before using. Drain brisket; discard marinade. In a smoker, arrange preheated coals, drained wood chunks, and water pan according to the manufacturer's directions. Pour water into pan. Place brisket on the grill rack over the water pan. Cover and smoke for 5 to 6 hours or until tender. Add additional coals and water as needed to maintain temperature and moisture. To serve, thinly slice brisket across grain; serve with Black Bean and Corn Salsa.

Black Bean and Corn Salsa: In a large bowl, combine 3 cups chopped, seeded tomatoes; one 15-ounce can black beans, rinsed and drained; 1 cup frozen whole kernel corn, thawed; ¹/₄ cup thinly sliced green onions; 3 tablespoons snipped fresh cilantro; 2 tablespoons cooking oil; 2 tablespoons lime juice; ¹/₂ teaspoon salt; ¹/₄ teaspoon ground cumin; ¹/₄ teaspoon ground black pepper; and 1 fresh jalapeño chile pepper, seeded and finely chopped. Cover and chill for 6 to 24 hours.
Per Serving: 381 cal., 17 g fat (5 g sat. fat), 83 mg chol., 429 mg sodium, 17 g carbo., 4 g fiber, 40 g pro.

pair 'em up!

Experiment with different foods and smoking woods to find flavor combinations you like. Look for a variety of wood chips, wood chunks, and grilling planks where smoker and grill accessories are sold. Here's a simple chart to get you started with some perfect pairings.

WOOD TYPE	CHARACTERISTICS	PAIR WITH
Alder	delicate	pork, poultry, fish
Cedar	strong, hearty, smoky	brisket, ribs, game, pork
Fruitwood (apple or cherry)	delicate, mildly sweet, fruity	veal, pork, poultry
Hickory	strong, hearty, smoky	brisket, ribs, game, pork
Mesquite	pungent, earthy	most meats, vegetables
Oak	assertive, versatile	beef, pork, poultry
Pecan	similar to hickory but a bit more subtle	pork, poultry, fish

applewood-smoked pork chops

applewood-smoked pork chops

When you choose a purchased rub, select one without a lot of sugar.
Rubs high in sugar tend to overbrown during long cooking.
Prep: 30 minutes   Chill: 2 hours   Soak: 1 hour
Smoke: 1³/₄ hours   Makes: 4 servings

4	boneless pork top loin chops, cut 1¹/₂ inches thick
2	tablespoons purchased barbecue spice rub
6	to 8 apple, cherry, or orange wood chunks
1	tablespoon butter
1	medium apple, peeled, cored, and chopped
¹/₄	cup chopped onion
1	small clove garlic, minced
3	tablespoons bourbon or apple juice
1	tablespoon apple cider vinegar
²/₃	cup chicken stock or broth
¹/₃	cup yellow mustard
1	tablespoon Dijon-style mustard
2	tablespoons honey
	Salt and ground black pepper
	Apple cut into julienne strips (optional)

1. Trim fat from chops. Place chops in a single layer in a shallow dish. Sprinkle some of the spice rub evenly over both sides of each chop; rub in with your fingers. Cover and chill for 2 to 4 hours.

2. For at least 1 hour before smoke cooking, soak the wood chunks in enough water to cover. Drain before using. In a smoker, arrange preheated coals, drained wood chunks, and water pan according to the manufacturer's directions. Pour water into pan. Place chops on the grill rack over water pan. Cover and smoke for 1³/₄ to 2¹/₄ hours or until the juices run clear (160°F). Add additional coals and water as needed to maintain temperature and moisture.

3. Meanwhile, for mustard sauce, in a medium skillet, melt butter over medium heat. Add chopped apple, onion, and garlic. Cook about 5 minutes or until onion is tender, stirring occasionally. Add bourbon and vinegar. Cook and stir over medium heat until liquid is reduced by half, about 1 minute. Add chicken stock; bring to boiling. Cook, uncovered, until liquid is reduced by half, about 3 to 4 minutes. Stir in yellow mustard and Dijon-style mustard. Bring to boiling; reduce heat. Simmer, uncovered, for 1 minute, stirring often. Remove from heat; add honey. Season to taste with salt and black pepper. Carefully add sauce to a food processor or blender. Cover and process or blend until smooth. Serve warm sauce over chops. If desired, top with apple strips.

Per Serving: 594 cal., 21 g fat (8 g sat. fat), 178 mg chol., 1,066 mg sodium, 20 g carbo., 2 g fiber, 71 g pro.

cognac-brined salmon

cognac-brined salmon

Cognac, with its full-throttle flavor, combines with water, honey, and salt in a brine that leaves salmon with whispers of the rich brandy. When using a brine, be sure to marinate only as long as the time recommended in the recipe. Otherwise, the flavors become overwhelming and the texture turns mushy.

Prep: 15 minutes   Chill: 1 hour   Marinate: 3 hours   Soak: 1 hour
Smoke: 45 minutes   Makes: 4 servings

- 1   1$^1/_2$-pound fresh or frozen salmon fillet (with skin), about 1 inch thick
- 2   cups water
- $^1/_2$ cup cognac
- $^1/_2$ cup honey
- 2   tablespoons coarse salt or 1 tablespoon salt
- 2   tablespoons coarsely cracked black pepper
- 6   to 8 alder or apple wood chunks
   Red Onion and Caper Sauce

1. Thaw salmon, if frozen. For brine, in a medium saucepan, combine the water, cognac, honey, salt, and pepper. Cook and stir over medium heat just until the honey and salt dissolve. Transfer brine to a medium bowl. Cover and chill for 1 hour.

2. Rinse the salmon. Place salmon in a large resealable plastic bag set in a shallow dish. Pour the chilled brine over salmon. Seal bag. Marinate in the refrigerator for 3 to 4 hours, turning bag occasionally. Drain salmon, discarding brine. Pat salmon dry with paper towels.

3. For at least 1 hour before smoke cooking, soak wood chunks in enough water to cover. Drain before using. In a smoker, arrange preheated coals, drained wood chunks, and water pan according to the manufacturer's directions. Pour water into pan. Place salmon, skin side down, on the grill rack over water pan. Cover and smoke for 45 to 60 minutes or until fish flakes easily with a fork. Serve salmon with Red Onion and Caper Sauce.

Red Onion and Caper Sauce: In a small bowl, stir together $^1/_2$ cup dairy sour cream, 3 tablespoons finely chopped red onion, and 2 tablespoons drained capers.

Per Serving: 417 cal., 23 g fat (7 g sat. fat), 110 mg chol., 842 mg sodium, 11 g carbo., 0 g fiber, 35 g pro.

the weather effect

The ideal conditions for smoke cooking are 60°F and above and no wind—in other words, a perfect spring or fall day in most parts of the country. You can certainly smoke-cook on a cold or windy day, but you may need to allow for a longer cooking time than specified in the recipe.

lemon-infused planked walleye

Prep: 20 minutes   Soak: 1 hour   Grill: 18 minutes
Makes: 4 servings

- 4   6- to 8-ounce fresh or frozen boneless walleye fillets with skin
- 4   individual or 2 medium (15×7×$^1/_2$-inch) maple, cherry, or cedar grilling planks
   Mashed Potatoes
- $^1/_2$ teaspoon salt
- 3   tablespoons lemon juice
- 3   tablespoons garlic-infused olive oil or olive oil
- 2   tablespoons snipped fresh dill or 1 teaspoon dried dill weed
- 4   teaspoons garlic-pepper seasoning
- 1   tablespoon packed brown sugar
- 2   teaspoons lemon-pepper seasoning
- $^1/_2$ teaspoon paprika
- 2   tablespoons butter, melted

1. Thaw fish, if frozen. For at least 1 hour before grilling, soak planks in enough water to cover. Place weights on the planks so they stay submerged during soaking. Prepare the Mashed Potatoes; set aside.

2. Rinse fish; pat dry with paper towels. Sprinkle fish with the salt. In a small bowl, combine the lemon juice, oil, dill, garlic-pepper seasoning, brown sugar, lemon-pepper seasoning, and paprika. Brush flesh side of each fillet with lemon-oil mixture. Drain planks.

3. For a charcoal grill, place the planks on the grill rack directly over medium coals. Heat, uncovered, about 5 minutes or until planks begin to crackle and smoke. Carefully arrange each fillet, skin side down, on a plank. Spoon or pipe about $^3/_4$ cup of the Mashed Potatoes on plank around each fillet. Lightly drizzle potatoes with melted butter. Grill, covered, for 18 to 22 minutes or until fish flakes easily when tested with a fork. (For a gas grill, preheat grill. Reduce heat to medium. Preheat plank. Place fish and potatoes on plank over heat. Cover and grill as above.)

4. To serve, bring planks to table and set each on a large serving plate. Serve immediately.

Mashed Potatoes: In a medium covered saucepan, cook 3 medium peeled and quartered baking potatoes (about 1$^1/_2$ pounds) and $^1/_2$ teaspoon salt in enough boiling water to cover for 20 to 25 minutes or until tender; drain. Mash with a potato masher or beat with an electric mixer on low speed. Add 2 tablespoons butter, $^1/_2$ teaspoon salt, and $^1/_4$ teaspoon ground black pepper. Gradually beat in 1 to 2 tablespoons milk to make mixture light and fluffy. Let cool for 5 minutes. If you like, spoon mixture into a pastry bag with a large star tip.

Per Serving: 473 cal., 24 g fat (9 g sat. fat), 177 mg chol., 1,875 mg sodium, 28 g carbo., 2 g fiber, 36 g pro.

maple-smoked chicken

Prep: 30 minutes   Soak: 1 hour   Smoke: 1 1/2 hours
Makes: 6 servings

6	to 8 maple wood chunks
6	whole chicken legs (thigh-drumstick portion)
3/4	cup ketchup
1/3	cup maple syrup
2	tablespoons cider vinegar
1	tablespoon bottled steak sauce
1	tablespoon yellow mustard or Dijon-style mustard
1/2	teaspoon ground cinnamon
1/4	teaspoon ground allspice
1/4	teaspoon black pepper
	Dash ground cloves
	Several dashes bottled hot pepper sauce
	Tomato slices (optional)

1. For at least 1 hour before smoke cooking, soak wood chunks in enough water to cover. Drain before using.

2. In a smoker, arrange preheated coals, drained wood chunks, and water pan according to the manufacturer's directions. Pour water into pan. Place chicken on the grill rack over water pan. Cover; smoke for 1 1/2 to 2 hours or until juices run clear (180°F). Add additional coals and water as needed to maintain temperature and moisture.

3. Meanwhile, for sauce, in a small saucepan, stir together ketchup, maple syrup, vinegar, steak sauce, mustard, cinnamon, allspice, pepper, cloves, and hot pepper sauce. Bring to boiling; reduce heat. Simmer, uncovered, for 10 minutes. Brush some of the sauce over the chicken during the last 10 minutes of cooking. Remove chicken from the smoker. Generously brush some of the warm sauce over chicken. Serve remaining sauce with chicken. If desired, garnish chicken with tomato slices.

Per Serving: 535 cal., 29 g fat (8 g sat. fat), 186 mg chol., 725 mg sodium, 25 g carbo., 2 g fiber, 43 g pro.

chili-rubbed drumsticks

Prep: 5 minutes   Soak: 1 hour   Smoke: 2 1/2 hours
Makes: 6 servings

6	to 8 hickory wood chunks
1	tablespoon chili powder
1	tablespoon finely shredded lime peel
1 1/2	teaspoons ground cumin
1/2	teaspoon salt
6	small turkey drumsticks (8 to 12 ounces each)
	Bottled salsa or barbecue sauce (optional)

1. For at least 1 hour before smoke cooking, soak wood chunks in enough water to cover. Drain before using.

2. For rub, in a small bowl, combine chili powder, lime peel, cumin, and salt. Sprinkle mixture evenly over turkey; rub in with your fingers.

3. In a smoker, arrange preheated coals, drained wood chunks, and water pan according to the manufacturer's directions. Pour water into pan. Place drumsticks on the grill rack over water pan. Cover; smoke for 2 1/2 to 3 hours or until juices run clear (180°F). Add additional coals and water as needed to maintain temperature and moisture. If desired, serve the turkey with salsa.

Per Serving: 178 cal., 9 g fat (3 g sat. fat), 80 mg chol., 269 mg sodium, 1 g carbo., 1 g fiber, 22 g pro.

caribbean smoked chops

Prep: 20 minutes   Soak: 1 hour   Smoke: 1 3/4 hours
Stand: 15 minutes   Makes: 4 servings

6	to 8 pecan or cherry wood chunks
4	pork loin chops, cut 1 1/2 inches thick
2	to 3 teaspoons Jamaican jerk seasoning
1	medium mango, peeled, seeded, and finely chopped (about 1 cup)
1/4	cup sliced green onions (2)
2	tablespoons snipped fresh cilantro or parsley
1/2	teaspoon finely shredded orange peel
2	teaspoons orange juice
1/4	teaspoon Jamaican jerk seasoning
	Fresh cilantro or parsley sprigs (optional)

1. For at least 1 hour before smoke cooking, soak wood chunks in enough water to cover. Drain before using.

2. Trim fat from chops. Sprinkle the 2 to 3 teaspoons jerk seasoning evenly over chops; rub it in with your fingers.

3. In a smoker, arrange preheated coals, drained wood chunks, and water pan according to the manufacturer's directions. Pour water into pan. Place chops on the grill rack over water pan. Cover; smoke for 1 3/4 to 2 1/4 hours or until the juices run clear (160°F). Add additional coals and water as needed to maintain temperature and moisture.

4. Meanwhile, for sauce, in a medium bowl, stir together mango, green onions, cilantro, orange peel, orange juice, and the 1/4 teaspoon jerk seasoning. Let stand at room temperature for 15 to 20 minutes to blend flavors. Serve the sauce over chops. If desired, garnish chops with cilantro sprigs.

Per Serving: 347 cal., 11 g fat (4 g sat. fat), 138 mg chol., 224 mg sodium, 11 g carbo., 1 g fiber, 49 g pro.

chili-rubbed drumsticks

chicken stuffed with mushrooms and prosciutto

Although the Italian-style ham known as prosciutto offers big flavor to the chicken, you can use cooked ham instead.

Prep: 30 minutes   Soak: 1 hour   Cool: 10 minutes
Grill: 20 minutes   Makes: 4 servings

- 1   15×7×¹/₂-inch cedar or alder grilling plank
- ¹/₂   cup sliced fresh mushrooms
- ¹/₄   cup finely chopped onion
- 1   clove garlic, minced
- 1   tablespoon olive oil
- ³/₄   cup chopped fresh spinach
- ¹/₂   cup shredded Fontina or Gouda cheese (2 ounces)
- 1   ounce prosciutto, chopped
- 4   medium chicken breast halves with skin and bone
  Freshly ground black pepper
  Fresh Herbed Pasta

1. For at least 1 hour before grilling, soak plank in enough water to cover. Place a weight on plank so it stays submerged during soaking. Drain plank.

2. In a medium skillet, cook mushrooms, onion, and garlic in hot oil until tender. Remove from heat. Let stand 5 minutes to cool slightly. Stir in spinach, cheese, and prosciutto. Remove bones from chicken breasts, leaving skin attached. Spoon mushroom mixture between the skin and flesh of each breast half. Brush chicken with additional *olive oil* and sprinkle with pepper.

3. For a charcoal grill, place plank on grill rack directly over medium coals. Heat, uncovered, about 5 minutes or until plank begins to crackle and smoke. Place chicken, skin sides up, on plank. Grill, covered, about 20 minutes or until chicken is no longer pink (170°F). (For a gas grill, preheat grill. Reduce heat to medium. Preheat plank. Place chicken on plank over heat. Cover and grill as above.)

4. Remove chicken from grill. Let chicken stand for 5 minutes. Slice chicken diagonally and serve over Fresh Herbed Pasta.

Fresh Herbed Pasta: Cook 6 ounces dry linguine according to package directions; drain. Meanwhile, in a large skillet, cook ¹/₄ cup finely chopped shallots and 2 cloves garlic, minced, in 2 tablespoons hot olive oil over medium heat until tender. Add ¹/₂ cup chicken broth and 2 tablespoons dry white wine. Bring to boiling; reduce heat. Simmer, uncovered, until mixture is reduced to ¹/₃ cup. Remove from heat. Add drained pasta, ¹/₂ cup coarsely chopped bottled roasted red sweet peppers, and ¹/₃ cup snipped fresh basil and/or Italian (flat-leaf) parsley. Toss until combined. Sprinkle with ¹/₃ cup finely shredded Parmesan cheese. Sprinkle with freshly ground black pepper to taste.

Per Serving: 759 cal., 41 g fat (12 g sat. fat), 12 mg chol., 651 mg sodium, 38 g carbo., 2 g fiber, 56 g pro.

---

sweet smoke

If you want great smoked barbecue, you need to follow two rules.

1. Cook low and slow.
2. Keep your smoke sweet. If smoke is stale or acrid, the food absorbs a strong—or even bitter— taste.

To keep your smoke sweet:

1. Maintain a constant heat source.
2. Keep air flowing through the smoker.
3. Use seasoned, high-quality wood. Alder, cedar, hickory, mesquite, oak, pecan, and fruitwood all give foods excellent flavor.

---

plank-smoked pork tenderloins

Prep: 30 minutes   Soak: 1 hour   Grill: 30 minutes
Makes: 6 servings

- 1   12×6×³/₄-inch cedar or alder grilling plank
- 2   12-ounce pork tenderloins
- 2   tablespoons Dijon-style mustard
  Salt
  Ground black pepper
- 2   tablespoons snipped fresh sage
- 2   tablespoons snipped fresh thyme
- 1   tablespoon snipped fresh rosemary
  Apple-Cherry Salad

1. For at least 1 hour before grilling, soak plank in enough water to cover. Place a weight on plank so it stays submerged during soaking. Drain plank.

2. Trim fat from pork. Brush pork with mustard; sprinkle with salt and pepper. Combine fresh herbs and sprinkle evenly over pork; rub in.

3. For a charcoal grill, place plank on the grill rack directly over medium coals. Heat, uncovered, about 5 minutes or until plank begins to crackle and smoke. Place tenderloins on plank. Grill, covered, for 30 to 40 minutes or until an instant-read thermometer registers 160°F. (For a gas grill, preheat grill. Reduce heat to medium. Preheat plank. Place tenderloins on plank over heat. Cover and grill as above.) Serve with Apple-Cherry Salad.

Apple-Cherry Salad: In a medium bowl, combine 2 Granny Smith apples, cored and chopped; ¹/₄ cup coarsely chopped walnuts, toasted; 1 ounce crumbled blue cheese; 2 tablespoons snipped dried tart red cherries; 2 tablespoons Calvados apple brandy or applejack; and 1 tablespoon extra virgin olive oil. Just before serving, stir in 3 slices bacon, cooked, drained, and crumbled.

Per Serving: 280 cal., 12 g fat (3 g sat. fat), 80 mg chol., 345 mg sodium, 10 g carbo., 2 g fiber, 27 g pro.

*plank-smoked
pork tenderloins*

fresh sides

When produce spills from farmer's market stalls and backyard gardens, load your basket with fruits and veggies. Make the most of nature's abundance with simple recipes that capture the essence of the fresh-picked goodness. This creative collection includes tried-and-true recipes, some new picnic salads that flaunt the crisp and crunchy textures of vegetables, and fun, not fancy, grilled specialties that boast bold and beautiful hues.

buttery mixed-veggie kabobs
(recipe, page 126)

Team this Asian-style salad of cool and crunchy cucumber slices with anything, from grilled burgers to chicken to salmon.

basil-cucumber salad

basil-cucumber salad

Prep: 10 minutes   Stand: 15 minutes   Makes: 5 servings

- 2 medium cucumbers, peeled
- 3 tablespoons rice vinegar
- 2 teaspoons sugar
- 1/2 teaspoon salt
- 1/2 teaspoon finely shredded lime peel
- 1/2 teaspoon grated fresh ginger
- 1/4 teaspoon crushed red pepper
- 2 tablespoons thinly sliced fresh basil

1. Using a vegetable peeler, peel thin strips of peel from cucumbers. Halve cucumbers lengthwise. Seed cucumbers and slice crosswise into 1/4-inch-thick slices.

2. In a medium bowl, combine cucumbers, rice vinegar, sugar, salt, lime peel, ginger, and crushed red pepper. Toss to mix. Let stand for 15 minutes. Stir in basil. Serve with a slotted spoon.

Per Serving: 30 cal., 0 g fat (0 g sat. fat), 0 mg chol., 235 mg sodium, 7 g carbo., 1 g fiber, 1 g pro.

summer strawberry salad

Hold back on adding the banana if you opt to chill the greens mixture. Add the banana, freshly peeled and sliced, when you toss the salad with the dressing.

Start to Finish: 20 minutes   Makes: 6 to 8 servings

- 6 cups chopped romaine lettuce
- 3 cups sliced fresh strawberries
- 2 cups cubed fresh pineapple
- 1 banana, sliced
- 1/4 cup water
- 1/4 cup cream of coconut
- 2 tablespoons lemon juice
- 1 tablespoon yellow mustard
- 1/2 teaspoon ground ginger
- 1/4 cup sliced almonds, toasted (optional)

1. In an extra-large bowl, toss together romaine, strawberries, pineapple, and banana. If desired, cover and chill for up to 1 hour.

2. For dressing, in a small bowl, whisk together the water, cream of coconut, lemon juice, mustard, and ginger. If desired, cover and chill until ready to serve.

3. To serve, drizzle dressing over greens mixture; toss gently to coat. If desired, sprinkle with almonds.

Per Serving: 111 cal., 4 g fat (3 g sat. fat), 0 mg chol., 35 mg sodium, 20 g carbo., 4 g fiber, 2 g pro.

summer vegetable pasta salad

To make enough salad for more than one meal, double the ingredient amounts and cut preparation time needed for another meal.
Prep: 30 minutes   Makes: 4 to 6 servings

- 8 ounces dried campanelle, penne, or mostaccioli pasta (2 1/3 cups)
- 1 tablespoon extra virgin olive oil
- 6 to 8 cloves garlic, thinly sliced
- 1 medium zucchini (8 ounces), trimmed and cut into matchstick-size strips (2 cups)
- 8 ounces sugar snap peas, strings removed
- 2 cups cherry or grape tomatoes, halved
- 3 tablespoons finely chopped shallot (1)
- 1 tablespoon sherry vinegar or white wine vinegar
- 1 tablespoon Dijon-style mustard
- 1/2 teaspoon salt
- 1/4 teaspoon ground black pepper
- 1/4 cup extra virgin olive oil
- 3 tablespoons chopped fresh parsley
  Finely shredded Asiago cheese (optional)

1. Bring a large pot of lightly salted water to boiling; add pasta and cook according to package directions. Drain and rinse pasta under cold water; drain again. Transfer pasta to a large bowl.

2. In a large nonstick skillet, heat 1 tablespoon oil over medium-high heat. Add garlic; cook and stir for 30 seconds. Add zucchini; cook and stir for 1 minute. Add snap peas; cook and stir 30 seconds. Stir in tomatoes; cook about 30 seconds or until tomatoes begin to soften. Transfer vegetable mixture to pasta bowl; toss to mix.

3. For shallot-mustard dressing,* in a small bowl, combine shallot, vinegar, mustard, salt, and pepper. Slowly whisk in 1/4 cup oil; stir in parsley. Pour dressing over pasta mixture, tossing to coat. Serve immediately or cover and chill for 4 hours or up to 3 days. Before serving, sprinkle each serving with Asiago cheese.

*Tip: To cut preparation time, use 1/3 cup bottled vinaigrette salad dressing in place of shallot-mustard dressing.

Per Serving: 434 cal., 18 g fat (2 g sat. fat), 0 mg chol., 404 mg sodium, 57 g carbo., 5 g fiber, 12 g pro.

tomato-squash salad

Cubed zucchini or yellow summer squash make a good substitute if baby squash aren't available.

Prep: 15 minutes Cook: 5 minutes Cool: 10 minutes
Makes: 8 servings

- 8 ounces baby pattypan squash and/or baby zucchini (about 2 cups)
- 4 cups red and/or yellow currant tomatoes
- 1 to 2 cups fresh arugula or romaine lettuce, coarsely torn
- 2 tablespoons snipped fresh basil, tarragon, and/or chives
- 1/4 cup olive oil
- 1/4 cup red wine vinegar or champagne vinegar
- 1 tablespoon lime juice or lemon juice
- 1/4 teaspoon salt
- 1/8 teaspoon ground black pepper

1. In a large saucepan, place squash in enough lightly salted boiling water to cover. Cook, covered, about 5 minutes or until tender. Drain. Cool squash by adding cold water and ice cubes to pan. Drain well.

2. In a serving bowl, combine squash, tomatoes, arugula, and herb.

3. For dressing, in a screw-top jar, combine oil, vinegar, lime juice, salt, and pepper. Cover and shake well. Add half of the dressing to the vegetables; toss to coat. Season to taste with additional salt and pepper. Serve remaining dressing on the side.

Per Serving: 82 cal., 7 g fat (1 g sat. fat), 0 mg chol., 57 mg sodium, 5 g carbo., 2 g fiber, 1 g pro.

two-tone coleslaw

If you plan to chill this salad for more than two hours, toss the apple slices in a little lemon juice to keep them crisp and fresh-looking.

Prep: 20 minutes Chill: 2 hours Makes: 12 servings

- 2/3 cup light mayonnaise
- 3 tablespoons cider vinegar
- 1 tablespoon snipped fresh dill or 1 teaspoon dried dill weed
- 1/2 teaspoon salt
- 1/2 teaspoon coarsely ground black pepper
- 7 cups shredded green cabbage
- 3 medium apples, cored and thinly sliced
- 1 cup chopped sweet onions
   Fresh dill sprig (optional)

1. For dressing, in an extra-large bowl, stir together mayonnaise, vinegar, snipped dill, salt, and pepper. Stir in cabbage, apples, and onions. Cover and chill at least 2 hours or up to 48 hours, stirring occasionally. If desired, garnish with fresh dill.

Per Serving: 78 cal., 5 g fat (1 g sat. fat), 5 mg chol., 195 mg sodium, 10 g carbo., 2 g fiber, 1 g pro.

pickled dilled green beans

Green beans vary in size from tiny French haricots verts to foot-long Chinese long beans to familiar string beans. Regardless of the size you choose, select beans that snap when bent.

Prep: 40 minutes   Cook: 3 minutes   Cool: 1¹/₂ hours
Chill: 4 hours   Makes: 40 servings

3	pounds green beans and/or yellow wax beans
3	cups water
3	cups cider vinegar
1	tablespoon pickling salt
3	tablespoons snipped fresh dill
¹/₂	teaspoon cayenne pepper
6	cloves garlic, sliced

1. Wash beans; drain. If desired, trim ends. Place enough water to cover beans in an 8-quart Dutch oven or kettle. Bring to boiling. Add beans. Cook, uncovered, for 3 minutes. Drain. Place beans in an extra-large bowl.

2. In a large saucepan, combine the 3 cups water, the vinegar, pickling salt, dill, cayenne pepper, and garlic. Bring to boiling. Pour mixture over beans in bowl. Cool to room temperature. Transfer bean mixture to a glass container. Cover and chill at least 4 hours before serving. Store in the refrigerator for up to 2 weeks.
Per Serving: 14 cal., 0 g fat (0 g sat. fat), 0 mg chol., 148 mg sodium, 2 g carbo., 1 g fiber, 1 g pro.

corn salad

To enjoy summertime flavors in the wintertime, substitute 3 cups frozen whole kernel corn, thawed, for the fresh corn.

Start to Finish: 25 minutes   Makes: 9 servings

¹/₄	cup lime juice
1	tablespoon honey
1	fresh jalapeño chile pepper, seeded and finely chopped*
3	tablespoons snipped fresh cilantro
¹/₄	teaspoon salt
6	fresh ears of sweet corn
1¹/₂	cups fresh baby spinach
1	large tomato, seeded and chopped
³/₄	cup seeded and chopped cucumber
	Small fresh chile peppers (optional)

1. For dressing, in a large nonreactive bowl, whisk together lime juice and honey until combined. Stir in jalapeño pepper, cilantro, and salt.

2. Using a sharp knife, carefully cut corn kernels off the cobs. Add corn to dressing in bowl. Stir in spinach, tomato, and cucumber. Serve immediately or cover and chill for up to 1 hour. If desired, garnish with whole peppers.

*Note: Because hot chile peppers, such as jalapeños, contain volatile oils that can burn your skin and eyes, avoid direct contact with chiles as much as possible. When working with chile peppers, wear plastic or rubber gloves. If your bare hands do touch the chile peppers, wash your hands well with soap and water.
Per Serving: 59 cal., 1 g fat (0 g sat. fat), 0 mg chol., 78 mg sodium, 13 g carbo., 2 g fiber, 2 g pro.

asian coleslaw with basil

Start to Finish: 30 minutes   Makes: 8 to 10 servings

- 1/2 cup thinly sliced shallots
- 4 teaspoons cooking oil
- 1/4 cup lime juice
- 2 tablespoons rice vinegar
- 2 teaspoons packed brown sugar
- 1 teaspoon soy sauce
- 1 teaspoon grated fresh ginger
- 3/4 teaspoon salt
- 1/8 teaspoon ground black pepper
- 1 small head napa cabbage or green cabbage (1 1/2 pounds), thinly sliced
- 1 cup coarsely shredded carrots
- 1 cup shredded fresh basil or 1 cup snipped fresh parsley plus 1 teaspoon dried basil, crushed
- 1/3 cup dry roasted peanuts, chopped

1. In a microwave-safe pie plate, combine shallots and 1 teaspoon of oil; toss gently to coat. Microwave on 100% power (high) about 3 minutes or until shallots are crisp-tender.

2. In an extra-large bowl, combine lime juice, vinegar, brown sugar, soy sauce, ginger, salt, pepper, and remaining 3 teaspoons oil. Add cabbage, carrots, basil, and shallots; toss gently to coat. If desired, cover and chill for up to 2 hours.

3. Before serving, sprinkle the coleslaw with peanuts.
Per Serving: 91 cal., 6 g fat (1 g sat. fat), 0 mg chol., 280 mg sodium, 9 g carbo., 2 g fiber, 3 g pro.

the cabbage patch

Here is a rundown of slaw-friendly cabbages you're likely to find in the produce section of your supermarket.

 ✳ **Green Cabbage** Also called white cabbage, this popular variety of cabbage has a round, firm head of thick, smooth leaves.

 ✳ **Red Cabbage** Actually more purple than red in color, this cabbage is rich in antioxidants.

 ✳ **Napa Cabbage** Also known as Chinese cabbage, this variety features a loosely packed, elongated head. The leaves are crinkly, thin, delicate, and mild-tasting.

 ✳ **Savoy Cabbage** An Italian favorite, Savoy cabbage is considered the most tender and sweet cabbage available.

honey-mustard slaw

Prep: 25 minutes   Chill: 2 hours   Makes: 8 servings

- 8 cups shredded red and/or green cabbage (about 1 head)
- 2 cups snow pea pods or sugar snap pea pods, halved crosswise
- 2 medium carrots, shredded
- 1/2 cup chopped red onion
- 1/3 cup coarse-grain brown mustard
- 1/4 cup lemon juice
- 1/4 cup salad oil
- 1/4 cup honey
- 2 cloves garlic, minced
- 3 tablespoons chopped nuts

1. In an extra-large bowl, combine cabbage, pea pods, carrots, and red onion; toss gently to combine. For dressing, in a screw-top jar, combine mustard, lemon juice, oil, honey, and garlic. Cover and shake well.

2. Pour dressing over cabbage mixture; toss gently to coat. Cover and chill for 2 to 8 hours. Before serving, stir cabbage mixture. Sprinkle with nuts.
Per Serving: 168 cal., 9 g fat (1 g sat. fat), 0 mg chol., 273 mg sodium, 19 g carbo., 3 g fiber, 2 g pro.

three-pepper slaw

Prep: 20 minutes   Chill: 2 hours   Makes: 4 servings

- 3 medium red, yellow, orange, and/or green sweet peppers, seeded and cut into thin strips
- 1 cup shredded cabbage
- 1/4 cup dried currants or raisins
- 1/4 cup sliced green onions (2)
- 1/4 cup white wine vinegar
- 3 tablespoons salad oil
- 2 to 3 tablespoons sugar
  Few dashes bottled hot pepper sauce (optional)

1. In a large bowl, combine sweet peppers, cabbage, currants, and green onions.

2. For dressing, in a screw-top jar, combine vinegar, oil, sugar, and, if desired, hot pepper sauce. Cover and shake well.

3. Pour dressing over sweet pepper mixture; toss gently to coat. Cover and chill for 2 to 24 hours. Stir before serving.
Per Serving: 175 cal., 11 g fat (1 g sat. fat), 0 mg chol., 9 mg sodium, 20 g carbo., 3 g fiber, 2 g pro.

savoy cabbage and fennel slaw

savoy cabbage and fennel slaw

Prep: 20 minutes   Chill: 2 hours   Makes: 8 servings

1	medium fennel bulb with leafy tops
1/3	cup olive oil
1/3	cup white balsamic vinegar or white wine vinegar
1	tablespoon coarse-grain brown mustard or Dijon-style mustard
1	to 2 teaspoons sugar
1/2	teaspoon salt
1/4	teaspoon ground black pepper
8	cups thinly sliced savoy cabbage (about 1 small head) or one 16-ounce package shredded cabbage with carrot (coleslaw mix)
1	small zucchini, cut into thin bite-size strips

1. Cut off stalks from fennel; reserve tops and discard stalks. Discard any wilted outer layers from fennel and cut a thin slice from base of bulb. Quarter fennel bulb lengthwise; slice very thinly. Set aside. Chop enough of the reserved fennel tops to make 1 tablespoon; set aside along with a few sprigs of the feathery leaves.

2. For vinaigrette, in a small screw-top jar, combine the 1 tablespoon chopped fennel tops, the oil, vinegar, mustard, sugar, salt, and pepper. Cover and shake well.

3. In a very large serving bowl, combine sliced fennel, cabbage, and zucchini; toss gently to combine. Pour vinaigrette over cabbage mixture; toss gently to coat. Cover and chill for 2 to 24 hours.

4. To serve, garnish the slaw with the reserved sprigs of feathery fennel leaves.

Per Serving: 121 cal., 9 g fat (1 g sat. fat), 0 mg chol., 200 mg sodium, 9 g carbo., 3 g fiber, 2 g pro.

grilled panzanella

grilled cheesy potatoes

buttery mixed-veggie kabobs

It's risky business to hold corn in your hand and try to skewer it. Instead, place corn pieces on end on a cutting board. Push each metal skewer downward into the corn. Pictured on page 115.

Prep: 25 minutes   Grill: 15 minutes   Makes: 4 servings

1   small zucchini and/or yellow squash, cut into 1-inch slices
8   baby pattypan squash, halved or quartered, or 1 small yellow squash, halved lengthwise and cut into eight 1-inch slices
8   red pearl onions or cipollini
2   fresh ears of sweet corn, husked, cleaned, and cut crosswise into 4 pieces each
1/3   cup butter, melted
1   clove garlic, minced
1   tablespoon finely chopped onion
1   tablespoon snipped fresh oregano or 1/4 teaspoon dried oregano, crushed
1/4   teaspoon ground chipotle chile powder or cayenne pepper

1. On eight 10- to 12-inch metal skewers, alternately thread the zucchini, pattypan squash, onions, and corn. In a small bowl, combine butter, garlic, chopped onion, oregano, and chipotle chile powder. Brush mixture evenly over vegetables. Transfer skewers to a baking pan.

2. For a charcoal grill, place skewers on the grill rack directly over medium coals. Grill, uncovered, for 15 to 18 minutes or until vegetables are tender and brown, turning and brushing occasionally with butter mixture. (For a gas grill, preheat grill. Reduce heat to medium. Place skewers on grill rack over heat. Cover and grill as above.)

Per Serving: 194 cal., 16 g fat (10 g sat. fat), 40 mg chol., 121 mg sodium, 13 g carbo., 2 g fiber, 3 g pro.

zucchini pancakes

These golden dinnertime treats flavored with Parmesan cheese and onion make great party nibbles, too.

Prep: 20 minutes   Stand: 15 minutes   Cook: 4 minutes per batch
Oven: 300°F   Makes: about 30 pancakes

4   to 5 medium zucchini (about 11/2 pounds)
3/4   teaspoon salt
4   eggs
1   clove garlic, minced
3/4   cup all-purpose flour
1/2   cup grated Parmesan cheese
1   tablespoon finely chopped onion
1/4   teaspoon ground black pepper
    Dairy sour cream (optional)

1. Trim and coarsely shred zucchini (you should have about 5 cups). In a large bowl, toss zucchini with salt. Place zucchini in a colander. Place a plate or 9-inch pie plate on top of zucchini; weigh down with cans. Let drain for 15 minutes. Discard liquid.

2. Preheat oven to 300°F. In the large bowl, beat together eggs and garlic. Stir in flour, Parmesan cheese, onion, and pepper until just moistened (batter should be lumpy). Stir in zucchini until just combined.

3. For each zucchini pancake, spoon 1 heaping tablespoon batter onto a hot lightly oiled griddle or heavy skillet, spreading to form a 3-inch circle. Cook over medium heat for 2 to 3 minutes on each side or until the pancake is golden brown. (Reduce heat to medium-low if pancakes brown too quickly.) Keep pancakes warm in the preheated oven while cooking remaining pancakes.

4. If desired, serve pancakes topped with a spoonful of sour cream.

To Make Ahead: Prepare and cook pancakes as directed. Cool completely. Place pancakes in a freezer container, separating layers with waxed paper; cover. Freeze for up to 3 months. To reheat, preheat oven to 425°F. Place frozen pancakes in a single layer on a greased baking sheet. Bake, uncovered, for 8 to 10 minutes or until hot and slightly crisp.

Per Pancake: 31 cal., 1 g fat (0 g sat. fat), 29 mg chol., 90 mg sodium, 3 g carbo., 0 g fiber, 2 g pro.

choosing zucchini

Lightly squeeze a zucchini to test for freshness. It should give just a bit, and you should be able to easily pierce the skin. Choose medium to small zucchini, heavy for their size, with vibrant color.

AKES

zucchini pancakes

grilled green tomatoes
with garden herb salad

grilled green tomatoes
with garden herb salad

The smokiness of grilled tomatoes complements their tanginess.
Prep: 40 minutes Grill: 6 minutes Makes: 4 servings

- 3/4 cup loosely packed fresh Italian (flat-leaf) parsley leaves
- 3/4 cup loosely packed fresh cilantro leaves
- 1/2 cup cut-up fresh chives
- 1 clove garlic, minced
- 1/2 cup olive oil
- 3 large green tomatoes or a mix of tomatoes
  Coarse (kosher) salt
  Ground black pepper
- 4 leaves iceberg lettuce, cut into thin bite-size strips
- 1/4 cup hazelnuts (filberts), toasted and coarsely chopped
- 1/4 cup slivered almonds, toasted and coarsely chopped
- 1/4 cup pistachio nuts, toasted and coarsely chopped
- 1/4 cup golden raisins
- 2 tablespoons sherry or white balsamic vinegar

1. For herb oil, on a cutting board, toss together parsley, cilantro, and chives. Coarsely chop all the herbs together. In a medium bowl, combine herb mixture and garlic. Stir in olive oil; set aside.

2. Using a serrated knife, slice tomatoes into 1/2-inch slices. Generously season with salt and pepper.

3. For a charcoal grill, place tomato slices on the grill rack directly over medium coals . Grill, uncovered, for 6 to 8 minutes or until tomatoes are tender, turning once halfway through grilling. (For a gas grill, preheat grill. Reduce heat to medium. Place tomato slices on grill rack over heat. Cover and grill as above.) Transfer tomatoes to a platter or shallow serving bowl, arranging slices in a single layer. Spoon some of the herb oil over tomatoes; turn slices over and spoon on remaining herb oil.

4. In a separate bowl, combine the lettuce, hazelnuts, almonds, pistachios, and raisins. Season to taste with salt and pepper. Drizzle vinegar over lettuce mixture; toss lightly to coat evenly. Spoon lettuce mixture over tomatoes.
Per Serving: 445 cal., 40 g fat (5 g sat. fat), 0 mg chol., 182 mg sodium, 20 g carbo., 5 g fiber, 7 g pro.

moroccan-style carrots

The microwave oven makes quick work of these tangy marinated carrots. Their Mediterranean flavor goes especially well with grilled lamb chops or beef steaks.
Prep: 10 minutes Microwave: 6 minutes Stand: 1 hour
Makes: 6 servings

- 1 pound carrots, bias-cut into 1/2-inch-thick slices
- 2 tablespoons water
- 1 tablespoon olive oil
- 1 tablespoon cider vinegar
- 1/2 to 3/4 teaspoon ground cumin
- 1/2 teaspoon kosher salt or 1/4 teaspoon salt
- 1/4 teaspoon ground coriander
  Dash cayenne pepper
- 1 cup sliced sweet onion
- 1/4 cup snipped fresh cilantro

1. In a large microwave-safe bowl, combine carrot slices and the water. Cover and microwave on 100% power (high) for 6 to 9 minutes or until crisp-tender, stirring once. Transfer carrots to a bowl filled with ice water. Let stand for 5 minutes. Drain and pat carrots dry with a paper towel.

2. In the same large bowl, combine oil, vinegar, cumin, salt, coriander, and cayenne pepper. Stir in carrots, sweet onion, and cilantro; toss to combine. Let stand at room temperature for 1 hour before serving.

To Make Ahead: Prepare as directed through Step 2, excluding the standing time. Cover and refrigerate for up to 24 hours. Let stand at room temperature for 1 hour before serving.
Per Serving: 58 cal., 2 g fat (0 g sat. fat), 0 mg chol., 212 mg sodium, 9 g carbo., 2 g fiber, 1 g pro.

At the market, sort through the selection of tomatoes and go beyond green. Select a colorful combination of tomatoes to add interest to the fresh herb salad combo.

corn-mango salad

Be sure to heat the cast-iron skillet on the grill before adding the kernels of sweet corn. Once they hit the hot pan, the sugars in the corn start cooking into yummy goodness.

Prep: 20 minutes   Grill: 8 minutes   Makes 6 servings

4	medium fresh ears of sweet corn, cleaned
2	to 3 large mangoes
1	medium red onion
1	teaspoon olive oil
4	tablespoons olive oil
2	tablespoons fresh lemon juice
1	teaspoon sugar
1/2	teaspoon curry powder
1/2	teaspoon salt
1/8	teaspoon ground black pepper
6	cups fresh arugula

1. Cut corn kernels from cobs. Seed and peel mangoes; cut in 12 slices. Peel onion; cut in six wedges, leaving root end intact.

2. For a charcoal grill, place a 9- to 10-inch cast-iron skillet on the grill rack directly over medium-hot coals. Heat for 3 minutes. Add corn and the 1 teaspoon oil. Cook and stir for 2 to 4 minutes. Remove from grill; transfer kernels to six serving bowls. Set aside. (For gas grill, preheat grill. Reduce heat to medium-hot. Place cast-iron skillet on rack directly over heat for 3 minutes. Add corn and oil. Cover and grill as above.)

3. In a bowl, combine mango slices and onion wedges; drizzle with 1 tablespoon of the olive oil. Toss. For a charcoal grill, place mango slices and onion wedges on the grill rack directly over medium coals. Grill mango slices, uncovered, for 3 to 5 minutes, turning often. Grill onion wedges, uncovered, for 6 to 8 minutes, turning often. Transfer mango and onion to bowl. (For a gas grill, reduce heat to medium. Place mango and onion on grill rack directly over heat. Cover and grill as above.)

4. For dressing, in a bowl, combine lemon juice, sugar, curry, salt, and pepper. Whisk in remaining 3 tablespoons oil until combined. Add 1 tablespoon dressing to mango mixture; toss. Spoon mango mixture on top of corn in bowls. Drizzle arugula with remaining dressing; toss. Add arugula to bowls.

Per Serving: 190 cal., 11 g fat (2 g sat. fat), 0 mg chol., 206 mg sodium, 25 g carbo., 3 g fiber, 2 g pro.

grilled corn
with cumin-lime butter

Another time, try one of the trendy toppings, opposite, on your grilled corn instead of the citrusy butter.

Prep: 30 minutes   Soak: 1 hour   Grill: 25 minutes
Makes: 6 servings

6	fresh ears of sweet corn with husks
2	quarts cold tap water
1	tablespoon coarse (kosher) salt
	Cumin-Lime Butter

1. Carefully peel the cornhusks down to the bottom of each ear without detaching. Remove and discard the silks. Gently rinse the corn. Carefully fold husks back around ears. Tie husk tops with 100-percent-cotton kitchen string to secure.

2. In an extra-large bowl or tub, combine the cold water and salt, stirring until salt mostly dissolves. Place corn in the water. Put a pan on top of corn to keep all ears submerged for 1 hour before grilling. Drain corn; pat dry.

3. For a charcoal grill, place corn on the grill rack directly over medium coals. Grill, covered, for 25 to 30 minutes or until kernels are tender, turning and rearranging with long-handled tongs three times. (For a gas grill, preheat grill. Reduce heat to medium. Place corn on grill rack over heat. Cover and grill as above.)

4. To serve, remove string from corn; discard string. Peel back husks. Serve corn with Cumin-Lime Butter.

Cumin-Lime Butter: In a small cast-iron or heavy skillet, cook and stir 1 tablespoon cumin seeds over low heat for 1 minute. Add 1 teaspoon coarse (kosher) salt and 1/4 teaspoon ground chipotle chile pepper. Cook and stir about 1 minute more or until seeds become fragrant and lightly colored. Remove from heat; shake skillet for 1 minute. Place cumin mixture in a spice or coffee grinder. Cover and pulse until ground. In a small bowl, stir together 1 cup butter, softened; cumin mixture; and 2 teaspoons finely shredded lime peel. Serve on grilled sweet corn. Refrigerate any remaining butter in tightly covered container for up to 3 days.

Per Serving: 354 cal., 32 g fat (20 g sat. fat), 81 mg chol., 877 mg sodium, 18 g carbo., 3 g fiber, 3 g pro.

corn on the cob

Season up summer's best side dish by blending these ingredients.

1. **Hummus,** roasted red pepper, olive tapenade
2. **Fresh sage,** rosemary leaves, butter
3. **Guacamole,** freshly squeezed lime juice
4. **Cinnamon,** granulated sugar, melted butter
5. **Curry powder,** chopped pistachios, melted butter
6. **Coarse sea salt,** cracked pepper, cumin seeds, olive oil
7. **Mayonnaise,** Mexican Cotija cheese, ground chili powder
8. **Pesto sauce,** freshly grated Parmesan cheese
9. **Fruit chutney,** melted butter
10. **Herbed pepper seasoning blend,** butter

bbq bash

Whether it's for a Stars and Stripes holiday, an annual block party, or simply a summertime get-together, pull out this one-of-a-kind barbecue menu and start the celebration. Designed to feed crowds of 12, 25, or 50, this All-American spread filled with traditional classics is neither too fancy nor labor-intensive. Follow the step-by-step timetable to guide you through and you'll find all you need is a little time, smoke, and organization to pull off a party showcasing fireworks of flavors.

beef brisket
(recipe, page 137)

BEEF
BRISKET

menu

✱ Beef Brisket and/or Pulled Pork Shoulder
✱ Kohlrabi Coleslaw
✱ Pan-Baked Beans
✱ Corn Bread
✱ Assorted cookies: Peanut Butter Cookies, Cherry and Chocolate Chip Cookies, and/or Star Sugar Cookies
✱ Assorted cool beverages

pulled pork shoulder

Set out a big pan or platter of these tender meat slices and let guests dish up their own.

beef brisket

To keep the underside of brisket from charring, smoke the meat on foil.
Pictured on page 133.
Prep: 1 hour   Smoke: 5 hours   Stand: 15 minutes
Makes: 12 servings

6	to 8 hardwood chunks such as mesquite or hickory wood
1/2	cup Dry Rub (see recipe, page 135)
1	5-pound fresh beef brisket
	Brisket Barbecue Sauce (see recipe, opposite)

1. For at least 1 hour before smoke cooking, soak wood chunks in enough water to cover. Drain before using.

2. Sprinkle Dry Rub evenly over all sides of brisket; rub in with your fingers. Cut a sheet of foil slightly larger than the brisket. Poke several holes in the foil. Place brisket on foil.

3. In a smoker, arrange preheated coals, about half the drained wood chunks, and a water pan according to the manufacturer's directions. Pour hot water into pan. Place brisket and foil on the grill rack over water pan. Cover and smoke for 5 to 6 hours or until brisket is tender. Test tenderness by inserting a fork into center of brisket and twisting. When fork twists easily, brisket is ready. Add additional coals, wood chunks, and water as needed. (Do not add wood after the first 2 hours of smoking. Too much smoke makes meat bitter.)

4. Remove brisket from smoker. Cover and let stand for 15 minutes. Meanwhile, if needed, reheat Brisket Barbecue Sauce in a saucepan over low heat. To serve brisket, trim away crusty outer layer; serve separately. Thinly slice brisket across the grain. Serve meat with Brisket Barbecue Sauce.

Charcoal Grill Instructions: For at least 1 hour before grilling, soak 6 to 8 wood chunks in enough water to cover. Prepare grill for indirect grilling. Arrange lit coals around a drip pan. Add half the wood chunks to coals. Place brisket on foil on grill rack over the drip pan. Cover and grill for 2 1/2 hours. Turn brisket and continue grilling for 1 1/2 to 2 hours or until brisket is tender. Add additional coals and wood as needed to maintain temperature and smoke. (Do not add additional wood after the first 2 hours of grilling. Too much smoke makes meat bitter.) Test by inserting fork into center of brisket and twisting. When fork twists easily, brisket is ready. Serve as directed above.

Gas Grill Instructions: Start with a full tank of propane. Preheat grill. Reduce heat to medium-low. Adjust for indirect cooking. Add soaked wood chunks according to manufacturer's directions. Or wrap the wood chunks in foil and add to grill.* Place a small can or pan of hot water on the side of the grill rack over a lit burner. Place brisket, fat side up, on a rack in a roasting pan; set pan on grill rack over unlit burner. Cover and grill for 2 1/2 hours or until brisket is very dark brown. Wrap brisket in foil, return to grill directly on grill rack. Cook for 1 1/2 to 2 hours more or until brisket is tender. Serve as directed at left.

For 25 servings: Double the recipe for both Dry Rub and Brisket Barbecue Sauce and use two 5- to 5 1/2-pound fresh beef briskets. Prepare each brisket as directed at left. Wrap each in heavy foil after slicing; refrigerate for up to 2 days.**

For 50 servings: Quadruple the recipe for both Dry Rub and Barbecue Sauce and use four 5- to 5 1/2-pound fresh beef briskets. Prepare briskets as directed at left, smoking two at a time. Wrap each in heavy foil after slicing; refrigerate for up to 2 days.**

Note: To make foil packet for smoking on a gas grill, place half the soaked wood chunks in the center of a 12×8-inch sheet of heavy aluminum foil. Bring up two opposite edges of foil and make a pouch with an opening in the top of packet for smoke to escape. Repeat with remaining wood and a second sheet of foil. Place the packets directly over heat on lava rocks, ceramic briquettes, or grates above the burner.

**Reheating instructions:* To reheat brisket on a charcoal grill, arrange medium-hot coals around the edge of the grill. Test for medium heat in the center of the grill. Place chilled brisket packets in the center of the grill rack, not over the heat. Cover and grill about 30 minutes or until heated through. For a gas grill, preheat grill. Reduce heat to medium. Adjust for indirect cooking. Grill as above. Packets also may be reheated in a 350°F oven about 30 minutes.

Per Serving: 423 cal., 18 g fat (6 g sat. fat), 145 mg chol., 1,249 mg sodium, 13 g carbo., 2 g fiber, 51 g pro.

pan-baked beans

pan-baked beans

For 50 servings, prepare two 25-serving batches so you don't burn beans at the bottom of the pot.

Prep: 40 minutes   Stand: 1 hour   Cook: 1³⁄₄ hours
Makes: 10 to 12 servings

1	pound dry navy beans
1	pound sliced bacon, cut up
2	cups chopped onions (2 large)
1	cup ketchup
1	cup molasses
3	tablespoons yellow mustard
2	teaspoons dried oregano, crushed (optional)
¹⁄₂	teaspoon salt
¹⁄₂	teaspoon ground black pepper

1. Rinse and drain beans. In a 4- to 6-quart Dutch oven, combine beans and 8 cups water. Bring to boiling; reduce heat. Simmer, uncovered, for 2 minutes. Remove from heat. Cover and let stand for 1 hour. (Or place beans and water in Dutch oven. Cover and let soak in a cool place for 6 to 8 hours or overnight.) Drain and rinse beans.

2. In the Dutch oven, cook bacon and onions until bacon is crisp. Drain off fat. Add the beans and 6 cups *fresh* water to Dutch oven. Bring to boiling; reduce heat. Simmer, covered, for 1¹⁄₄ to 1¹⁄₂ hours or until beans are tender, stirring occasionally. Stir in the ketchup, molasses, mustard, oregano (if desired), salt, and pepper. Bring to boiling; reduce heat. Simmer, uncovered, for 30 to 45 minutes more or until beans are desired consistency, stirring occasionally.

For 25 servings: Prepare as directed above with the following exceptions: Double amounts of all ingredients. Boil and soak beans in 12 cups water in an 8- to 10-quart pot. Cook half the onions and bacon at a time. In Step 2, stir in 10 cups of *water.* Cook, uncovered, for 1 to 1¹⁄₄ hours, stirring frequently.

For 50 servings: Prepare the 25-serving recipe twice (do not double the recipe).

Per Serving: 429 cal., 11 g fat (4 g sat. fat), 21 mg chol., 788 mg sodium, 62 g carbo., 12 g fiber, 16 g pro.

kohlrabi coleslaw

Prep: 30 minutes Makes: 12 servings

- 3/4 cup mayonnaise
- 1/4 cup white vinegar
- 2 tablespoons sugar
- 2 teaspoons celery seeds (optional)
- 1/2 teaspoon salt
- 1/4 teaspoon ground black pepper
- 9 cups chopped or finely shredded green cabbage
- 1 cup finely shredded carrots (2 medium)
- 1 cup shredded kohlrabi, jicama, or radishes
- 1 cup snipped Italian (flat-leaf) parsley

1. For dressing, in a small bowl, stir together mayonnaise, vinegar, sugar, celery seeds, salt, and pepper. Set aside.

2. In an extra-large bowl, combine the cabbage, carrots, kohlrabi, and parsley. Stir in the dressing; mix well. Cover and chill until serving time or for up to 24 hours. Serve with a slotted spoon.

For 25 servings: Double the 12-serving recipe above.

For 50 servings: Prepare the 25-serving recipe twice.
Per Serving: 124 cal., 11 g fat (2 g sat. fat), 5 mg chol., 209 mg sodium, 7 g carbo., 2 g fiber, 1 g pro.

peanut butter cookies

Double this classic recipe to make about 72 cookies.
Prep: 40 minutes Chill: 1 hour Bake: 8 minutes per batch
Oven: 375° F Makes: about 36 cookies

- 1/2 cup peanut butter
- 1/2 cup butter, softened
- 1/2 cup granulated sugar
- 1/2 cup packed brown sugar
- 1/2 teaspoon baking soda
- 1 egg
- 1/2 teaspoon vanilla
- 1 1/4 cups all-purpose flour

1. In a large bowl, beat peanut butter and butter with electric mixer on medium speed for 30 seconds. Add sugars, soda, and 1/4 teaspoon *salt*. Beat until combined. Beat in egg and vanilla until combined. Beat in as much of the flour as you can. Stir in any remaining flour. Cover and chill dough about 1 hour or until easy to handle.

2. Preheat oven to 375°F. Shape dough into 1-inch balls. Place balls 2 inches apart on ungreased cookie sheets. Flatten the balls by making crisscross marks with a fork, dipping fork in sugar before flattening each ball. Bake in the preheated oven 8 minutes or until edges are lightly browned. Transfer cookies to wire racks; let cool.

To Store: Arrange cookies in an airtight container; cover. Store at room temperature for up to 3 days or freeze for up to 3 months.
Per Cookie: 82 cal., 4 g fat (2 g sat. fat), 13 mg chol., 71 mg sodium, 9 g carbo., 0 g fiber, 2 g pro.

timetable

Up to 6 months ahead:
* Stir together the Dry Rub. Store at room temperature.

Up to 3 months ahead:
* Make and bake your choice of Peanut Butter Cookies, Cherry and Chocolate Chip Cookies, and/or Star Sugar Cookies. Place in airtight containers and freeze.

Up to 1 month ahead:
* Prepare Brisket Barbecue Sauce. Transfer pureed sauce to an airtight container and store it in refrigerator.
* Make and bake Corn Bread. Cool completely, then cover tightly with foil. Store in the freezer.

1 week ahead:
* Prepare Vinegar Barbecue Sauce; store in the refrigerator.

Up to 3 days ahead:
* Smoke the pork shoulder roast(s). Pull the meat into strands, mix in some of the Vinegar Barbecue Sauce to moisten, and place meat mixture in an airtight container to store in the refrigerator.

Up to 2 days ahead:
* Smoke the Beef Brisket. Thinly slice the briskets across the grain, wrap tightly in foil, and place in the refrigerator.

1 day ahead:
* Stir together the Kohlrabi Coleslaw. Cover and chill slaw, stirring it occasionally to redistribute the dressing.
* If desired, start soaking the beans for Pan-Baked Beans.

3 hours ahead:
* Begin cooking the Pan-Baked Beans.
* Remove cookies from the freezer to thaw.

30 minutes ahead:
* Reheat the beef and/or pork according to the recipes.
* Cut the Corn Bread into squares.

Just before serving:
* Arrange cookies in baskets or on platters.
* Stir coleslaw; add a slotted spoon.
* Spoon the beans into a serving bowl.
* Pour remaining Brisket Barbecue Sauce and/or Vinegar Barbecue Sauce in a bowl or a small pitcher.
* Arrange beef slices on a platter and/or transfer the shredded pork to a bowl.

corn bread

This recipe serves 24, but you can serve 12 people and have leftovers.
Toasted corn bread with honey and butter tastes great for breakfast.
Prep: 10 minutes Bake: 35 minutes Oven: 350°F
Makes: 24 servings

2¹/₂ cups all-purpose flour
2 cups yellow cornmeal
¹/₂ cup sugar
4 teaspoons baking powder
1 teaspoon salt
3 eggs
2¹/₄ cups whole milk
¹/₂ cup butter, melted

1. Preheat oven to 350°F. Grease a 13×9×2-inch disposable foil pan or coat the pan with nonstick cooking spray; set aside.

2. In an extra-large bowl, stir together the flour, cornmeal, sugar, baking powder, and salt. In a medium bowl, mix together eggs, milk, and melted butter. Add egg mixture to the flour mixture and stir until just combined. Do not overmix. Pour batter into the prepared pan, spreading evenly.

3. Bake in the preheated oven for 35 to 40 minutes or until a toothpick inserted in the center comes out clean. Using a serrated knife, cut the corn bread into 24 squares.*

For 50 servings: Prepare the 24-serving recipe twice (do not double recipe).

*Tip: The corn bread is better made one day ahead. Cover bread tightly with foil; store at room temperature. Or bake it up to 2 months ahead; wrap, label, and freeze.
Per Serving: 190 cal., 7 g fat (4 g sat. fat), 47 mg chol., 219 mg sodium, 28 g carbo., 1 g fiber, 5 g pro.

cherry and chocolate chip cookies

Be sure to snip the dried cherries into smaller pieces before tossing them in the bowl. Each little cherry piece adds yummy sweetness to the soft-centered rounds.
Prep: 25 minutes Bake: 9 minutes per batch Oven: 375°F
Makes: about 48 cookies

1 cup butter, softened
1 cup granulated sugar
1 cup packed brown sugar
1 teaspoon baking soda
1 teaspoon salt
2 eggs
1¹/₂ teaspoons vanilla
3 cups all-purpose flour
1 12-ounce package semisweet chocolate pieces
1 cup snipped dried cherries

1. Preheat oven to 375°F. In a large bowl, beat butter with an electric mixer on medium to high speed for 30 seconds. Add granulated sugar, brown sugar, baking soda, and salt. Beat until combined, scraping bowl occasionally. Beat in eggs and vanilla until combined. Beat in as much of the flour as you can with the mixer. Stir in any remaining flour. Stir in chocolate pieces and cherries.

2. Drop dough by tablespoons 2 inches apart onto ungreased cookie sheets. Bake in the preheated oven about 9 minutes or until edges are lightly browned. Transfer cookies to wire racks; let cool.

To Store: Arrange baked cookies in layers separated by waxed paper in an airtight container; cover. Store at room temperature for up to 3 days or freeze for up to 3 months.
Per Cookie: 136 cal., 6 g fat (4 g sat. fat), 19 mg chol., 206 mg sodium, 20 g carbo., 1 g fiber, 2 g pro.

star sugar cookies

star sugar cookies

If you like cakelike cookies, roll the dough to $\frac{1}{4}$-inch thickness and increase the baking time to 8 to 9 minutes. Because you double the thickness, you'll get half as many cookies.

Prep: 45 minutes Chill: 1 hour Bake: 5 minutes per batch
Oven: 375°F Makes: about 108 cookies

1	cup butter, softened
1	cup sugar
1$\frac{1}{2}$	teaspoons baking powder
$\frac{1}{2}$	teaspoon salt
$\frac{1}{4}$	teaspoon ground nutmeg
1	egg
2	tablespoons milk
1	teaspoon vanilla
3	cups all-purpose flour
	Sugar, red- and/or blue-colored sugar, or sprinkles

1. In a large bowl, beat butter with electric mixer on medium to high speed for 30 seconds. Add sugar, baking powder, salt, and nutmeg. Beat until combined, scraping bowl occasionally. Beat in egg, milk, and vanilla until combined. Beat in as much flour as you can with the mixer. Stir in any remaining flour. Divide dough in half. Wrap each dough portion in clear plastic wrap and chill about 1 hour or until easy to handle.

2. Preheat oven to 375°F. On a lightly floured surface, roll one portion of dough to a $\frac{1}{8}$-inch thickness. Keep remaining dough chilled until ready to roll. With a 1$\frac{1}{2}$-, 2-, 3-, and/or 3$\frac{1}{2}$-inch star-shape cookie cutter, cut dough. Place cutouts 1 inch apart on ungreased cookie sheets. Sprinkle with sugar.

3. Bake in the preheated oven for 5 to 6 minutes or until edges are light brown. Transfer cookies to wire racks; let cool.

To Store: Arrange baked cookies in layers separated by waxed paper in an airtight container; cover. Store at room temperature for up to 3 days or freeze for up to 3 months.
Per 3-inch Cookie: 35 cal., 2 g fat (1 g sat. fat), 7 mg chol., 73 mg sodium, 4 g carbo., 0 g fiber, 0 g pro.

pick-me-ups

Sandwiches, often considered the quintessential brown-bag food, don't need to be boring. When something grilled lands between bread, the sandwich erupts with deliciousness. An entrée that demands casualness, sandwiches let you relax while you assemble them and have fun while you eat them. When you crave a fancy-free meal, turn to this assortment of pick-me-ups perfect for lunch, picnics, or backyard gatherings.

blue cheese and steak sandwiches
(recipe, page 149)

*pork wraps with
corn-tomato relish*

pork wraps with
corn-tomato relish

When you expect an evening with a dinner-hour rush, grill the pork and stir together the relish the night before. These wraps taste just as delicious served chilled.

Prep: 50 minutes   Grill: 30 minutes   Stand: 15 minutes
Makes: 10 wraps

  2   1-pound pork tenderloins
      Salt
      Freshly ground black pepper
  2   tablespoons honey
  2   tablespoons Dijon-style mustard
 1/8 teaspoon ground cumin
      Shredded napa cabbage (optional)
      Corn-Tomato Relish
 10   8- to 10-inch plain or flavored flour tortillas

1. Trim fat from meat. Sprinkle meat with salt and black pepper. For glaze, in a small bowl, stir together honey, mustard, and cumin; set aside.

2. For a charcoal grill, arrange hot coals around a drip pan. Test for medium-hot heat above pan. Place meat on the grill rack over the drip pan. Grill, covered, for 30 to 35 minutes or until an instant-read thermometer registers 155°F, brushing with honey-mustard mixture the last 5 to 10 minutes of grilling. (For gas grill, preheat grill. Reduce heat to medium-high. Adjust for indirect cooking. Place meat on grill rack. Cover and grill as above.) Cover meat and let stand 15 minutes (meat temperature will rise to 160°F). Slice meat into thin bite-size strips.

3. To serve, divide meat, cabbage (if desired), and Corn-Tomato Relish among tortillas. Roll up each tortilla.

Corn-Tomato Relish: Thaw one 16-ounce package frozen whole kernel corn; drain well and pat dry with paper towels or use 3 cups fresh whole kernel corn. In a large skillet, heat 2 tablespoons olive oil over medium heat. Add corn, 1/2 cup finely chopped red onion and/or green onions, 1/4 cup finely chopped celery or green sweet pepper, 1 teaspoon minced garlic, 3/4 teaspoon salt, 1/2 teaspoon ground cumin or chili powder, and 1/8 teaspoon cayenne or ground black pepper. Cook about 10 minutes or until vegetables are tender, stirring occasionally. Remove from heat. Stir in 3/4 cup finely chopped and seeded tomatoes, 1/4 cup snipped fresh parsley, 1/4 cup mayonnaise, and 1 tablespoon lime juice. Cover and chill for at least 1 hour or up to 24 hours.

Per Wrap: 323 cal., 12 g fat (3 g sat. fat), 62 mg chol., 501 mg sodium, 30 g carbo., 2 g fiber, 23 g pro.

lemon-and-dill fish sandwiches with tartar sauce

Prep: 1 hour   Grill: 10 minutes   Makes: 6 sandwiches

- 24 to 36 ounces fresh or frozen skinless, boneless walleye pike, haddock, sole, tilapia, or cod fillets, 3/4 inch thick
  Salt and freshly ground black pepper
- 2 teaspoons finely shredded lemon peel
- 3 tablespoons lemon juice
- 3 tablespoons olive oil
- 2 tablespoons snipped fresh dill or 1 teaspoon dried dill weed
- 4 cloves garlic, minced
- 1/4 to 1/2 teaspoon bottled hot pepper sauce
- 4 large lemons, cut into 1/4-inch slices
- 12 slices country wheat bread, lightly buttered; or 6 hoagie buns or other crusty rolls, split and lightly buttered
- 3 cups packaged shredded cabbage with carrot (coleslaw mix) or packaged mixed salad greens
- 6 tomato slices
  Tartar Sauce

1. Thaw fish, if frozen. Rinse fish; pat dry with paper towels. Sprinkle both sides of each fillet with salt and black pepper. In a small bowl, combine lemon peel and juice, oil, dill, garlic, and hot pepper sauce.

2. Grease an unheated grill rack. For a charcoal grill, arrange a bed of lemon slices on the greased grill rack directly over medium coals. Arrange fish on lemon slices. Brush with the lemon-oil mixture. Grill, covered, for 10 to 12 minutes or until fish flakes easily when tested with a fork (do not turn fish). (For a gas grill, preheat grill. Reduce heat to medium. Arrange lemon slices and fish on greased grill rack over heat [line grill rack with foil if grids are too wide to hold lemon slices]. Brush fish with lemon-oil mixture. Cover and grill as above.) Place bread or buns, cut sides down, next to fish the last 2 minutes of grilling or until toasted, turning bread slices once.

3. To serve, using a large spatula, transfer fish pieces to six bread slices or bun bottoms topped with shredded cabbage mix and tomato slices. Top with Tartar Sauce and remaining bread or bun tops. Discard lemon slices.

Tartar Sauce: In a medium bowl, combine 1 cup mayonnaise, 2 tablespoons finely chopped sweet or dill pickle, 1 tablespoon finely chopped green onion, 1 tablespoon snipped fresh parsley, 1/2 teaspoon finely shredded lemon peel, 2 teaspoons lemon juice, 1 1/2 teaspoons snipped fresh dill or 1/2 teaspoon dried dill weed, and 1/2 teaspoon paprika. Cover and chill any remaining Tartar Sauce for up to 1 week.

Per Sandwich: 586 cal., 39 g fat (7 g sat. fat), 111 mg chol., 642 mg sodium, 29 g carbo., 3 g fiber, 28 g pro.

chicken sandwiches with roasted pepper and goat cheese spread

The creamy spread makes these focaccia sandwiches look and taste like a trattoria specialty.

Prep: 30 minutes   Marinate: 1 hour   Grill: 11 minutes
Makes: 4 sandwiches

- 4 skinless, boneless chicken breast halves
- 1/4 cup balsamic vinegar
- 2 tablespoons olive oil
- 1 tablespoon snipped fresh rosemary
- 2 cloves garlic, minced
  Salt and ground black pepper
- 1 10- to 12-inch rosemary or garlic Italian flatbread (focaccia)
  Roasted Pepper and Goat Cheese Spread
- 1/2 of a medium red onion, thinly sliced
- 1 cup baby spinach leaves or small romaine leaves

1. Place a chicken breast half between two pieces of plastic wrap. Using the flat side of a meat mallet, pound the chicken lightly to about 1/2-inch thickness. Remove plastic wrap. Repeat with remaining chicken pieces.

2. Place chicken in a large resealable plastic bag set in a shallow dish. For marinade, combine vinegar, oil, rosemary, and garlic. Pour over chicken; seal bag. Marinate in the refrigerator for 1 to 2 hours, turning bag occasionally.

3. Drain chicken, discarding marinade. Sprinkle chicken lightly with salt and pepper. For a charcoal grill, place chicken on the grill rack over medium coals. Grill, uncovered, for 9 to 11 minutes or until chicken is no longer pink (170°F), turning once halfway through grilling. (For a gas grill, preheat grill. Reduce heat to medium. Place chicken on the grill rack over heat. Cover and grill as above.)

4. To serve, cut flatbread into four wedges. Slice each wedge in half horizontally. Grill wedges, cut sides down, directly over medium heat about 2 minutes or until lightly toasted. Spread toasted sides of bread with Roasted Pepper and Goat Cheese Spread. If necessary, cut chicken breasts to fit bread. Divide chicken, onion slices, and spinach among half of the bread wedges. Add top bread wedges.

Roasted Pepper and Goat Cheese Spread: Drain 1/4 cup roasted red sweet peppers, reserving 1 teaspoon liquid. In a food processor, combine sweet peppers, reserved liquid, 4 ounces soft goat cheese (chèvre), and 1 teaspoon snipped fresh rosemary. Process until nearly smooth. (Or finely chop the sweet pepper and stir mixture together with a wooden spoon.)

Per Sandwich: 321 cal., 12 g fat (5 g sat. fat), 96 mg chol., 392 mg sodium, 11 g carbo., 1 g fiber, 40 g pro.

grilled italian panini

grilled italian panini

You can find capocollo (an Italian ham coated with peppery spices) at Italian delis and in some supermarkets. Substitute prosciutto or cured deli ham if capocollo isn't available.

Prep: 20 minutes Grill: 8 minutes Makes: 4 servings

  1 16-ounce loaf unsliced ciabatta or Italian bread
  6 ounces thinly sliced provolone cheese
 1/4 cup mayonnaise
  1 tablespoon purchased basil pesto
  4 ounces thinly sliced capocollo or cooked ham
  4 ounces thinly sliced salami
     Red Onion Relish
  1 cup arugula
  1 tablespoon olive oil

1. Carefully trim off and discard the top crust of the bread to make a flat surface. Turn bread over; trim off and discard bottom crust. Cut remaining bread in half horizontally to form two 1/2-inch slices.

2. Place half of the provolone cheese on one slice of bread. Combine mayonnaise and pesto in a small bowl; spread over cheese. Top with capocollo, salami, Red Onion Relish, arugula, remaining cheese, and the other slice of bread. Brush both sides of panini with oil.

3. Grease an unheated grill rack. For a charcoal grill, place panini on the greased grill rack directly over medium coals. Put a 13×9×2-inch baking pan on top of sandwich; weigh down pan with several baking potatoes or a foil-wrapped brick. Grill, uncovered, 5 minutes or until sandwich is lightly browned. Use hot pads to remove baking pan. Use a spatula to carefully turn over sandwich. Place weighted baking pan back on sandwich; grill about 3 minutes more or until cheese melts. (For a gas grill, preheat grill. Reduce heat to medium. Place sandwich on grill rack over heat. Place pan on sandwich; cover and grill as above.)

Red Onion Relish: Combine 1 medium red onion, halved and thinly sliced (1 cup); 2 tablespoons olive oil; 1 tablespoon red wine vinegar; and 1 teaspoon snipped fresh oregano in a small bowl. Sprinkle with salt and ground black pepper to taste. Cover; let stand at room temperature for up to 2 hours.

Per Serving: 840 cal., 51 g fat (15 g sat. fat), 77 mg chol., 2,118 mg sodium, 62 g carbo., 4 g fiber, 33 g pro.

honey-citrus pork quesadillas

A splash of fresh lime juice and a touch of honey make these quesadillas a fantastic grilled treat.

Prep: 30 minutes Marinate: 20 minutes Grill: 9 minutes
Makes: 6 servings

 1/2 cup lime juice
 1/4 cup snipped fresh cilantro
  1 tablespoon honey
  2 cloves garlic, thinly sliced
  1 pound boneless pork loin chops, cut 3/4 inch thick
  1 medium red onion, sliced 1/2 inch thick
  1 medium green sweet pepper, seeded and cut lengthwise into quarters
  3 tablespoons lime juice
  2 green onions, thinly sliced
  8 ounces Monterey Jack cheese with jalapeño peppers, shredded
 12 6-inch flour tortillas
     Dairy sour cream and/or bottled salsa (optional)

1. Place chops in a large resealable plastic bag set in a shallow dish. Combine the 1/2 cup lime juice, 2 tablespoons cilantro, honey, and garlic. Pour marinade over pork. Seal bag; turn to coat. Marinate in the refrigerator for 20 minutes. Drain pork; discard marinade.

2. For a charcoal grill, place pork, red onion slices, and pepper quarters on the rack directly over medium coals. Grill vegetables, uncovered, for 5 to 7 minutes or until crisp-tender, turning to brown evenly. Grill pork chops for 7 to 9 minutes or until pork is slightly pink in the center (160° F), turning once halfway through grilling. (For a gas grill, preheat grill. Reduce heat to medium. Place pork, onion, and sweet pepper on grill rack over heat. Cover and grill as above.)

3. Meanwhile, in a large bowl, combine 3 tablespoons lime juice, 2 tablespoons cilantro, the green onions, 1/4 teaspoon each salt and black pepper. Chop pork, onion, and sweet peppers; add to green onion mixture.

4. Spoon cheese evenly onto one half of each tortilla. Top cheese with pork mixture. Fold plain half of tortilla over filling. For a charcoal grill, place half of filled tortillas on the rack directly over medium coals. Grill, uncovered, 2 to 3 minutes or until tortillas are lightly browned, turning once halfway through grilling. (For a gas grill, place folded tortillas on the grill rack directly over medium heat. Cover and grill as above.) Transfer quesadillas to a platter; cover with foil to keep warm. Repeat with remaining filled tortillas.

5. Cut each quesadilla into 3 wedges and, if desired, serve with sour cream and/or salsa.

Per Serving: 316 cal., 16 g fat (7 g sat. fat), 52 mg chol., 526 mg sodium, 25 g carbo., 1 g fiber, 18 g pro.

grilled brats with black bean salsa

grilled brats
with black bean salsa

The classic German sausage goes Mexican. Dress up your brat with salsa, or serve the salsa on the side with garlic tortilla chips.

Prep: 15 minutes Cook: 20 minutes Grill: 20 to 25 minutes
Makes: 10 servings

10	uncooked bratwursts (about 4 ounces each)
10	hoagie buns, split
2	medium onions, halved and thinly sliced (1 cup)
1	tablespoon cooking oil
2	14-ounce cans chicken broth
1	12-ounce can beer
	Black Bean Salsa

1. Pierce brats in several places with tines of fork. For a charcoal grill, arrange medium-hot coals around a drip pan. Test for medium heat above pan. Place brats on the grill rack over drip pan. Grill, covered, for 20 to 25 minutes or until juices run clear, turning occasionally. Add the hoagie buns to the grill rack, cut sides down; grill about 1 minute, or until toasted. (For a gas grill, preheat grill. Reduce heat to medium. Adjust for indirect grilling. Place brats on grill rack. Cover and grill as above. Place buns on grill rack the last minute of grilling.)

2. Meanwhile, cook onion in hot oil in a Dutch oven until tender. Stir in broth and beer. Bring to boiling; reduce heat. Simmer, uncovered, for 20 minutes. Add cooked bratwursts; heat through.

3. Serve bratwursts on buns with onions. Top with Black Bean Salsa.

Black Bean Salsa: In a medium bowl, combine one 15-ounce can black beans, rinsed and drained; 1 medium cucumber, peeled, seeded, and chopped; 1 medium tomato, seeded and chopped; 1/2 cup sliced green onions; 1/4 cup lime juice; 1 tablespoon snipped fresh cilantro; 1 tablespoon olive oil, 1/2 teaspoon ground cumin; 1/8 teaspoon salt; and 1/8 teaspoon cayenne pepper. Cover and chill for 4 to 24 hours.

Per Serving: 465 cal., 36 g fat (17 g sat. fat), 68 mg chol., 1,519 mg sodium, 15 g carbo., 5 g fiber, 17 g pro.

Add some sizzle to your tailgating adventures by serving these two-handed specialties.

blue cheese and steak sandwiches

These hefty sandwiches make great picnic or tailgate fare. Prepare meat with rub, stir together spread, and clean or cut arugula and pepper at home. Then grill the steak and buns at the picnic and assemble the sandwiches. Pictured on page 143.
Prep: 30 minutes Chill: up to 2 days Grill: 17 minutes
Stand: 10 minutes Makes: 4 sandwiches

- 1   tablespoon packed brown sugar
- 2   teaspoons ground cumin
- 2   teaspoons garlic powder
- 1   teaspoon onion powder
- $1/2$ teaspoon salt
- $1/4$ teaspoon ground black pepper
- 1   1$3/4$-pound flank steak
- 4   sourdough or ciabatta buns, sliced
- $1/3$ cup crumbled blue cheese
- $1/3$ cup mayonnaise
- 1   teaspoon Worcestershire sauce
- 1   teaspoon white wine vinegar
- $1/2$ cup fresh arugula
- $1/2$ cup bottled roasted red sweet pepper cut into strips

1. For rub, in a small bowl, combine brown sugar, cumin, garlic powder, onion powder, salt, and black pepper. Sprinkle rub mixture evenly over both sides of steak; rub in with your fingers. Wrap steak in plastic wrap and chill for up to 2 days.

2. For a charcoal grill, place steak on the grill rack directly over medium coals. Grill, uncovered, for 17 to 21 minutes for medium doneness (160°F), turning once halfway through grilling. Add the sourdough buns to the grill rack, cut sides down; grill about 1 minute or until toasted. (For a gas grill, preheat grill. Reduce heat to medium. Place steak on the grill rack over heat. Cover and grill as above. Place buns on grill rack the last minute of grilling.)

3. Transfer steak to a cutting board and let stand, loosely covered with aluminum foil, for 10 minutes. Thinly slice steak diagonally across the grain.

4. In a small bowl, stir together blue cheese, mayonnaise, Worcestershire sauce, and vinegar. Spread the toasted side of bun bottoms with blue cheese mixture. Layer with sliced steak, arugula, and roasted pepper; add bun tops. Secure with wooden picks.
Per Sandwich: 684 cal., 29 g fat (9 g sat. fat), 80 mg chol., 1,092 mg sodium, 48 g carbo., 1 g fiber, 53 g pro.

beer-braised brat sandwiches

The unusual topping of drunken onions and tart cranberry relish adds a new twist to a traditional grilled favorite.
Prep: 30 minutes Grill: 20 minutes Makes: 10 sandwiches

- 10   uncooked bratwursts (about 2$1/2$ pounds total)
- 10   hoagie buns, bratwurst buns, or other crusty rolls, split and toasted
- $1/4$ cup butter
- 1   large onion, halved and cut into thin slices
- 2   12-ounce bottles or cans dark German beer
- 2   tablespoons packed brown sugar
- 2   tablespoons vinegar
- 1   teaspoon caraway seeds
- 1   teaspoon dried thyme, crushed
- 1   teaspoon Worcestershire sauce
-      Easy Cranberry-Pickle Relish

1. Pierce bratwursts with fork. For a charcoal grill, arrange medium-hot coals around a drip pan. Test for medium heat above pan. Place bratwursts on the grill rack over drip pan. Grill, covered, for 20 to 30 minutes or until an instant-read thermometer inserted into bratwursts registers 160°F, turning once halfway through grilling time. Add the hoagie buns to the grill rack, cut sides down; grill about 1 minute, or until toasted. (For a gas grill, preheat grill. Reduce heat to medium. Adjust for indirect cooking. Place brats on grill rack. Cover and grill as above. Place buns on grill rack the last minute of grilling.)

2. Meanwhile, in a Dutch oven, heat butter over medium heat. Add onion; cook and stir about 5 minutes or until tender. Add beer, brown sugar, vinegar, caraway seeds, thyme, and Worcestershire sauce. Bring to boiling; reduce heat. Place bratwursts in beer mixture; keep warm until serving time.

3. To serve, place grilled bratwursts in buns. Using a slotted spoon, top with some cooked onion slices and Easy Cranberry-Pickle Relish.

Easy Cranberry-Pickle Relish: In a small bowl, stir together 1 cup canned whole cranberry sauce and $1/2$ cup sweet pickle relish.
Per Sandwich: 682 cal., 33 g fat (12 g sat. fat), 76 mg chol., 1,341 mg sodium, 70 g carbo., 3 g fiber, 20 g pro.

beef-spinach sandwiches

Prep: 20 minutes Marinate: 4 hours Grill: 17 minutes
Makes: 6 sandwiches

1/4	cup champagne vinegar or white wine vinegar
2	tablespoons Dijon-style mustard
1/4	cup olive oil
2	teaspoons finely chopped shallots or sweet onion
1	teaspoon sugar
1/2	teaspoon salt
1/4	teaspoon ground black pepper
1	1 1/2-pound beef flank steak
6	hoagie buns, hamburger buns, or sourdough rolls, split
3	cups baby spinach
2	ounces goat cheese or feta cheese, crumbled
1/2	cup roasted red sweet pepper strips*

1. For marinade, in a small bowl, stir together vinegar and mustard until mixture is smooth in a small bowl. Stir in olive oil, shallots, sugar, salt, and ground black pepper. Score both sides of steak in a diamond pattern by making shallow diagonal cuts at 1-inch intervals. Place steak in a resealable plastic bag set in a shallow dish. Pour marinade over steak; seal bag. Chill in refrigerator 4 to 24 hours, turning bag occasionally. Drain steak; discard marinade.

2. For a charcoal grill, place steak on the grill rack directly over medium coals. Grill, uncovered, 17 to 21 minutes for medium doneness (160°F), turning once halfway through grilling. Add the hoagie buns to the grill rack, cut side down; grill about 1 minute or until toasted. (For a gas grill, preheat grill. Reduce heat to medium. Place steaks on grill rack. Cover and grill as above. Place buns on grill rack the last 1 minute of grilling.)

3. Slice steaks across the grain into thin strips. Arrange spinach, steak, and cheese on bottom half of each grilled bun. Top with red pepper strips and bun tops.

To roast red pepper strips: quarter a medium red sweet pepper. Remove stems, seeds, and membranes. Place pepper quarters, skin sides down, on grill rack directly over medium coals. Grill for 10 to 12 minutes or until skins are charred. Wrap peppers in foil and let stand 5 minutes. Use a sharp knife to loosen the skin edges; gently and slowly pull the skin from the pepper quarters. Discard skin. Cut pepper quarters into strips or 3/4-inch pieces. (Or use purchased red sweet peppers; drain and cut into strips.)
Per Sandwich: 487 cal., 20 g fat (5 g sat. fat), 42 mg chol., 739 mg sodium, 51 g carbo., 2 g fiber, 26 g pro.

smoked roast beef sandwiches

To reduce last minute prep time, smoke the sirloin roast ahead of time and refrigerate it for up to one week. And there's a bonus: beef is easier to slice when it is cold.
Prep: 30 minutes Grill: 1 1/2 hours Chill: 24 hours
Makes: 12 sandwiches

2	cups mesquite wood chips
1	3 to 4 pound boneless beef sirloin roast
2	teaspoons chipotle chili powder
1/2	teaspoon salt
1/2	teaspoon ground black pepper
1/2	teaspoon ground cumin
2/3	cup purchased onion jam or onion relish
2	tablespoons prepared horseradish or mustard
12	sourdough and/or whole wheat mini rolls, split and, if desired, toasted
1	cup roasted red and/or yellow peppers, cut into strips
2	cups arugula leaves, rinsed and dried (optional)

1. For at least 1 hour before grilling, soak wood chips in enough water to cover. Drain wood chips.

2. Trim fat from sirloin roast. For rub, in a small bowl, combine chipotle chili powder, salt, ground black pepper, and cumin. Sprinkle rub evenly over roast; rub in with your fingers. Insert a meat thermometer into the thickest part of the meat.

3. For a charcoal grill, arrange medium-hot coals around a drip pan. Test for medium heat above the pan. Sprinkle drained wood chips over coals. Place beef roast on grill rack over drip pan. Cover and grill for 1 1/2 to 2 hours or until the meat reaches desired doneness (140°F for medium-rare or 155°F for medium). Add more coals and wood chips as needed to maintain temperature and smoke. (For a gas grill, preheat grill. Reduce heat to medium. Adjust for indirect cooking. Grill as above adding wood chips according to manufacturer's directions.)

4. Cover the beef roast with foil. Let stand 15 minutes before carving. (The meat's temperature will rise 5°F during standing.) Thinly slice the beef. Cover and refrigerate for up to 24 hours.

5. In a small bowl, combine the onion jam and horseradish. Spread mixture over cut sides of roll tops. Place sliced roast beef on roll bottoms. Top with roasted red pepper strips and, if desired, arugula. Top with bun tops.
Per Sandwich: 453 cal., 6 g fat (2 g sat. fat), 54 mg chol., 682 mg sodium, 63 g carbo., 1 g fiber, 35 g pro.

smoked roast beef
sandwiches

beyond basic burgers

Forget the ketchup and dill pickle—
There's much more to put on—and in—a burger. Unique seasonings, flavorful toppings, and creative additions make these burgers far from ordinary.

grilled poblano burgers

Pictured at left.

Prep: 25 minutes Roast: 20 minutes Stand: 20 minutes
Grill: 14 minutes Oven: 425°F Makes: 4 burgers

- 2 fresh medium poblano chile peppers
- 1 egg, lightly beaten
- 3/4 cup soft bread crumbs (1 slice)
- 1/2 cup shredded carrot
- 2 tablespoons water
- 1 teaspoon dried oregano, crushed
- 2 cloves garlic, minced
- 1/2 teaspoon salt
- 1/4 teaspoon ground black pepper
- 1 pound lean ground beef
- 4 kaiser rolls, split
- 4 slices red and/or yellow tomato
  Frozen guacamole (optional)

1. Preheat oven to 425°F. To roast chiles, halve peppers lengthwise and remove stems, seeds, and membranes. Place peppers, cut sides down, on a foil-lined baking sheet. Roast for 20 to 25 minutes in preheated oven. Wrap peppers in foil and let stand 20 minutes. Using a paring knife, gently and slowly pull skins off peppers and discard. Chop roasted peppers.

2. In a large bowl, combine roasted peppers, egg, bread crumbs, carrot, the water, oregano, garlic, salt, and black pepper. Add ground beef; mix well. Shape mixture into four 3/4-inch-thick patties.

3. For a charcoal grill, place patties on the grill rack directly over medium coals. Grill, uncovered, for 14 to 18 minutes or until done (160°F), turning once halfway through grilling. Toast kaiser rolls on grill. (For a gas grill, preheat grill. Reduce heat to medium. Place patties, then kaiser rolls, on grill rack over heat. Cover and grill as above.)

4. Serve burgers in kaiser rolls with tomato and, if desired, thawed guacamole.
Per Burger: 478 cal., 21 g fat (7 g sat. fat), 130 mg chol., 751 mg sodium, 41 g carbo.,

old-world burgers

Explore old-world flavors by using veal instead of beef and rye instead of white.

Prep: 20 minutes Grill: 14 minutes Makes: 4 burgers

- 1 egg, lightly beaten
- 2 tablespoons beer or water
- 3/4 cup soft rye bread crumbs (1 slice)
- 1/2 teaspoon caraway seeds
- 1/2 teaspoon dried marjoram, crushed
- 1 clove garlic, minced
- 1/4 teaspoon salt
- 1/4 teaspoon ground black pepper
- 1 pound ground veal or lean ground beef
- 8 slices rye bread
- 4 slices Swiss cheese (4 ounces)
- 3 tablespoons German-style mustard

1. In a large bowl, combine egg and beer. Stir in bread crumbs, caraway seeds, marjoram, garlic, salt, and pepper. Add ground veal; mix well. Using hands, shape mixture into four 3/4-inch-thick patties.

2. For a charcoal grill, place patties on the grill rack directly over medium coals. Grill, uncovered, for 14 to 18 minutes or until done (160°F), turning once halfway through grilling. (For a gas grill, preheat grill. Reduce heat to medium. Place patties on grill rack over heat. Cover and grill as above.)

3. When burgers are nearly done, add rye bread slices to the grill. Grill for 1 to 2 minutes or until bottoms are lightly browned. Turn bread slices; place cheese on four of the bread slices. Grill for 1 to 2 minutes more.

4. Place burgers on the cheese-topped bread slices. Spread the plain bread slices with mustard; place on top of burgers.
Per Burger: 492 cal., 19 g fat (7 g sat. fat), 172 mg chol., 1,056 mg sodium, 37 g carbo., 4 g fiber, 37 g pro.

old-world burgers

double-beef burgers

These burgers use most of the ingredients of the American deli's most famous invention—the Reuben.

Prep: 15 minutes   Grill: 14 minutes   Makes: 4 burgers

- 1   egg, lightly beaten
- 1   2^1/$_2$-ounce package very thinly sliced corned beef, chopped
- ^{1}/$_3$ cup finely chopped cabbage
- ^{1}/$_4$ cup soft rye bread crumbs (about ^{1}/$_2$ slice)
- ^{1}/$_2$ teaspoon caraway seeds
- ^{1}/$_4$ teaspoon salt
- 1   pound lean ground beef
- 1   large red onion, sliced
- 4   kaiser rolls, split
- 3   tablespoons horseradish mustard

1. In a medium bowl, combine egg, corned beef, cabbage, bread crumbs, caraway seeds, and salt. Add ground beef; mix well. Shape mixture into four ^{3}/$_4$-inch-thick patties.

2. For a charcoal grill, place patties on the grill rack directly over medium coals. Grill, uncovered, for 14 to 18 minutes or until done (160°F), turning once halfway through grilling. Add onion slices to the grill during the last 10 to 12 minutes or until tender, turning once halfway through grilling. Toast kaiser rolls on the grill until golden brown. (For a gas grill, preheat grill. Reduce heat to medium. Place patties, then onion slices and kaiser rolls on grill rack over heat. Cover and grill as above.)

3. Spread kaiser rolls with horseradish mustard. Serve burgers in rolls with onion slices.

Per Burger: 479 cal., 22 g fat (7 g sat. fat), 138 mg chol., 861 mg sodium, 36 g carbo., 2 g fiber, 33 g pro.

garden burgers

No ketchup and mustard required: A vinegar-oil dressing adds a little zing to the saladlike toppings.

Prep: 20 minutes   Grill: 14 minutes   Makes: 4 burgers

- 2   tablespoons olive oil
- 2   tablespoons red wine vinegar
- 1   teaspoon snipped fresh thyme
- ^{1}/$_4$ teaspoon cracked black pepper
- 1   pound 90% lean ground beef
- ^{1}/$_4$ teaspoon salt
- ^{1}/$_4$ teaspoon ground black pepper
- 2   medium yellow summer squash, cut lengthwise into ^{1}/$_4$- to ^{1}/$_2$-inch-thick slices
- 4   hamburger buns, split and toasted
     Lettuce or arugula
- 2   to 4 ounces blue cheese, cut in wedges
     Tomato slices (optional)
     Red onion slices (optional)

1. For the dressing, in a screw-top jar, combine olive oil, vinegar, thyme, and cracked black pepper. Cover and shake well. Set aside.

2. In a bowl, combine ground beef, salt, and ground black pepper; mix well. Shape ground beef into four ^{3}/$_4$-inch-thick patties. Brush squash slices with some of the dressing. Set remaining dressing aside.

3. For a charcoal grill, place patties on the grill rack directly over medium coals. Grill, uncovered, for 14 to 18 minutes or until done (160°F), turning once halfway through grilling. Place squash slices alongside beef patties. Grill over medium coals for 7 to 10 minutes or until tender, turning once. (For a gas grill, preheat grill. Reduce heat to medium. Place patties and then squash slices on the grill rack over heat. Cover and grill as above.)

4. To serve, divide lettuce among bottoms of buns. Top with burgers. Top burgers with squash and blue cheese. If desired, add tomato and red onion. Drizzle cut sides of bun tops with remaining dressing. Add bun tops to sandwiches.

Per Burger: 426 cal., 24 g fat (8 g sat. fat), 82 mg chol., 592 mg sodium, 24 g carbo., 2 g fiber, 28 g pro.

Just a handful of flavorful additions takes ordinary burgers to extraordinary. Be adventuresome! Create your own signature burger.

juicy tips

The colors, aromas, and flavors of fresh meats are greatly enhanced when the meats are seared or browned. To perfectly sear burgers, use these tips.

* **Use ground meat** that contains at least 20 percent fat.

* **If you prefer lower-fat burgers,** decrease the surface moisture on your lower-fat patties by leaving them uncovered for 1 to 2 hours on a plate in the refrigerator, by patting them with paper towels, or even by blow-drying them with a hair dryer.

* **Use rubs.** Not only do rubs add new flavors to meat, but they also aid browning. Be careful when using rubs that contain sugar because they burn quickly.

* **Use correct temperatures.** A good rule of thumb is that low temperatures work best for thick burgers and high temps create the best thin ones. NOTE: When cooking over low temperatures, turn patties several times.

garden burgers

black bean burgers
with sweet corn salsa

Prep: 45 minutes   Stand: 1 hour   Grill: 37 minutes
Makes: 6 burgers

1½	cups walnuts, toasted
⅔	cup chopped onion
⅔	cup snipped fresh cilantro
2	teaspoons ground cumin
3	cloves garlic
½	teaspoon dried oregano, crushed
½	teaspoon dried basil, crushed
2	15-ounce cans black beans, rinsed and drained
¼	cup canned diced green chile peppers, drained
2	eggs, lightly beaten
¾	cup fine dry bread crumbs
¼	teaspoon ground black pepper
2	fresh ears corn (with husks)
1	medium tomato, chopped
¼	cup finely chopped onion
¼	cup snipped fresh cilantro
1	teaspoon finely shredded lime peel
2	tablespoons lime juice
2	tablespoons olive oil
½	of a small fresh jalapeño chile pepper, seeded and finely chopped*
¼	teaspoon salt
¼	teaspoon ground black pepper
6	English muffins, split

1. In a food processor fitted with a metal blade,** combine walnuts, the ⅔ cup onion, the ⅔ cup cilantro, the cumin, garlic, oregano, and basil. Cover and process with several on/off turns just until combined. Add black beans and green chiles. Cover and process with several on-off turns just until combined. Transfer mixture to a large bowl. Stir in eggs, bread crumbs, and ¼ teaspoon black pepper. Using damp hands, shape mixture into six ¾-inch-thick patties. Place patties on a baking sheet, cover, and chill until ready to grill.

2. Carefully peel back cornhusks but do not remove. Using a stiff brush or your fingers, remove corn silks. Fold husks back around corn. If necessary, tie husk tops with 100-percent-cotton kitchen string. Soak corn in enough water to cover for at least 1 hour.

3. While corn soaks, start preparing salsa. In a medium bowl, combine tomato, the ¼ cup onion, the ¼ cup cilantro, the lime peel, lime juice, 1 tablespoon of the oil, the jalapeño pepper, salt, and ¼ teaspoon black pepper. Cover and chill until needed.

4. Drain corn; shake to remove excess water. Brush corn kernels with the remaining 1 tablespoon oil. For a charcoal grill, place corn (with husks) on the rack of a grill with a cover directly over medium coals. Cover and grill for 25 to 30 minutes or until corn kernels are tender, turning corn several times. (For a gas grill, preheat grill. Reduce heat to medium. Place corn [with husks] on grill rack over heat. Cover and grill as above.) Carefully remove string and husks. Cut the corn kernels off cobs. Stir corn into salsa.

5. For charcoal grill, place patties on the grill rack directly over medium coals. Grill, uncovered, for 12 to 14 minutes or until done (160°F), turning once halfway through grilling. Toast English muffins on the grill. (For gas grill, place patties, then English muffins on grill rack over medium heat. Cover and grill as above.)

6. Serve burgers between English muffin halves with salsa.

*Note: Because chile peppers contain volatile oils that can burn your skin and eyes, avoid direct contact with them as much as possible. When working with chile peppers, wear plastic or rubber gloves. If your bare hands do touch the peppers, wash your hands and nails well with soap and warm water.

**Tip: If you do not have a food processor, finely chop the walnuts, the ⅔ cup onion, the ⅔ cup cilantro, and the garlic. In a large bowl, combine walnuts, onion, cilantro, garlic, cumin, oregano, and basil. Stir in beans and green chile peppers. Using a potato masher, mash the bean mixture slightly. Stir in eggs, bread crumbs, and ¼ teaspoon black pepper. Shape into patties as directed.

Per Burger: 595 cal., 28 g fat (3 g sat. fat), 71 mg chol., 973 mg sodium, 70 g carbo., 12 g fiber, 22 g pro.

*black bean burgers
with sweet corn salsa*

jerk burgers with mango salsa

jerk burgers
with mango salsa

Prep: 20 minutes   Grill: 10 minutes   Makes: 4 burgers

1	tablespoon cooking oil
1	cup chopped green sweet pepper
1/4	cup chopped red sweet pepper
1/4	cup finely chopped onion
1	teaspoon grated fresh ginger
1	medium mango, seeded, peeled, and chopped
1/4	cup apple jelly
1	tablespoon lime juice
	Dash salt
1	egg, lightly beaten
1/3	cup bottled jerk sauce
1/4	cup fine dry bread crumbs
1	pound lean ground beef
4	ciabatta rolls or hamburger buns, split
1	cup shredded Monterey Jack cheese (4 ounces)

1. For salsa, in a medium saucepan, heat oil over medium heat. Add sweet peppers, onion, and ginger; cook and stir for 3 minutes. Add mango, jelly, lime juice, and salt; cook and stir until jelly melts. Set aside.

2. In a large bowl, combine egg, 1/4 cup of the jerk sauce, and the bread crumbs. Add ground beef; mix well. Using hands, shape mixture into four 1/2-inch-thick patties.

3. For a charcoal grill, place patties on the grill rack directly over medium coals. Grill, uncovered, for 10 to 13 minutes or until done (160°F), turning and brushing once with the remaining jerk sauce halfway through grilling. If desired, toast ciabatta rolls on the grill. (For a gas grill, preheat grill. Reduce heat to medium. Place patties, then ciabatta rolls, if desired, on grill rack over heat. Cover and grill as above.)

4. Divide cheese among bottoms of rolls. Serve burgers in rolls with some of the salsa. Serve remaining salsa on the side.

Per Burger: 808 cal., 50 g fat (20 g sat. fat), 167 mg chol., 740 mg sodium, 60 g carbo., 3 g fiber, 31 g pro.

pizza burgers

Easy-to-make, juicy, and always satisfying, these dressed-up burgers may be the season's greatest grilling pleasures.

pizza burgers

Prep: 20 minutes   Grill: 14 minutes   Makes: 4 burgers

1	egg, lightly beaten
1/3	cup canned mushroom stems and pieces, drained and chopped
1/4	cup seasoned fine dry bread crumbs
2	tablespoons milk
1	teaspoon dried Italian seasoning
1/4	teaspoon salt
1	pound lean ground pork
8	1/2-inch-thick slices French bread
1	8-ounce can pizza sauce
1/4	cup sliced pitted ripe olives
1/4	cup shredded mozzarella cheese

1. In a medium bowl, combine egg, mushrooms, bread crumbs, milk, Italian seasoning, and salt. Add ground pork; mix well. Using hands, shape mixture into four 3/4-inch-thick patties.

2. For a charcoal grill, place patties on the grill rack directly over medium coals. Grill, uncovered, for 14 to 18 minutes or until done (160°F), turning once halfway through grilling. Toast bread slices on the grill. (For a gas grill, preheat grill. Reduce heat to medium. Place patties, then bread slices on grill rack over heat. Cover and grill as above.)

3. For sauce, in a small saucepan, combine pizza sauce and olives; heat through.

4. Serve burgers between grilled bread slices with sauce and cheese.
Per Burger: 546 cal., 23 g fat (9 g sat. fat), 133 mg chol., 1,133 mg sodium, 48 g carbo., 4 g fiber, 37 g pro.

bull's-eye onion burgers

Served on hearty bread and dripping with Swiss cheese, this unusual onion burger is sure to hit your taste-bud target with each and every bite. With the addition of kale, the sandwich also hits a nutritional mark with a bit of vitamin K.

Prep: 20 minutes   Grill: 10 minutes   Makes: 4 burgers

1	large sweet onion
1	pound lean ground beef
1 1/2	teaspoons garlic powder
1/2	teaspoon salt
1/4	teaspoon ground black pepper
4	slices Swiss cheese
8	red and/or green kale leaves, stems removed
2	teaspoons olive oil
4	slices 3/4-inch-thick hearty bread or Texas toast

1. Peel and cut onion into four 1/4-inch-thick slices; refrigerate remaining onion for another use. Using hands, shape meat loosely into four 1/2-inch-thick patties; sprinkle with garlic powder, salt, and ground black pepper. Press one onion slice into the center of each patty and shape meat around onion until top of onion is flush with the surface of the meat patty.

2. For a charcoal grill, place meat, onion side up, on the rack directly over medium coals. Grill, uncovered, for 10 to 13 minutes or until meat is done (160°F), turning once halfway through grilling. Top with cheese before the last minute of grilling. Toast bread slices on the grill. (For a gas grill, preheat grill. Reduce heat to medium. Place patties, then bread slices on grill rack over heat. Cover and grill as above.) Brush kale leaves lightly with oil and add to grill the last 1 to 1 1/2 minutes of grilling.

3. To serve, place two kale leaves atop each bread slice. Top with a burger, onion side up.
Per Burger: 624 cal., 18 g fat (3 g sat. fat), 85 mg chol., 1,101 mg sodium, 67 g carbo., 7 g fiber, 46 g pro.

currant-glazed pork burgers

Sweet and sour and gorgeous to boot, these burgers use many of the same ingredients as Cumberland sauce.

Prep: 15 minutes Grill: 14 minutes Makes: 4 burgers

- 1/4 cup currant jelly
- 3 tablespoons ketchup
- 1 tablespoon cider vinegar
- 1/8 teaspoon ground cinnamon
  Dash ground cloves
- 1 egg, lightly beaten
- 3 tablespoons fine dry bread crumbs
- 2 tablespoons chopped onion
- 2 tablespoons milk
- 1/4 teaspoon salt
- 1/4 teaspoon dried thyme, crushed
- 1/8 teaspoon ground black pepper
- 1 pound lean ground pork
- 4 whole wheat hamburger buns, split
- 4 lettuce leaves (optional)

1. For sauce, in a small saucepan, combine currant jelly, ketchup, vinegar, cinnamon, and cloves. Cook and stir just until boiling. Remove from heat; cover to keep warm.

2. In a medium bowl, combine egg, bread crumbs, onion, milk, salt, thyme, and pepper. Add ground pork; mix well. Using hands, shape mixture into four 3/4-inch-thick patties.

3. For a charcoal grill, place patties on the grill rack directly over medium coals. Grill, uncovered, for 14 to 18 minutes or until done (160°F), turning once halfway through grilling. Toast hamburger buns on the grill. (For a gas grill, preheat grill. Reduce heat to medium. Place patties, then hamburger buns on grill rack over heat. Cover and grill as above.)

4. Serve burgers in buns with sauce and, if desired, lettuce.

Per Burger: 347 cal., 11 g fat (4 g sat. fat), 107 mg chol., 612 mg sodium, 43 g carbo., 3 g fiber, 21 g pro.

fish burgers
with green cabbage slaw

Prep: 30 minutes Grill: 10 minutes Makes: 6 burgers

- 1 1/2 pounds fresh or frozen tuna and/or salmon fillets
- 1/4 cup snipped fresh cilantro
- 2 tablespoons lime juice
- 2 tablespoons olive oil
- 1 tablespoon pickled sushi ginger, finely chopped
- 1 tablespoon Asian chili sauce
- 1 to 2 teaspoons prepared wasabi paste
- 2 cloves garlic, minced
- 1/4 teaspoon salt
- 1/4 teaspoon ground black pepper
- 3 pita bread rounds, quartered
  Green Cabbage Slaw
  Coarsely chopped tomato (optional)

1. Thaw fish, if frozen. Rinse fish; pat dry with paper towels. Finely chop fish.* In a large bowl, combine fish, cilantro, lime juice, 4 teaspoons of the oil, the ginger, chili sauce, wasabi paste, garlic, salt, and pepper. Shape mixture into six 3/4-inch-thick patties.

2. Grease an unheated grill rack. For a charcoal grill, place patties on the greased grill rack directly over medium coals. Grill, uncovered, for 10 to 12 minutes or until done (160°F), turning once halfway through grilling. Brush pita quarters with remaining oil. Toast pita quarters on grill. (For gas grill, preheat grill. Reduce heat to medium. Place patties, then pita quarters on greased grill rack over heat. Cover and grill as above.)

3. Serve burgers between pita quarters with Green Cabbage Slaw and, if desired, chopped tomato.

Green Cabbage Slaw: In a food processor or blender, combine 1/2 cup plain low-fat yogurt; 2 tablespoons snipped fresh parsley; 2 tablespoons snipped fresh dill; 1 tablespoon lime juice; 1 to 2 cloves garlic, minced; 1/8 teaspoon salt; and 1/8 teaspoon ground black pepper. Cover and process or blend until smooth. In a large bowl, combine 3 cups finely shredded Napa cabbage and the yogurt mixture; toss gently to coat. Cover and chill for up to 24 hours.

*Tip: If you like, add the fish, a little at a time, to a food processor; cover and process with on/off turns until finely chopped.

Per Burger: 318 cal., 11 g fat (2 g sat. fat), 44 mg chol., 408 mg sodium, 22 g carbo., 1 g fiber, 31 g pro.

fish burgers with green cabbage slaw

hot dog!

Whether you're at the ballpark, a bonfire, or picnic, hot dogs are one of America's most popular sandwiches. And, depending on the region where you live, there's a traditional way to top them. So grab a juicy dog and check out this roundup of dressed-up regional versions of the summertime favorite.

chicago-style dog

Grill hot dogs as directed for Basic Hot Dog on page 165. Place hot dogs in poppy seed hot dog buns. Top with yellow mustard, chopped onion, sweet pickle relish, thinly sliced roma tomato wedges, thinly sliced and halved cucumber, chopped jalapeño pepper, and celery salt.

coney island dog

Grill hot dogs as directed for Basic Hot Dog on page 165. Place hot dogs in hot dog buns. Top with Coney Island Chili.

Coney Island Chili: In a large skillet, cook 12 ounces ground beef, 1 cup chopped onion, and 3 minced garlic cloves over medium-high heat until meat is browned; drain fat. Stir in one 14 1/2-ounce can diced tomatoes, one 4-ounce can diced green chile peppers, 1 tablespoon chili powder, 1 tablespoon yellow mustard, 1 teaspoon sugar, 1 teaspoon paprika, 1 teaspoon Worcestershire sauce, 1/2 teaspoon ground cumin, 1/2 teaspoon celery seeds, 1/4 teaspoon salt, and 1/4 teaspoon ground black pepper. Bring to boiling; reduce heat. Simmer, uncovered, for 20 minutes.

new york city dog

Grill hot dogs as directed for Basic Hot Dog on page 165. Place hot dogs in hot dog buns. Spread each hot dog with 1 teaspoon Dijon-style mustard. Top with New York City Onion Sauce and warmed sauerkraut.

New York City Onion Sauce: In a large skillet, cook 2 onions, thinly sliced, in 1 tablespoon hot oil over medium heat for 15 minutes or until tender and golden, stirring occasionally (reduce heat to medium-low if necessary). Stir in 1 teaspoon chili powder and 1/2 teaspoon ground cinnamon. Cook and stir for 1 minute more. Stir in 1/3 cup ketchup, 1/3 cup water, 1 teaspoon bottled hot pepper sauce, 1/4 teaspoon salt, and 1/4 teaspoon freshly ground black pepper.

kansas city dog

Grill hot dogs as directed for Basic Hot Dog on page 165. Place hot dogs in toasted sesame seed hot dog buns. Immediately top hot dogs with warmed sauerkraut and Swiss cheese slices.

Create your own favorite: Grab some toppings or condiments to crown a sizzling hot dog.

tex-mex dog

Grill hot dogs as directed for Basic Hot Dog, opposite. Place hot dogs in hot dog buns. Top with purchased or Homemade Pico de Gallo, chopped or sliced jalapeño peppers, and shredded Monterey Jack cheese.

Homemade Pico de Gallo: In a small bowl, stir together 2 medium tomatoes, chopped; 2 tablespoons finely chopped onion; 2 tablespoons snipped fresh cilantro; 1 serrano pepper, finely chopped; and a dash of sugar.

southern dog

Grill hot dogs as directed for Basic Hot Dog, opposite. Place hot dogs in hot dog buns. Top with purchased or homemade coleslaw.

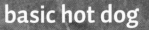

basic hot dog

Stick to this basic grilling method when you prepare any of the regional dogs on pages 162–165 with the exception of the Baltimore and Texas Dogs: To grill hot dogs on a charcoal grill, place 8 hot dogs on the grill rack directly over medium coals. Grill, uncovered, for 3 to 7 minutes or until heated through, turning occasionally. (For a gas grill, preheat grill. Reduce heat to medium; cover and grill as above.)

baltimore dog

Brush 2 onions, sliced $1/2$ inch thick, with olive oil. For a charcoal grill, place sliced onions on the grill rack directly over medium coals. Grill, uncovered, about 12 minutes or until browned, turning once. (For a gas grill, preheat grill. Reduce heat to medium. Place onions on grill rack. Cover and grill as above.) In a large heavy skillet, heat $1/2$ inch vegetable oil over medium-high heat until a drop of water sizzles in oil. Reduce heat. Split hot dogs lengthwise halfway through. Cook, uncovered, for 4 to 7 minutes. Drain on paper towels. Place hot dogs in hot dog buns and immediately top with cheddar cheese slices and grilled onion rings.

texas dog

Prepare 8 refrigerated or frozen corn dogs according to package directions. Serve with mustard and ketchup.

shortcake

Stack up three yummy treats— a baked biscuit, whipped cream, and a fruit—and you get a classic shortcake. But start mixing vibrantly colorful fruits, whipped cream with sweet additions, and flavorfully accented shortcake, and your delicious creations evolve into fabulous desserts beyond compare. Turn the page for five sweet shortcake combinations.

cherry-berry poppy seed shortcakes
(recipe, page 169)

plum-topped peanut shortcakes

plum-topped peanut shortcakes

Prep: 35 minutes   Bake: 10 minutes   Cool: 10 minutes
Grill: 3 minutes   Oven: 425°F   Makes: 6 servings

4	cups all-purpose flour
1/4	cup granulated sugar
4	teaspoons baking powder
1	teaspoon salt
2/3	cup creamy honey-roasted peanut butter
1/4	cup shortening
1 1/3	cups milk
	Milk
	Demerara or turbinado sugar
2	tablespoons butter, melted
1/4	teaspoon ground ginger
6	plums, halved and pitted
3	cups vanilla ice cream
1/3	cup chopped honey-roasted peanuts

1. Preheat oven to 425°F. Lightly grease a baking sheet; set aside. Stir together flour, sugar, baking powder, and salt. Using a pastry blender, cut in peanut butter and shortening until mixture resembles coarse crumbs. Make a well in the center of the flour mixture. Add 1 1/3 cups milk all at once to flour mixture. Using a fork, stir just until moistened.

2. Turn dough out onto a lightly floured surface. Knead dough by folding and gently pressing dough for four to six strokes or just until dough holds together. Pat or lightly roll dough to a 3/4- to 1-inch thickness. Cut the dough with a floured 3-inch round cutter, rerolling dough as needed to make 6 biscuits. Brush tops with additional milk and sprinkle with demerara sugar.

3. Place biscuits 1 inch apart on a lightly greased baking sheet. Bake in the preheated oven for 10 to 12 minutes or until lightly browned. Cool shortcakes on a wire rack for 10 minutes.

4. Meanwhile, in a small bowl, stir together melted butter and ginger. Brush mixture onto plum halves. For a charcoal grill, place plum halves, cut sides down, on the grill rack directly over medium coals. Grill, uncovered, for 3 to 4 minutes or until lightly browned. (For a gas grill, preheat grill. Reduce heat to medium. Place plum halves, cut sides down, on grill rack over heat. Cover and grill as above.) Remove plums from grill and cut into thin wedges.

5. To serve, split six biscuits in half horizontally (save any remaining for another use). Place biscuit bottoms in six shallow dessert dishes. Top each with plum wedges and a scoop of ice cream. Sprinkle with peanuts and replace shortcake tops. Serve immediately.
Per Serving: 776 cal., 41 g fat (18 g sat. fat), 112 mg chol., 576 mg sodium, 88 g carbo., 4 g fiber, 17 g pro.

A sprinkling of sugar over the cakes before they bake gives each one a sweet, crunchy top.

strawberry-walnut shortcakes

Prep: 35 minutes   Bake: 8 minutes   Cool: 10 minutes
Oven: 450°F   Makes: 8 to 10 servings

5	to 6 cups sliced fresh strawberries
1/4	cup sugar
2	cups all-purpose flour
1/4	cup sugar
2	teaspoons baking powder
1/2	teaspoon salt
1/2	cup cold butter, cut up
1	egg, lightly beaten
2/3	cup milk
1	teaspoon finely shredded orange peel
1/2	cup chopped black walnuts or English walnuts
	Whipped Cream
	Chopped black walnuts or English walnuts (optional)

1. In a medium bowl, stir together the sliced strawberries and 1/4 cup sugar; set aside.

2. Preheat oven to 450°F. In a medium bowl, stir together the flour, 1/4 cup sugar, baking powder, and salt. Using a pastry blender, cut in butter until mixture resembles coarse crumbs. Make a well in the center of the flour mixture. In a small bowl, combine egg, milk, and orange peel. Add egg mixture to flour mixture. Using a fork, stir just until moistened. Stir in the 1/2 cup walnuts.

3. Drop the dough into eight to 10 mounds on an ungreased baking sheet; flatten each mound slightly with the back of the spoon. Bake in the preheated oven for 8 to 10 minutes or until golden. Cool shortcakes on a wire rack for 10 minutes.

4. To serve, using a serrated knife, cut each shortcake in half horizontally. Carefully lift off shortcake tops. Place bottoms on dessert plates. Spoon half of the strawberries and Whipped Cream over bottoms. Replace shortcake tops. Top with any remaining Whipped Cream and spoon remaining strawberries around the shortcakes. If desired, sprinkle each serving with additional walnuts. Serve immediately.

Whipped Cream: In a chilled medium mixing bowl, beat 1 cup whipping cream, 2 tablespoons sugar, and 1/2 teaspoon vanilla with an electric mixer on medium speed until soft peaks form (tips curl).
Per Serving: 475 cal., 29 g fat (15 g sat. fat), 100 mg chol., 317 mg sodium, 49 g carbo., 3 g fiber, 8 g pro.

cherry-berry poppy seed shortcakes

Pictured on page 167.
Prep: 45 minutes   Bake: 10 minutes   Cool: 10 minutes
Oven: 425°F   Makes: 6 servings

2	cups fresh or frozen unsweetened blueberries
1	cup fresh or frozen unsweetened raspberries
1	cup fresh or frozen unsweetened pitted sweet cherries
1/4	cup granulated sugar
3	cups packaged biscuit mix
1	tablespoon poppy seeds
1 1/2	teaspoons finely shredded lemon peel
1/4	cup cold butter, cut up
1/2	to 2/3 cup half-and-half, light cream, or whole milk
1	tablespoon granulated sugar
1	cup whipping cream
1	3-ounce package cream cheese, softened and cut up
1/3	cup powdered sugar

1. Thaw fruit, if frozen. In a large bowl, stir together blueberries, raspberries, cherries, and 1/4 cup granulated sugar; set aside.

2. Preheat oven to 425°F. In a large bowl, stir together biscuit mix, poppy seeds, and 1 teaspoon of the lemon peel. Cut in butter until mixture resembles coarse crumbs. Make a well in center of mixture. Add half-and-half all at once to flour mixture. Using a fork, stir just until moistened.

3. Drop dough into six mounds on an ungreased baking sheet; flatten each mound by hand or with the back of a spoon until about 3/4 inch thick. Lightly sprinkle each mound with some of the 1 tablespoon granulated sugar. Bake in the preheated oven for 10 to 12 minutes or until golden. Cool shortcakes on a wire rack for 10 minutes.

4. Meanwhile, in a chilled medium mixing bowl, beat whipping cream with an electric mixer on medium speed until soft peaks just begin to form. Add cream cheese, powdered sugar, and the remaining 1/2 teaspoon lemon peel. Beat until fluffy.

5. To serve, split warm shortcakes in half horizontally. Lift off shortcake tops. Place bottoms on a serving platter or in six shallow dessert dishes. Spoon whipped cream mixture over bottoms. Spoon fruit over whipped cream. Replace tops. Serve immediately.
Per Serving: 604 cal., 35 g fat (18 g sat. fat), 86 mg chol., 855 mg sodium, 67 g carbo., 4 g fiber, 7 g pro.

don't short the cake

Light, tender, high-rising shortcakes are a breeze to make if you follow these basic techniques.

✳ **Stir the dry ingredients** well to distribute the baking powder and/or baking soda.

✳ **When a recipe calls for butter,** make sure it's cold when you begin.

✳ **Stir in the liquid ingredients** just until the dough is moistened.

✳ **If the dough is to be kneaded,** fold and press the dough gently and only enough to distribute the moisture and form a soft dough.

✳ **When you first roll out the dough,** cut out as many shortcakes as possible. A second rolling and the additional flour that gets added make the resulting shortcakes a bit tougher.

✳ **Remove shortcakes** from the oven when the top and bottom crusts are evenly golden.

sweet corn shortcakes with summer berries

vanilla dream floats
(recipe, page 174)

sherbet pops

vanilla dream floats

You can purchase cream soda in an amber shade or clear in color. The amber shade contrasts with the light color of the ice cream. Pictured on page 173.

Prep: 10 minutes   Makes: 4 servings

1¹⁄₂ pints cookie dough ice cream
  2 12-ounce cans or bottles cream soda

1. Place two large scoops of ice cream in the bottom of each of four 8-ounce glasses. Fill each glass with cream soda.

Per Serving: 333 cal., 14 g fat (8 g sat. fat), 38 mg chol., 112 mg sodium, 48 g carbo., 0 g fiber, 5 g pro.

sherbet pops

Lick fast! On a hot summer day, this refreshing, fruity dessert on a stick drips with sweetness.

Prep: 20 minutes   Freeze: 6 hours   Makes: 10 pops

10 5-ounce paper cups
  3 peeled and chopped kiwifruits
  1 tablespoon sugar
  1 quart raspberry, tangerine, and/or lime sherbet
  2 to 4 tablespoons orange juice
10 flat wooden crafts sticks

1. Arrange cups on a baking pan. Combine kiwifruits and sugar. Divide kiwifruits among cups. In a bowl, beat sherbet and orange juice with an electric mixer on low speed until combined and mixture is spoonable. Spoon sherbet mixture over kiwifruits, filling cups.

2. Cover each cup with a square of foil. Use a knife to make a small hole in center of each foil square. Slide a crafts stick through each hole and into fruit mixture in cup. Freeze at least 6 hours or overnight.

3. To serve, remove foil; tear away paper cups. Serve immediately.

Per Pop: 129 cal., 2 g fat (1 g sat. fat), 0 mg chol., 36 mg sodium, 28 g carbo., 3 g fiber, 1 g pro.

Clear a space in your freezer so the frozen treats sit flat and don't take a tumble.

double-melon bowls

Create a sweet-salty taste sensation by sprinkling sea salt over the frosty fruit delight.

Prep: 25 minutes Freeze: 2 hours + overnight Stand: 20 minutes
Makes: 6 to 8 servings

- 2 cups cubed, seeded watermelon
- 1 medium cantaloupe (about 3 pounds), halved and seeded
- 1 quart vanilla frozen yogurt or vanilla ice cream, softened
- Sea salt or kosher salt (optional)

1. Place watermelon cubes in a single layer on a tray or in a shallow baking pan; freeze for 2 to 3 hours or until firm. Transfer cubes to a freezer bag or container until needed.

2. With a large spoon, remove flesh from cantaloupe, leaving a 1/4-inch shell; set fruit aside. Using a sharp knife, cut a thin slice from the bottom of each shell so the shell sits flat. Place shells, upside down, on a tray lined with paper towels; set aside.

3. Place cantaloupe fruit in a food processor or blender; cover and blend or process until smooth. Place fruit puree in a fine-mesh sieve set over a bowl. Let stand for 5 minutes to remove excess liquid; discard liquid. You should have about 1 cup puree.

4. In a large bowl, gently fold the puree into the softened ice cream until just combined. Divide the ice cream mixture evenly between the cantaloupe shells. Place shells on a baking sheet or tray. Cover and freeze overnight until very firm.

5. Before serving, let shells stand at room temperature for 20 to 30 minutes to soften ice cream slightly. Top melon bowls with watermelon cubes; if desired, sprinkle watermelon lightly with sea salt. Scoop mixture from melon bowls into serving bowls.

Per Serving: 188 cal., 4 g fat (2 g sat. fat), 13 mg chol., 59 mg sodium, 36 g carbo., 1 g fiber, 4 g pro.

double-chocolate ice cream cake

To cut the cake with ease, warm a long knife by holding it under hot running water and then wipe it dry before cutting.

Prep: 45 minutes Freeze: 6 hours Stand: 30 minutes
Makes: 12 servings

- 3 cups packaged chocolate cookie crumbs
- 1 cup miniature semisweet chocolate pieces
- 2/3 cup butter, melted
- 1/2 cup finely chopped toasted pecans
- 1 pint chocolate ice cream, softened
- 1 pint vanilla ice cream, softened
- 1 8-ounce container frozen whipped dessert topping, thawed
- 1/2 cup coarsely chopped toasted pecans

1. Place a 9-inch round sheet of parchment paper or waxed paper over the base of an 8-inch springform pan. Attach sides of pan to base, clamping the paper in place. Set pan aside.

2. In a large bowl, stir together cookie crumbs, chocolate pieces, butter, and finely chopped pecans. Press one-third of the cookie crumb mixture onto the bottom of the prepared pan. Using the back of a large spoon, carefully spread the softened chocolate ice cream over the cookie crumb layer. Cover and freeze for 1 hour.

3. Sprinkle half of the remaining cookie crumb mixture over the chocolate ice cream, pressing gently to form a crust. Carefully spread the vanilla ice cream over the cookie crumb layer using the back of a large spoon. Sprinkle remaining crumb mixture over the vanilla ice cream, pressing gently to form a crust. Cover and freeze for 1 hour.

4. Remove sides of pan; lift cake from bottom of pan and peel paper off bottom of cake. Place frozen cake on a serving platter. Frost with whipped dessert topping. Top with coarsely chopped pecans. Loosely cover and freeze cake for 4 to 24 hours or until firm. Let stand at room temperature 30 minutes before serving.

Per Serving: 480 cal., 32 g fat (15 g sat. fat), 59 mg chol., 289 mg sodium, 46 g carbo., 4 g fiber, 6 g pro.

jumbo peanut butter and oatmeal sandwiches

jumbo peanut butter and oatmeal sandwiches

Prep: 30 minutes Freeze: 1 hour Bake: 10 minutes
Stand: 1 minute Oven: 375°F Makes: 8 or 9 sandwiches

1	pint vanilla ice cream
1	pint chocolate ice cream
3/4	cup peanut butter
1/2	cup butter, softened
3/4	cup packed brown sugar
1/2	cup granulated sugar
1/2	teaspoon baking powder
1/4	teaspoon baking soda
2	eggs
1	teaspoon vanilla
1 1/4	cups all-purpose flour
2 1/2	cups regular rolled oats
1 1/2	cups raisins and/or semisweet chocolate pieces

1. Line a baking pan or tray with waxed paper. Using a small ice cream scoop, place 48 to 54 scoops of vanilla and chocolate ice cream on prepared tray. Cover with waxed paper and freeze for 1 hour.

2. Meanwhile, preheat oven to 375°F. Lightly grease large cookie sheets; set aside.

3. In a large mixing bowl, beat the peanut butter and butter with an electric mixer on medium to high speed for 30 seconds. Add the brown sugar, granulated sugar, baking powder, and baking soda. Beat on medium speed until mixture is fluffy. Add the eggs and the vanilla; beat well. On low speed, beat in the flour. Using a wooden spoon, stir in the rolled oats and the raisins.

4. Using 1/4 cup dough for each cookie, drop the dough 3 inches apart onto prepared cookie sheets. Press the dough into 4-inch circles.

5. Bake in the preheated oven about 10 minutes or until the edges are golden. Let the cookies stand for 1 minute. Transfer the cookies to wire racks and cool completely.

6. To assemble sandwiches, place two scoops of vanilla and two scoops of chocolate ice cream between two cookies. Place each sandwich on a dessert plate and top with another scoop of each flavor of ice cream.

Per Sandwich: 848 cal., 36 g fat (16 g sat. fat), 110 mg chol., 334 mg sodium, 117 g carbo., 8 g fiber, 21 g pro.

soften the ice cream

When a recipe calls for softened ice cream, place the ice cream in a large bowl. Let it stand for 5 minutes, then stir the ice cream with a wooden spoon until softened.

old-fashioned ice cream sundae cake

Prep: 45 minutes Bake: 25 minutes Cool: 10 minutes
Freeze: 13 hours Stand: 20 minutes Oven: 350°F
Makes: 16 servings

2	cups all-purpose flour
2	teaspoons baking powder
3/4	teaspoon salt
3/4	cup shortening
1 1/2	cups sugar
1	tablespoon vanilla
1	cup whole milk
5	egg whites
1	pint chocolate ice cream, softened
2/3	cup finely chopped firm banana (1 small)
1	pint vanilla ice cream, softened
1	8-ounce can crushed pineapple, well-drained
1	pint strawberry ice cream, softened
2/3	cup finely chopped strawberries
1	12-ounce carton frozen whipped dessert topping, thawed
1/2	cup shredded coconut, toasted

1. Preheat oven to 350°F. Grease and lightly flour two 9×1 1/2-inch round baking pans. In a small bowl, combine flour, baking powder, and salt; set aside. In a large bowl, beat shortening with an electric mixer on medium speed for 30 seconds. Add sugar and vanilla; beat until combined. Alternately add flour mixture and milk, beating on low to medium speed after each addition just until combined. Wash beaters. In another large bowl, beat egg whites on medium to high speed until stiff peaks form (tips stand straight). Gently fold egg whites into beaten mixture. Pour batter into prepared pans.

3. Bake in the preheated oven 25 to 30 minutes or until a toothpick inserted in centers comes out clean. Cool in pans on wire racks for 10 minutes. Remove from pans; cool completely on racks. Using a long-blade serrated knife, slice each cake layer in half horizontally.

4. Place a 9-inch springform pan in a baking pan. Place one cake layer in springform pan. Stir together chocolate ice cream and banana; spread over cake in pan. Cover and freeze 30 minutes. Top with a second cake layer. Gently stir together vanilla ice cream and pineapple; spread over second cake layer. Cover and freeze 30 minutes. Top with a third cake layer. Stir together strawberry ice cream and strawberries; spread over third cake layer. Top with remaining cake layer. Cover and freeze for 12 to 24 hours.

5. To serve, remove cake from springform pan and place on a serving platter. Frost top and sides with dessert topping. Sprinkle with coconut. Let stand 20 minutes before serving. Cut into wedges.

Per Serving: 431 cal., 21 g fat (11 g sat. fat), 29 mg chol., 203 mg sodium, 55 g carbo., 1 g fiber, 5 g pro.

butterscotch crunch squares

german chocolate ice cream cupcakes

For a super shortcut, start with 12 bakery cupcakes or make cupcakes from a cake mix. Then top each cupcake with a circle of frosty ice cream and embellishments.

Prep: 25 minutes   Freeze: 4 hours   Bake: 25 minutes
Cool: 1 hour   Oven: 350°F   Makes: 12 servings

Chocolate-Pecan Ice Cream "Frosting"
- 1 cup all-purpose flour
- 1/2 teaspoon baking soda
- 1/4 teaspoon salt
- 2 ounces sweet baking chocolate
- 1/4 cup water
- 1/2 cup butter, softened
- 1/2 cup sugar
- 2 eggs
- 1/2 teaspoon vanilla
- 1/2 cup buttermilk or sour milk*
- 2/3 cup coconut, toasted
- Caramel-flavor ice cream topping

1. Prepare Chocolate-Pecan Ice Cream "Frosting." Cover and freeze. Line twelve 2 1/2-inch muffin cups with paper bake cups. Set aside.

2. Preheat oven to 350°F. In a small bowl, stir together flour, baking soda, and salt; set aside.

3. In a small saucepan, cook and stir chocolate and the water over low heat until chocolate melts. Remove from heat; cool about 10 minutes.

4. In a large bowl, beat butter with an electric mixer on medium to high speed for 30 seconds. Beat in sugar until fluffy. Add eggs and vanilla; beat on low speed until combined, then beat on medium speed for 1 minute. Beat in chocolate mixture. Add the flour mixture and buttermilk alternately to beaten mixture, beating on low speed after each addition just until combined. Spoon batter into prepared muffin cups, filling each cup about two-thirds full.

5. Bake in the preheated oven about 25 minutes or until a wooden toothpick inserted in a cupcake comes out clean. Cool in pan on wire rack for 10 minutes. Remove from pan. Cool thoroughly.

6. Just before serving, heat ice cream topping until warm. Remove wrappers from cupcakes; place cupcakes on plates or in shallow bowls. Top each cupcake with a round of the Chocolate-Pecan Ice Cream "Frosting." Top with toasted coconut and drizzle with warm caramel ice cream topping.

Chocolate-Pecan Ice Cream "Frosting": Line a baking sheet with waxed paper; set aside. Slice 1 half gallon brick-style chocolate ice cream into sheets about 2 inches thick. Use a cookie cutter to cut 12 rounds that are just larger than a cupcake from the frozen ice cream. Place cutouts on prepared baking sheet. Press 3/4 to 1 cup toasted pecan pieces into ice cream, letting pecans protrude from the ice cream. Cover and freeze at least 4 hours or overnight.

*Note: If you don't have buttermilk, make sour milk by combining 1 teaspoon lemon juice or vinegar with enough milk to make 1/2 cup total liquid; stir. Let the mixture stand for 5 minutes before using it in the recipe.

Per Serving: 411 cal., 25 g fat (12 g sat. fat), 80 mg chol., 261 mg sodium, 43 g carbo., 2 g fiber, 6 g pro.

butterscotch crunch squares

Ice cream fanatics everywhere adore these easy fix-and-freeze dessert bars. To accommodate everyone's tastes, any flavor of ice cream can be sandwiched between layers of the crunchy crumb mixture.

Prep: 40 minutes   Bake: 10 minutes   Cool: 10 minutes
Freeze: 6 hours   Stand: 5 minutes   Oven: 400°F
Makes: 24 squares

- 2 cups all-purpose flour
- 1/2 cup quick-cooking rolled oats
- 1/2 cup packed brown sugar
- 1 cup butter
- 1 cup chopped pecans or walnuts
- 1 cup butterscotch-flavor or caramel-flavor ice cream topping
- 1 gallon butter brickle, butter pecan, or vanilla ice cream

1. Preheat oven to 400°F. In a large bowl, combine the flour, oats, and brown sugar. Using a pastry blender, cut in butter until mixture resembles coarse crumbs. Stir in nuts. Pat mixture lightly into an ungreased 15×10×1-inch baking pan. Bake in the preheated oven for 10 to 15 minutes. Remove from oven. Let cool 10 minutes. Stir nut mixture to crumble. Cool completely.

2. Spread half of the crumbs in a 13×9×2-inch pan; drizzle about half of the ice cream topping over crumbs in pan. Place ice cream in a chilled large bowl; stir with a wooden spoon to soften. Spoon softened ice cream carefully over topping-drizzled crumbs, spreading ice cream evenly with the back of a large spoon. Drizzle with remaining topping; sprinkle with the remaining crumbs. Cover and freeze at least 6 hours or until firm. Let stand at room temperature for 5 to 10 minutes before serving. Cut into 24 squares.

Per Square: 450 cal., 28 g fat (15 g sat. fat), 112 mg chol., 156 mg sodium, 46 g carbo., 1 g fiber, 5 g pro.

For smooth cutting, dip the knife in hot water between cuts.

neapolitan ice cream sundaes

The delicate baked crepe chips fracture easily, so handle them carefully.

Prep: 20 minutes Bake: 6 minutes Oven: 375°F
Makes 10 servings

1	tablespoon sugar
1/2	teaspoon ground cinnamon
1/2	of a 4- to 5-ounce package refrigerated ready-to-use crepes (5)
2	tablespoons butter, melted
1	half gallon brick-style Neapolitan ice cream
	Sweetened Whipped Cream
	Maraschino cherries
1	11.75-ounce jar hot fudge ice cream topping, warmed (optional)

1. Preheat oven to 375°F. Grease two large baking sheets; set aside. In a small bowl, stir together sugar and cinnamon. Brush both sides of each crepe with butter and sprinkle with sugar mixture. Cut each crepe into quarters and arrange pieces on prepared baking sheets. Bake, one baking sheet at a time, in the preheated oven for 3 to 4 minutes or until crepe pieces are lightly browned. Cool on baking sheets. Remove and set aside.

2. Using a long sharp knife, cut ice cream crosswise into 10 slices; halve slices crosswise again.

3. For each serving, layer two crepe pieces and two ice cream slices in a bowl. Add Sweetened Whipped Cream and cherries. If desired, serve with hot fudge ice cream topping.

Sweetened Whipped Cream: In a chilled large bowl, beat 1 cup whipping cream, 2 tablespoons powdered sugar, and 1/2 teaspoon vanilla with an electric mixer on medium speed until stiff peaks form (tips stand straight).

Per Serving: 254 cal., 13 g fat (8 g sat. fat), 55 mg chol., 113 mg sodium, 45 g carbo., 0 g fiber, 4 g pro.

grown-up s'mores torte

Work quickly to cut slices of this yummy marshmallow-topped dessert. It melts quickly because it's been quick-broiled to golden goodness.

Prep: 30 minutes Bake: 10 minutes Cool: 1 hour
Freeze: 13 hours Broil: less than 1 minute Oven: 350°F
Makes: 12 to 16 servings

10	whole cinnamon graham cracker squares
2/3	cup sliced almonds, toasted
1	tablespoon sugar
1/4	cup butter, melted
1	quart coffee ice cream, softened
1	cup chocolate-fudge-flavor ice cream topping
1	quart dulce de leche ice cream, softened
1	7-ounce jar marshmallow crème
2	cups tiny marshmallows
1	cup miniature semisweet chocolate pieces

1. Preheat oven to 350°F. In a food processor, combine graham crackers, toasted almonds, and sugar. Cover and pulse with several on/off turns until crackers are finely crushed. Add butter; cover and pulse until moist crumbs form. Press crumbs firmly into the bottom of a 9-inch springform pan. Bake crust in the preheated oven for 10 to 12 minutes or until edges begin to turn golden. Transfer pan to a wire rack and cool completely.

2. Using the back of a large spoon, spread softened coffee ice cream over crust in pan. Spread fudge topping over coffee ice cream. Freeze about 1 hour or until fudge topping sets.

3. Using the back of a large spoon, spread softened dulce de leche ice cream over fudge topping layer. Cover and freeze cake at least 12 hours or overnight.

4. Preheat broiler and arrange oven rack so top of torte will be about 4 inches from the heat. Place springform pan containing torte on a baking sheet. Quickly spread marshmallow crème over top of torte. Sprinkle top evenly with marshmallows and chocolate pieces.

5. Broil for 30 to 60 seconds or just until marshmallows turn golden brown. Run a warm knife around pan sides to loosen. Remove pan sides. Cut torte into wedges and serve immediately.

Per Serving: 535 cal., 24 g fat (13 g sat. fat), 40 mg chol., 252 mg sodium, 75 g carbo., 2 g fiber, 6 g pro.

grown-up s'mores torte

lemon drop shakes

lemon drop shakes

Start to Finish: 5 minutes   Makes: 6 (6-ounce) servings

- $^1/_2$ of a small lemon, thinly sliced
- 2   tablespoons crushed lemon drop candies
- 1   tablespoon sugar
- 1   quart vanilla ice cream
- $1^1/_2$ cups lemonade

1. Rub rims of 6 juice-size glasses with one lemon slice. In a shallow dish, combine crushed lemon drops and sugar. Dip glass rims in mixture; set aside.

2. In a blender, combine ice cream and lemonade. Cover and blend until smooth.

3. Pour ice cream mixture into glasses. Garnish with remaining lemon slices.

Per Serving: 403 cal., 23 g fat (15 g sat. fat), 131 mg chol., 108 mg sodium, 45 g carbo., 0 g fiber, 5 g pro.

frozen orange sorbet towers

Prep: 20 minutes   Freeze: 4 hours   Makes: 4 servings

- 2   pints orange or mango sorbet
- 2   tablespoons Grand Marnier or other orange liqueur
- 3   medium oranges and/or blood oranges, peeled

1. Line a 13×9×2-inch baking pan with plastic wrap, extending the plastic wrap over the sides. Place orange sorbet in a large bowl. Using a wooden spoon, stir sorbet to soften. Stir in liqueur. Transfer the sorbet to the prepared pan, spreading evenly. Freeze for 4 to 24 hours or until firm.

2. Using a sharp knife, slice each peeled orange crosswise into four rounds. Wrap and place oranges in the freezer until needed.

3. Holding the edges of the plastic wrap, carefully lift the sorbet from the pan. Using a 2- to $2^1/_2$-inch scalloped round cookie cutter (it should be the same diameter as an orange), cut sorbet into rounds (you should have at least 12 rounds). To serve, stack three rounds of sorbet alternately with three slices of orange. Place on individual dessert plates. Serve immediately.

Per serving: 80 cal., 0 g fat, 0 mg chol., 0 mg sodium, 80 g carbo., 4 g fiber, 1 g pro.

dulce de leche ice cream torte

Prep: 25 minutes   Freeze: 5 hours to overnight   Makes: 9 servings

- 2   cups finely crushed purchased shortbread or pecan shortbread cookies (about 10 ounces)
- 3   tablespoons butter, melted
- 2   pints dulce de leche ice cream
- $^2/_3$ cup roasted, lightly salted cashews, coarsely chopped
  Pineapple Topping

1. In a medium bowl, combine cookie crumbs and butter. Press half of the cookie crumb mixture (about 1 cup) evenly onto the bottom of an 8×8×1$^7/_8$-inch disposable foil pan* or a 9×9×2-inch baking pan. Set aside. Soften half of the ice cream (see tip, page 177). Carefully spread softened ice cream over the cookie crumb layer in the pan. Top with half of the cashews. Sprinkle the remaining cookie crumb mixture over the layers in the pan. Cover and freeze for 1 to 2 hours or until firm.

2. Soften remaining ice cream. Carefully spread ice cream over frozen layers in pan. Cover and freeze overnight or until very firm.

3. To serve, top with remaining cashews. Cut into squares* and serve with Pineapple Topping.

Pineapple Topping: In a large skillet, melt 2 tablespoons butter. Add 3 tablespoons packed brown sugar; cook and stir until sugar is dissolved. Add 2 cups peeled, cored, and cubed fresh pineapple; stir to coat. Serve at once or cover and chill up to 3 days; reheat before serving.

Per Serving: 440 cal., 25 g fat (10 g sat. fat), 41 mg chol., 349 mg sodium, 50 g carbo., 1 g fiber, 6 g pro.

Note: If using the foil pan, use a spatula to cut the ice cream torte into servings; a sharp knife will cut through the foil pan.

chocolate cupcake ice cream sandwiches

Prep: 10 minutes Freeze: 1 hour Makes: 6 servings

6	purchased or homemade unfrosted chocolate cupcakes
2	to 3 cups chocolate chip ice cream
1	10-ounce jar maraschino cherries, drained and chopped (1/2 cup)
1/3	cup chopped pecans, toasted
1/3	cup seedless raspberry jam

1. Remove papers, if present, and slice cupcakes in half horizontally. Place cupcakes on a tray or baking sheet lined with waxed paper. Cover with waxed paper; freeze for 1 hour. Line another tray or shallow baking pan with waxed paper. Using a miniature ice cream scoop (#60, about 2 teaspoons), place 18 to 24 scoops of ice cream on prepared tray. Cover with waxed paper; freeze for 1 hour.

2. Meanwhile, in small bowl, combine cherries, pecans, and jam.

3. For each serving, place cupcake bottom in a dessert dish. Top with 2 to 3 scoops of ice cream. Top with cherry mixture, cupcake top, and remaining scoops of ice cream.

Per Serving: 477 cal., 22 g fat (7 g sat. fat), 52 mg chol., 316 mg sodium, 66 g carbo., 2 g fiber, 6 g pro.

tropical treat ice cream sandwiches

Prep: 35 minutes Freeze: 5 hours Bake: 6 minutes/batch
Oven: 350°F Makes: 20 sandwiches

1	18-ounce package refrigerated sugar cookie dough
1/2	cup all-purpose flour
2	teaspoon milk
4	teaspoon coarse sugar or 1 teaspoon granulated sugar
1	1.75-quart container tropical fruit or rainbow sherbet

1. Preheat oven to 350°F.

2. Place cookie dough and flour in a large mixing bowl; knead with hands until combined. On a lightly floured surface, roll dough, half at a time, to a 14×10-inch rectangle. With fluted pastry wheel or pizza cutter, cut into 3 1/2 × 2-inch rectangles (you should have 40 rectangles). Place on ungreased cookie sheets. Prick each rectangle with a fork. Brush with milk and sprinkle with sugar.

3. Bake for 6 to 7 minutes or until edges are lightly browned. Cool on cookie sheet 1 minute. Transfer to wire racks; cool completely.

4. Place a large baking sheet or 15×10×1-inch pan in the freezer. Cut carton from sherbet using kitchen scissors and place sherbet on a cutting board. With a long sharp knife, cut in half lengthwise. Lay ice cream, cut sides down on, the cutting board. Cut crosswise into 1-inch slices. Halve each slice crosswise (you should have 20 slices*). Arrange the slices on the chilled baking sheet or pan. Cover and freeze for 1 hour or until firm. For each sandwich, place a sherbet slice between two cookies, sugar sides out. Wrap each sandwich in plastic wrap and freeze at least 4 hours or until firm.

5. Cookies may be frozen for up to 3 months.

Per Sandwich: 214 cal., 6 g fat (2 g sat. fat), 7 mg chol., 132 mg sodium, 38 g carbo., 0 g fiber, 2 g pro.

Note: The slices will have some rounded edges due to the shape of the carton.

chocolate cupcake ice cream sandwiches

tropical treat ice cream sandwiches

ice cream

Scoops of creamy vanilla ice cream piled high on a cone make a sure summertime bliss. But add a heap of chocolate or a variety of fruit, nut, or candy stir-ins and you get delicious versions of ice cream shop specialties.

homemade vanilla ice cream

homemade vanilla ice cream

Get churnin'! With more than a dozen delicious flavor options on these pages, you'll be making ice cream all summer.

Prep: 15 minutes Freeze: per manufacturer's directions
Ripen: 4 hours Makes: about 2 quarts (32 1/2-cup servings)

- 3 cups whipping cream
- 2 cups half-and-half or light cream
- 1 14-ounce can (1 1/4 cups) sweetened condensed milk, chilled
- 4 teaspoons vanilla

1. In a large bowl, combine whipping cream, half-and-half, sweetened condensed milk, and vanilla.

2. Pour cream mixture into the freezer can of a 4- to 5-quart ice cream freezer. Add the dasher; cover with the freezer can lid. Freeze according to the manufacturer's directions. Ripen 4 hours (see tip, below). (Ice cream becomes quite firm during ripening.)

Per Serving: 277 cal., 22 g fat, 81 mg chol., 61 mg sodium, 16 g carbo., 0 g fiber, 4 g pro.

vanilla ice cream variations

Cream Cheese Ice Cream: Gradually beat the 14-ounce can sweetened condensed milk into two 8-ounce packages softened cream cheese until mixture is smooth. Combine cream cheese mixture with other ice cream base ingredients and freeze.

Spiced Honey Ice Cream: Stir in 1/3 cup honey, 1 teaspoon ground cinnamon, 1/4 teaspoon ground nutmeg, and 1/8 teaspoon ground ginger into ice cream mixture before freezing.

Lemon Cream Ice Cream: Finely shred 2 teaspoons of peel from 1 lemon; set aside. Whisk one 10-ounce jar lemon curd and 1 tablespoon lemon juice into ice cream mixture before freezing. After freezing but before ripening, stir in the lemon peel.

Macadamia and White Chocolate Chip Ice Cream: Stir 1 cup white baking pieces and 3/4 cup chopped macadamia nuts into ice cream mixture before ripening.

Maraschino Cherry and Toasted Pecan Ice Cream: Stir 1 cup chopped red maraschino cherries and 3/4 cup chopped pecans, toasted, into ice cream mixture before ripening. If desired, stir in 3 tablespoons rum before freezing.

Peach Ice Cream: Place 4 cups fresh peeled and cut-up ripe peaches or apricots or 4 cups unsweetened frozen peaches in a blender or food processor. Cover and blend or process until smooth (you should have about 2 cups puree). If desired, add 2 tablespoons peach brandy or peach liqueur and 1/2 teaspoon ground nutmeg. Stir peach mixture into ice cream mixture before freezing.

Fresh Berry Ice Cream: Place 4 cups fresh raspberries, blackberries, blueberries, and/or cut-up strawberries in a blender or food processor. Cover and blend or process until smooth. Sieve berry puree and discard seeds (you should have about 2 cups sieved puree). Stir berry puree into ice cream mixture before freezing.

Dark Roast Coffee Ice Cream: Stir 1/2 cup chilled brewed espresso and 2 tablespoons coffee liqueur into ice cream mixture before freezing. If desired, stir 2/3 cup coarsely crushed chocolate-covered espresso beans and 2/3 cup toasted, chopped hazelnuts (filberts) into ice cream mixture before ripening.

Cookies-and-Cream Ice Cream: Stir 2 cups crumbled chocolate sandwich cookies with white filling into ice cream mixture before ripening.

Animal Tracks Ice Cream: Stir 10 coarsely chopped chocolate-covered peanut butter cups (1 3/4 cups) and 1 cup coarsely chopped chocolate fudge into ice cream mixture before ripening.

ready to ripen

Ripening is a hardening technique that improves an ice cream's texture and helps keep the mixture from melting too fast after you serve it. Although it improves the ice cream, ripening isn't required.

To ripen ice cream in a traditional-style ice cream freezer, after churning, remove the lid and dasher; cover the top of the freezer can with waxed paper or foil. Plug the hole in the lid with a cloth; replace the lid. Pack the outer freezer bucket with enough ice and rock salt to cover the top of the freezer (use 4 cups ice to 1 cup salt). Ripen the ice cream about 4 hours.

When using an ice cream freezer with an insulated freezer bowl, transfer the ice cream to a covered freezerproof container; ripen in refrigerator freezer about 4 hours.

Start with the Chocolate Ice Cream recipe and stir in a few goodies.

chocolate-mint ice cream, chocolate-peanut butter ice cream, and rocky trail ice cream

homemade chocolate ice cream

Prepare Homemade Vanilla Ice Cream as directed on page 187, except stir 1 cup chocolate-flavor syrup into ice cream mixture before freezing. (This ice cream will be a little softer after ripening than the vanilla.)

chocolate ice cream variations

Mocha Ice Cream: Stir 1 cup chilled strong brewed coffee or 1/2 cup brewed espresso and 2 tablespoons coffee liqueur into chocolate ice cream mixture before freezing. If desired, stir in 1 cup miniature semisweet chocolate pieces before ripening the ice cream.

Chocolaty Chocolate Chip Ice Cream: Stir 1 cup miniature semisweet chocolate pieces or 6 ounces of your favorite chocolate candy bar, coarsely chopped, into chocolate ice cream before ripening.

Chocolate-Almond Ice Cream: Stir 1 cup chopped almonds, toasted, into chocolate ice cream before ripening.

Chocolate-Peanut Butter Ice Cream: Whisk 1 cup creamy or chunky peanut butter into chocolate ice cream mixture before freezing; stir in 8 chocolate-covered peanut butter cups, coarsely chopped, before ripening the ice cream.

Chocolate-Mint Ice Cream: Stir 1 cup finely broken peppermint candies and ten 1 1/2-inch-diameter chopped chocolate-covered cream-filled mint patties into chocolate ice cream before ripening.

Chocolate-Toffee Ice Cream: Stir four 1.4-ounce bars chocolate-covered toffee candy, coarsely chopped, into chocolate ice cream before ripening.

Truffle Ice Cream: Stir 1 cup coarsely chopped chocolate truffles or your favorite chocolate candy and 1 cup chopped pecans, toasted, into chocolate ice cream before ripening.

Rocky Trail Ice Cream: Stir 1 cup chopped almonds, toasted, and 1 cup tiny marshmallows into chocolate ice cream before ripening.

Fudge Brownie Ice Cream: Stir 2 cups coarsely chopped fudge brownie bars into chocolate ice cream before ripening.

Chocolate Cookie Ice Cream: Stir 2 cups crumbled chocolate sandwich cookies with white filling or chocolate wafer cookies into chocolate ice cream before ripening.

index

index

What's for Dinner Tonight?

These days, time is short but home-cooked meals are still a must! Check out this ultimate collection of quick-to-the-table recipes, designed specifically for your busy life. Whether you're looking for a no-fuss slow-cooked dinner or a 20-minute eat-and-run supper, these flavorful recipe collections will help you eat right without slowing you down.

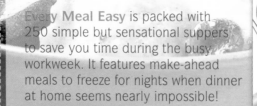

Every Meal Easy is packed with 250 simple but sensational suppers to save you time during the busy workweek. It features make-ahead meals to freeze for nights when dinner at home seems nearly impossible!

So-Easy Slow Cooker simmers up more than 120 rich and savory meals that require almost no prep. Just toss in the ingredients before work and let dinner slow-cook its way to dynamite flavor.

Quick-Fix Family Favorites serves up more than 250 fabulous family-friendly meals that can be on the table in mere minutes! You'll find dozens of five-ingredient favorites and easy off-the-shelf fix-ups perfect for even the littlest diners.